THE ASHES

THE ASHES

A GUIDE TO CRICKET'S MOST ENDURING RIVALRY

DEAN HAYES

SELECT
EDITIONS

This edition printed in 2005 for
Selectabook Ltd
Folly Road, Roundway, Devizes,
Wiltshire SN10 2HT

ISBN 1-84193-314-7

Printed in China

Book Design: Mike Reynolds

CONTENTS

Introduction

When those players representing England and Australia took to the field at Melbourne in March 1877, little could they have realised they were not just playing the first match between the two countries, but they were initiating one of the great sporting institutions. There may be other series that are more adventurous and entertaining, but none receive the attention and generate the same feeling as that between England and Australia, which from 1883, has been a battle for the Ashes.

The very existence of the Ashes themselves is proof of the importance of the series. It was considered a national disaster when England were beaten by Australia at The Oval in 1882. A mock memorial notice appeared in the *Sporting Times* "in remembrance of England cricket". It was said that "the body will be cremated and the Ashes taken to Australia". Ivo Bligh, captain of the England touring team bound for Australia the following winter, promised to bring back 'the Ashes' to England. When his team was successful some ladies in Melbourne burnt the bails in the deciding match and presented the Ashes to Bligh in an urn. Those Ashes remain at Lord's but are mythically played for in each series.

Though I was too young to be at Old Trafford for Jim Laker's record-breaking haul of 19 wickets in 1956, I was there some eight years later, travelling the short distance from my home in Bolton to witness the 'Old Trafford Bowling Massacre'. Four scored centuries – Simpson 311, Barrington 256, Dexter 174 and Lawry 106 and Booth missed becoming a fifth by just two runs.

That's how it all started for me. The Ashes. I've loved every series since. *The Ashes: A Guide To Cricket's Most Enduring Rivalry* is my contribution to this unique sporting occasion.

TO CRICKET LOVERS EVERYWHERE, I INVITE YOU TO JOIN ME IN RELIVING THE MAGIC OF ENGLAND – AUSTRALIA TEST HISTORY.

DEAN P. HAYES
PEMBROKESHIRE, OCTOBER 2004

1882-1900

THE 19th CENTURY

Australia could not hope to beat England at full strength on level terms; that was the view of English cricket followers up to the time of the first of all 'Test' matches played at Melbourne in March 1877. Yet Australia won a notable victory by 45 runs. The English touring party was all professional so it was not quite fully representative, but it was a strong team and few had doubted beforehand that it would be good enough to win.

Right from this first encounter no quarter was asked and none given. Charles Bannerman, whose hard-hitting innings of 165 set Australia on the road to victory, had his knuckles so badly bruised by the rising deliveries of Yorkshire's George Ulyett that he was eventually forced to retire. The English tourists won the return match but the Australians confirmed their new status as international cricketers at Melbourne in 1879 by beating another touring English side by 10 wickets.

THE OVAL 1880

Those three matches introduced some of the greatest of all names to Test cricket, especially on the Australian side: Charlie and Alec Bannerman, Billy Murdoch, later captain, the bearded wicket-keeper Blackham and the legendary Spofforth, first of the game's greatest fast bowlers. Those who maintained, despite these reverses, that England at full strength on their home ground would prove invincible, found confirmation of their view at The Oval in 1880 in the first Test match in England and the only one of that Australian tour. WG Grace's 152 in his first Test was bettered by Murdoch's 153 not out but not before Australia had followed on. England were left with only 57 to win, yet they lost five wickets in the process. GF (Fred) Grace took one of his-

THOSE THREE MATCHES INTRODUCED SOME OF THE GREATEST OF ALL NAMES TO TEST CRICKET

tory's most famous catches off a monster hit by the giant Bonnor – the batsmen were on their third run as the ball was safely caught. GF Grace died a fortnight later from a chill and lung congestion.

Another all-professional party visited Australia in 1881-82, a strong combination that included Ulyett, Barlow, Bates, Scotton, Shrewsbury, Emmett and Shaw, but it lost two of the four Tests played and failed to win any. These men must have been well aware what England would be up against in 1882 but belief in invincibility at home remained.

BACK AT THE OVAL, 1882

As in 1880, only one Test was played, at The Oval. Needing only 85 to win in a low-scoring match, England were bowled out for 77, a feat immortalised by the famous lament in the 'Sporting Times' on the death of English cricket. Grace's running out of Sammy Jones when the youngster left his crease to attend to a divot in the pitch did nothing to reduce the grim if seemingly optimistic determination of the Australians. The man chiefly responsible for the upset was Fred Spofforth whose figures of 14 for 90 were not to be beaten by an Australian player until 1972. One spectator died of heart failure during the tense closing ▶

Fred Spofforth
(Australia) 1878-82

When he arrived on his first tour of England in 1878, Fred Spofforth stunned both crowds and opposition. Quite simply they'd never seen anything quite like his bowling action, which consisted of a nine-pace run-up, a huge leap in the air and a devastatingly quick delivery. It earned him the nickname 'The Demon' and it's a fair assumption most of his 94 Test victims were scared out of their crease!

Against a strong MCC side at Lord's in 1878, Spofforth took 6 for 4 including a hat-trick in the first innings with just 23 balls and 4 for 36 in the second. The MCC were bowled out for 33 and 19 and beaten in a day. In the sole Test of 1878-79 at Melbourne against 'the Gentlemen of England' with Ulyett and Emmett, the two best professional cricketers of the day, Spofforth took 13 for 110 including Test cricket's first hat-trick. On Australia's tour of England in 1882, Spofforth at The Oval, in the only Test played, had taken 7 for 46 in England's first innings only to see Australia bundled out cheaply twice. England went out to bat in the final innings of the match needing just 85 runs to win with the strongest batting line-up it had ever fielded. The Demon had been enraged when WG Grace ran out Sammy Jones as he left his crease to pat down a bump on the pitch and he let all the Englishmen taste his fury. Spofforth finished with 7 for 44 and match figures of 14 for 90, the best by an Australian in England until Bob Massie's performance nine decades later. Spofforth, whose father emigrated to Australia from Yorkshire, later settled in England and played several games for Derbyshire before they became a first-class county. He was quite a businessman too, leaving £164,000 in his will when he died in 1926.

THE AUSTRALIA TEAM WHO TOURED ENGLAND IN 1882: (BACK ROW, L-R) GE PALMER, HF BOYLE, PS MCDONNELL, FR SPOFFORTH, T HORAN, SP JONES, WL MURDOCH; (FRONT ROW, L-R) CW BEAL, G GIFFEN, A BANNERMAN, TW GARRETT, HH MASSIE, GJ BONNOR

Hugh Trumble
(Australia) 1890-1902

Hugh Trumble, the genial Melbourne cricketer with oriental eyes, drooping moustache and cool bowling brain, which accounted for 141 English Test wickets in 31 matches, toured England five times from 1890 to 1902. Grace called him the 'best bowler Australia has sent us' and though he took only 17 wickets in his first eight Tests, he later came into his own. During his visits to England, there were some fine performances – at The Oval in 1896 he took 6 for 59 and 6 for 30; at Old Trafford in 1902 he picked up 10 wickets in a classic game which Australia won by three runs, while in the next match at The Oval he took 8 for 65 and 4 for 108 as England won by one wicket. During this match he also scored 64 to become the first Australian to take 10 wickets and score 50 in a Test match. Hugely successful in England, he was no less a match-winner in Australia.

In 1897-98 he took 19 wickets as Australia won the series. He captained Australia to victory in each of the last two Tests of the 1901-02 series and also performed the hat-trick in the last game at Melbourne. Persuaded to play in the second Test against England in 1903-04, he took 4 for 107 and 5 for 34. He continued for the remainder of the series and in his last game at Melbourne, Trumble ended his Test career with 7 for 28, bowling his side to victory and taking his second Test hat-trick. It was a fitting end to a wonderful career. In retirement, he became an astute writer on the game and was the secretary of the Melbourne Cricket Club for many years, but he is best remembered as Australia's finest off-spin bowler.

JOHNNY BRIGGS OF LANCASHIRE AND ENGLAND SQUARES UP TO THE CAMERA BEFORE EMBARKING ON AN ASHES TOUR

stages and another had bitten through his umbrella handle!

England regained the Ashes somewhat luckily in 1882-83 by winning two of a rubber of three matches. Australia squared the series by winning a fourth match but the fate of the Ashes was held to have been decided already. Following this somewhat hollow revenge, England went on to retain the Ashes for the next nine years but they were often fortunate to do so. Up to 1885, the Australians probably had the stronger side. Their great quartet of bowlers – Spofforth, Garrett, Palmer and Boyle – were more dangerous than any English combination, and their fielding had improved dramatically. It was only a tendency to rashness in the batting, and an indulgence in disputes that affected team selection, that allowed English teams to prevail.

After a disappointing tour of England in 1886, when several leading Australian players were absent and the quartet of bowlers ageing, Australian cricket went into decline. From 1886 to 1890, 11 Test matches were played and England, losing only once, won the other 10. This period coincided with the peak of the Surrey pace bowler George Lohmann and the emergence of the slow left-arm bowlers Johnny Briggs and Bobby Peel. Yet no pair of bowlers has ever been quite so destructive on English wickets as the Australians Turner and Ferris in 1888. Poorly supported, they often had to bowl at impossible targets because of batting displays that lacked the necessary skill and concentration and for all their effectiveness they could not triumph on their own over the all-round strength of the English teams of the period.

GEORGE GIFFEN'S RECORD PLACES HIM AMONG THE GREATEST OF AUSTRALIAN ALL-ROUNDERS

The recovery of Australian cricket came in 1891-92 when England sent a strong side led by WG Grace but lost the first two Tests of a rubber. Stonewaller Alec Bannerman was the great stumbling block, while Turner had found a new bowling partner in George Giffen. Giffen's record places him with Noble, Armstrong and Miller among the greatest of Australian all-rounders.

THREE IN A ROW FOR ENGLAND

England came back to win the next three series in 1893, 1894-95 and 1896, when they owed much to their batting strength. Shrewsbury, FS Jackson, William Gunn, Grace, Stoddart and Ranjitsinhji in particular, were outstanding. But the power that tipped the scales in this period was the fast bowling of Tom Richardson. His tally of 88 wickets in only 14 Tests places him still among those with the highest striking rates of wickets taken per Test match. It was not until his power began to wane that Australia won another series. But thanks in most part to the emergence of players of the calibre of Victor Trumper, Clem Hill, Monty Noble, Joe Darling, Hugh Trumble and Ernie Jones, Australia finished the 1890s strongly by winning the last two series. The Australian side of 1899, led by Darling, was by general consent the strongest seen in England since 1882 and is still considered one of the best ever. ●

THE RESULTS

ENGLAND v AUSTRALIA
Played at The Oval, 28-9 August 1882

AUSTRALIA

AC Bannerman	c Grace b Peate	9	c Studd b Barnes	13
HH Massie	b Ulyett	1	b Steel	55
WL Murdoch	b Peate	13	run out	29
GJ Bonnor	b Barlow	1	b Ulyett	2
T Horan	b Barlow	3	c Grace b Peate	2
G Giffen	b Peate	2	c Grace b Peate	0
J Mc Blackham	c Grace b Barlow	17	c Lyttleton b Peate	7
TW Garrett	c Read b Peate	10	not out	2
HF Boyle	b Barlow	2	b Steel	0
SP Jones	c Barnes b Barlow	0	run out	6
FR Spofforth	not out	1	b Peate	0
Extras		1		6
Total		**63**		**122**

Fall of wickets 1-6 2-21 3-22 4-26 5-30 6-30 7-48 8-50 9-59 10-63
2nd Innings   1-66 2-70 3-70 4-79 5-79 6-99 7-114 8-17 9-122 10-122

England Bowling (4-ball overs)

	O	M	R	W	O	M	R	W
Peate	38	24	31	4	21	9	40	4
Ulyett	9	5	11	1	6	2	10	1
Barlow	31	22	19	5	13	5	27	0
Steel	-	-	-	-	7	0	15	2
Barnes	-	-	-	-	11	5	15	1
Studd	-	-	-	-	4	1	9	0

ENGLAND

RG Barlow	c Bannerman b Spofforth	11	b Spofforth	0
WG Grace	b Spofforth	4	c Bannerman b Boyle	32
G Ulyett	st Blackham b Spofforth	26	c Blackham b Spofforth	11
AP Lucas	c Blackham b Boyle	9	b Spofforth	5
Hon A Lyttleton	c Blackham b Spofforth	2	b Spofforth	12
CT Studd	b Spofforth	0	not out	0
JM Read	not out	19	b Spofforth	0
W Barnes	b Boyle	5	c Murdoch b Boyle	2
AG Steel	b Garrett	14	c and b Spofforth	0
AN Hornby	b Spofforth	2	b Spofforth	9
E Peate	c Boyle b Spofforth	0	b Boyle	2
Extras		9		4
Total		**101**		**77**

Fall of wickets 1-13 2-18 3-56 4-59 5-60 6-63 7-70 8-96 9-101 10-101
2nd Innings   1-15 2-15 3-51 4-53 5-66 6-70 7-70 8-75 9-75 10-77

Australia Bowling (4-ball overs)

	O	M	R	W	O	M	R	W
Spofforth	36.3	18	46	7	28	15	44	7
Garrett	16	7	22	1	7	2	10	0
Boyle	19	7	24	2	20	11	19	3

AUSTRALIA WON BY 7 RUNS

1876-77
SERIES DRAWN 1-1

1st Test at Melbourne
March 15,16,17,19
AUSTRALIA 245 (C Bannerman 165 ret hurt) and 104 (A Shaw 5-38)
ENGLAND 196 (H Jupp 63 WE Midwinter 5-78) and 108 (T Kendall 7-55)

AUSTRALIA WON BY 45 RUNS

2nd Test at Melbourne
March 31 April 2,3,4
AUSTRALIA 122 (A Hill 4-27) and 259 (DW Gregory 43 N.Thompson 41, James Lillywhite 4-70 J.Southerton 4-46)
ENGLAND 261 (A Greenwood 49 A.Hill 49 T.Emmett 48 T.Kendall 4-82) and 122-6 (G Ulyett 63)

ENGLAND WON BY 4 WICKETS

1878-79
Only test at Melbourne
January 2,3,4
ENGLAND 113 (CA Absalom 52 FR Spofforth 6-48) and 160 (FR Spofforth 7-62)
AUSTRALIA 256 (AC Bannerman 73 T Emmett 7-68) and 19-0

AUSTRALIA WON BY 10 WICKETS

1880
Only test at The Oval
London,September 6,7,8
ENGLAND 420 (WG Grace 152 AP Lucas 55 Lord Harris 52 AG Steel 42) and 57-5
AUSTRALIA 149 (F Morley 5-56) and 327 (WL Murdoch 153* PS McDonnell 43)

ENGLAND WON BY 5 WICKETS

1881-82
AUSTRALIA WON SERIES 2-0

1st Test at Melbourne
December 31 January 2,3,4
ENGLAND 294 (G Ulyett 87 W Bates 58 J Selby 55) and 308 (J Selby 70 WH Scotton 50* W Bates 47 A Shaw 40 WH Cooper 6-120)
AUSTRALIA 320 (TP Horan 124) and 127-3

MATCH DRAWN

2nd Test at Sydney
February 17,18,20,21
ENGLAND 133 (GE Palmer 7-68) and 232 (G Ulyett 67 RG Barlow 62 GE Palmer 4-97 TW Garrett 4-62)
AUSTRALIA 197 (HH Massie 49 JM Blackham 40 W Bates 4-52) and 169-5 (WL Murdoch 49)

AUSTRALIA WON BY 5 WICKETS

3rd Test at Sydney
March 3,4,6,7
ENGLAND 188 (A Shrewsbury 82 GE Palmer 5-46) and 134 (A Shrewsbury 47 TW Garrett 6-78 GE Palmer 4-44)
AUSTRALIA 260 (PS McDonnell 147 AC Bannerman 70 E Peate 5-43) and 66-4

AUSTRALIA WON BY 6 WICKETS

4th Test at Melbourne
March 10,11,13,14 (no play)
ENGLAND 309 (G Ulyett 149 TW Garrett 5-80 and 234-2 (G Ulyett 64 RG Barlow 56 W Bates 52* J Selby 48*)
AUSTRALIA 300 (WL Murdoch 85 PS McDonnell 52 WE Midwinter 4-81)

MATCH DRAWN

1882
Only test at The Oval
London August 28,29
AUSTRALIA 63 (RG Barlow 5-19 E Peate 4-31) and 122 (HH Massie 55 E Peate 4-40)
ENGLAND 101 (FR Spofforth 7-46) and 77 (FR Spofforth 7-44)

AUSTRALIA WON BY 7 RUNS

1882-83
SERIES DRAWN 2-2

1st Test at Melbourne
December 30 January 1,2
AUSTRALIA 291 (GJ Bonnor 85, WL Murdoch 48, PS McDonnell 43) and 58-1
ENGLAND 177 (GE Palmer 7-65) and 169 (G Giffen 4-38)

AUSTRALIA WON BY 9 WICKETS

2nd Test at Melbourne
January 19,20,22
ENGLAND 294 (WW Read 75 W Bates 55 CFH Leslie 54 GE Palmer 5-103 G Giffen 4-89)
AUSTRALIA 14 (HH Massie 43 W Bates 7-28) and 153 (W Bates 7-74)

ENGLAND WON BY AN INNINGS AND 27 RUNS

3rd Test at Sydney
January 26,27,29,30
ENGLAND 247 (WW Read 66 EFS Tylecote 66 FR Spofforth 4-73) and 123 (FR Spofforth 7-44
AUSTRALIA 218 (AC Bannerman 94 G Giffen 41 F Morley 4-47) and 83 (RG Barlow 7-40)

ENGLAND WON BY 69 RUNS

4th Test at Sydney
February 17,19,20,21
ENGLAND 263 (AG Steel 135* CT Studd 48) and 197 (W Bates 48*)
AUSTRALIA 262 (GJ Bonnor 87 JM Blackham 57) and 199-6 (AC Bannerman 63 JM Blackham 58*)

AUSTRALIA WON BY 4 WICKETS

1884
ENGLAND WON SERIES 1-0

1st Test at Old Trafford
Manchester July 10(no play)11,12
ENGLAND 95 (A Shrewsbury 43 HF Boyle 6-42 FR Spofforth 4-42) and 180-9 (GE Palmer4-47)
AUSTRALIA 182

MATCH DRAWN

2nd Test at Lord's
July 21,22,23
AUSTRALIA 229 (HJH Scott 75 G Giffen 63 E Peate 6-85) and 145 (G Ulyett 7-36)

ENGLAND 379 (AG Steel 148 GE Palmer 6-111)

ENGLAND WON BY AN INNINGS AND 5 RUNS

3rd Test at The Oval
August 1,12,13
AUSTRALIA 551 (WL Murdoch 211 PS McDonnell 103 HJH Scott 102 Hon A Lyttleton 4-19)
ENGLAND 346 (WW Read 117 WH Scotton 90 GE Palmer 4-90) and 85-2

MATCH DRAWN

1884-85
ENGLAND WON SERIES 3-2

1st Test at Adelaide Oval
December 12,13,15,16
AUSTRALIA 243 (PS McDonnell 124 JM Blackham 66 W Bates 5-31) and 191 (PS McDonnell 83 G Giffen 47 R Peel 5-51)
ENGLAND 369 (W Barnes 134 WH Scotton 82 G Ulyett 68 GE Palmer 5-81) and 67-2

ENGLAND WON BY 8 WICKETS

2nd Test at Melbourne
January 1,2,3,5
ENGLAND 401 (J Briggs 121 A Shrewsbury 72 W Barnes 58 SP Jones 4-47) and 7-0
AUSTRALIA 279 (AH Jarvis 82 TP Horan 63 JW Trumble 59) and 126 (W Bruce 45 W Barnes 6-31)

ENGLAND WON BY 10 WICKETS

3rd Test at Sydney
February 20,21,23,24
AUSTRALIA 181 (TW Garrett 51* W Flowers 5-46 W Attewell 4-53) and 165 (W Bates 5-24)
ENGLAND 133 (TP Horan 6-40 FR Spofforth 4-54) and 207 (W Flowers 56 JM Read 56 FR Spofforth 6-90)

AUSTRALIA WON BY 6 RUNS

4th Test at Sydney
March 14,16,17
ENGLAND 269 (W Bates 64 W Barnes 50 JM Read 47 A Shrewsbury 40 G Giffen 7-117)and 77 (FR Spofforth 5-30 GE Palmer 4-32)
AUSTRALIA 309 (GJ Bonnor 128 AC Bannerman 51 SP Jones 40 W Barnes 4-61) and 38-2

AUSTRALIA WON BY 8 WICKETS

5th Test at Melbourne
March 21,23,24,25
AUSTRALIA 163 (FR Spofforth 50 G Ulyett 4-52) and 125
ENGLAND 386 (A Shrewsbury 105* W Barnes 74 W Bates 61 J Briggs 43)

ENGLAND WON BY AN INNINGS AND 98 RUNS

1886
ENGLAND WON SERIES 3-0

1st Test at Old Trafford
July 5,6,7
AUSTRALIA 205 (SP Jones 87 AH Jarvis 45 G Ulyett 4-46) and 123 (HJH Scott 47RG Barlow 7-44)
ENGLAND 223 (WW Read 51 FR Spofforth 4-82_ and 107-6

ENGLAND WON BY 4 WICKETS

2nd Test at Lord's
July 19,20,21
ENGLAND 353 (A Shrewsbury 164 W Barnes 58 FR Spofforth 4-73)
AUSTRALIA 121 (J Briggs 5-29) and 126 (GE Palmer 48 J Briggs 6-45)

ENGLAND WON BY AN INNINGS AND 106 RUNS

3rd Test at The Oval
August 12,13,14
ENGLAND 434 (WG Grace 170 WW Read 94 J Briggs 53 A Shrewsbury 44 FR Spofforth 4-65)
AUSTRALIA 68 (GA Lohmann 7-36) and 149 (G Giffen 47 G Lohmann 5-68)

ENGLAND WON BY AN INNINGS AND 217 RUNS

1886-87
ENGLAND WON SERIES 2-0

1st Test at Sydney
January 28,29,31
ENGLAND 45 (CTB Turner 6-15 JJ Ferris 4-27) and 184 (JJ Ferris 5-76)
AUSTRALIA 119 and 97 (W.Barnes 6-28)

ENGLAND WON BY 13 RUNS

2nd Test at Sydney
February 25,26,28, March 1
ENGLAND 151 (JJ Ferris 5-71 CTB Turner 5-41) and 154 (RG Barlow 42* JJ Ferris 4-69 CTB Turner 4-52)
AUSTRALIA 84 (GA Lohmann 8-35) and 150 (W Bates 4-26)

ENGLAND WON BY 71 RUNS

1887-88
Only test Sydney
February 10,1 (no play) 13 (no play) 14,15
ENGLAND 113 (A Shrewsbury 44 CTB Turner 5-44 JJ Ferris 4-60) and 137 (CTB Turner 7-43)
AUSTRALIA 42 (GA Lohmann 5-17 R Peel 5-18) and 82 (R Peel 5-40 GA Lohmann 4-35)

ENGLAND WON BY 126 RUNS

1888
ENGLAND WON SERIES 2-1

1st Test at Lord's
July 16,17
AUSTRALIA 16 (R Peel 4-36) and 60 (R Peel 4-14 GA Lohmann 4-33)
ENGLAND 53 (CTB Turner 5-27) and 62 (JJ Ferris 5-26 CTB Turner 5-36)

AUSTRALIA WON BY 61 RUNS

2nd Test at The Oval
August 13,14
AUSTRALIA 80 (J Briggs 5-25) and 100 (W Barnes 5-32 R Peel 4-49)
ENGLAND 317 (R Abel 70 W Barnes 62 GA Lohmann 62* CTB Turner 6-112)

ENGLAND WON BY AN INNINGS AND 137 RUNS

3rd Test at Old Trafford
August 30,31
ENGLAND 172 (CTB Turner 5-86)
AUSTRALIA 81 (R Peel 7-31) and 70 (R Peel 4-37)

ENGLAND WON BY AN INNINGS AND 21 RUNS

1890
ENGLAND WON SERIES 2-0

1st Test at Lord's
July 21,22,23
AUSTRALIA 132 (JJ Lyons 55 W Attewell 4-42) and 176 (JE Barrett 67*)
ENGLAND 173 (G Ulyett 74 JJ Lyons 5-30) and 137-3 (WG Grace 75*)

ENGLAND WON BY 7 WICKETS

2nd Test at The Oval
August 11, 12
AUSTRALIA 92 (F Martin 6-50) and 102 (F Martin 6-52)
ENGLAND 100 (JJ Ferris 4-25) and 95-8 (JJ Ferris 5-49)

ENGLAND WON BY 2 WICKETS

1891-92
AUSTRALIA WON SERIES 2-1

1st Test at Melbourne
January 1,2,4,5,6
AUSTRALIA 240 (W Bruce 57 AC Bannerman 45 JW Sharpe 6-84) and 236 (JJ Lyons 51 AC Bannerman 41 W Bruce 40)
ENGLAND 264 (WG Grace 50 G Bean 50 J Briggs 41 RW McLeod 5-55) and 158 (CTB Turner 5-51)

AUSTRALIA WON BY 54 RUNS

2nd Test at Sydney
January 29 30 February 1,2,3
AUSTRALIA 145 (JJ Lyons 41 GA Lohmann 8-58) and 391 (JJ Lyons 134 AC Bannerman 91 W Bruce 72 G Giffen 49 J Briggs 4-69)
ENGLAND 307 (R Abel 132* G Giffen 4-88) and 157 (AE Stoddart 69 G Giffen 6-72 CTB Turner 4-46)

AUSTRALIA WON BY 72 RUNS

3rd Test at Adelaide Oval
March 24,25,26,28
ENGLAND 499 (AE Stoddart 134 R Peel 83 WG Grace 58 W Attewell 43*)
AUSTRALIA 100 (J Briggs 6-49) and 169 (J Briggs 6-87)

ENGLAND WON BY AN INNINGS AND 230 RUNS

1893
ENGLAND WON SERIES 1-0

1st Test at Lord's
July 17,18,19
ENGLAND 334 (A Shrewsbury 106 FS Jackson 91 CTB Turner 6-67) and 234-8 dec (A Shrewsbury 81 W Gunn 77 G Giffen 5-43)
AUSTRALIA 269 (H Graham 107 SE Gregory 57 WH Lockwood 6-101)

MATCH DRAWN

2nd Test at The Oval
August 14,15,16
ENGLAND 483 (FS Jackson 103 AE Stoddart 83 WG Grace 68 A Shrewsbury 66, A Ward 55 WW Read 52 G Giffen 7-128)
AUSTRALIA 91 (J Briggs 5-34 WH Lockwood 4-37) and 349 (GHS Trott 92, AC Bannerman 55 G Giffen 53 H Graham 42 J Briggs 5-114 WH Lockwood 4-96)

ENGLAND WON BY AN INNINGS AND 43 RUNS

3rd Test at Old Trafford
August 24, 25,26
AUSTRALIA 204 (W Bruce 68 T.Richardson 5-49 J.Briggs 4-81) and 236 (AC Bannerman 60 T.Richardson 5-107)
ENGLAND 243 (W Gunn 102* WG Grace 40 G Giffen 4-113) and 18-4 (WG Grace 45 AE Stoddart 42)

MATCH DRAWN

1894-95
ENGLAND WON SERIES 3-2

1st Test at Sydney
December 14,15,17,18,19,20
AUSTRALIA 586 (SE Gregory 201 G Giffen 161 JM Blackham 74 T Richardson 5-181) and166 (J Darling 53 G Giffen 41 R Peel 6-67)
ENGLAND 325 (A Ward 75 J Briggs 57 W Brockwell 49 G Giffen 4-75) and 437 (A Ward 17 JT Brown 53 FGJ Ford 48 J Briggs 42 G Giffen 4-164)

ENGLAND WON BY 10 RUNS

2nd Test at Melbourne
December 29,31 January 1,2,3
ENGLAND 75 (CTB Turner 5-32) and 475 (AE Stoddart 173 R Peel 53 A Ward 41 G Giffen6-155)
AUSTRALIA 123 (T Richardson 5-57) and 333 (GHS Trott 95 FA Iredale 68 W Bruce 54 G Giffen 43 R Peel 4-77)

ENGLAND WON BY 94 RUNS

3rd Test at Adelaide Oval
January 11,12,14,15
AUSTRALIA 238 (G Giffen 58 GHS Trott 48 ST Callaway 41 T Richardson 5-75) and 411 (FA Iredale 140 W Brice 80 AE Trott 72* R Peel 4-96)
ENGLAND 124 (G Giffen 5-76 ST Callaway 5-37) and 143 (AE Trott 8-43)

AUSTRALIA WON BY 382 RUNS

4th Test at Sydney
February 1, 2 (no play) 4
AUSTRALIA 284 (H Graham 105 AE Trott 85* J Briggs 4-65)
ENGLAND 65 and 72 (G Giffen 5-26 CTB Turner 4-33)

AUSTRALIA WON BY AN INNINGS AND 147 RUNS

5th Test at Melbourne
March 1,2,4,5,6
AUSTRALIA 414 (J Darling 74 SE Gregory 70 G Giffen 57 JJ Lyons 55 GHS Trott 42 R Peel 4-14) and 267 (G Giffen 51 J Darling 50 GHS Trott 42 T Richardson 6-104)
ENGLAND 385 (AC MacLaren 120 R Peel 73 AE Stoddart 68 G Giffen 4-130 GHS Trott 4-71) and 298-4 (JT Brown 140 A Ward 93)

ENGLAND WON BY 6 WICKETS

1896
ENGLAND WON SERIES 2-1

1st Test at Lord's
June 22,23,24
AUSTRALIA 53 (T Richardson 6-39) and 347 (GHS Trott 143 SE Gregory 103 T Richardson 5-134 JT Hearne 5-76)
ENGLAND 292 (R Abel 94 WG Grace 66 FS Jackson 44) and 111-4

ENGLAND WON BY 6 WICKETS

2nd Test at Old Trafford
July 16,17,18
AUSTRALIA 412 (FA Iredale 108 G Giffen 80 GHS Trott 53 T Richardson 7-168) and 125-7 (T Richardson 6-76)
ENGLAND 231 (AFA Lilley 65* KS Ranjitsinhji 62) and 305 (KS Ranjitsinhji 154* AE Stoddart 41*)

AUSTRALIA WON BY 3 WICKETS

3rd Test at The Oval
August 10,11,12
ENGLAND 145 (FS Jackson 45 H Tumble 6-59) and 84 (H Trumble 6-30)
AUSTRALIA 19 (J Darling 47 JT Hearne 6-41) and 44 (R Peel 6-23)

ENGLAND WON BY 66 RUNS

1897-98
AUSTRALIA WON SERIES 4-1

1st Test at Sydney
December 13,14,15,16,17
ENGLAND 551 (KS Ranjitsinhji 175 AC MacLaren 109 TW Hayward 72 GH Hirst 62 W Storer 43) and 96-1 (AC MacLaren 50*)
AUSTRALIA 237 (H Trumble 70 CE McLeod 50* SE Gregory 46 JT Hearne 5-42) and 408 (J Darling 101 C Hill 96 JJ Kelly 46* JT Hearne 4-99)

ENGLAND WON BY 9 WICKETS

2nd Test at Melbourne
January 1,3,4,5
AUSTRALIA 520 (CE McLeod 112 FA Iredale 89 GHS Trott 79 SE Gregory 71 C Hill 58)
ENGLAND 315 (KS Ranjitsinhji 71 W Storer 51 J Briggs 46* NF Druce 44 H Trumble 4-54 and 150 (MA Noble 6-49 H Trumble 4-53)

AUSTRALIA WON BY AN INNINGS AND 55 RUNS

3rd Test at Adelaide Oval
January 14,15,17,18,19
AUSTRALIA 573 (J Darling 178 FA Iredale 84 C Hill 81 SE Gregory 52 T Richardson 4-164)
ENGLAND 278 (GH Hirst 85 TW Hayward 70 WP Howell 4-70) and 282 (AC MacLaren 124 KS Ranjitsinhji 77 MA Noble 5-84 CE McLeod 5-65)

AUSTRALIA WON BY AN INNINGS AND 13 RUNS

4th Test at Melbourne
January 29, 31 February 1,2
AUSTRALIA 323 (C Hill 188 H Trumble 46 JT Heane 6-98) and 115-2 (C McLeod 64*)
ENGLAND 174 (E Jones 4-56) and 263 (KS Ranjitsinhji 55 AC MacLaren 45)

AUSTRALIA WON BY 8 WICKETS

5th Test at Sydney
February 26, 28 March 1,2
ENGLAND 335 (AC MacLaren 65 NF Druce 64 E Wainwright 49 TW Hayward 47 W Storer 44 GH Hirst 44 E Jones 6-82) and 178 (TW Hayward 43 H Trumble 4-37)
AUSTRALIA 239 (CE McLeod 64 T Richardson 8-94) and 276-4 (J Darling 160 J Worrall 62)

AUSTRALIA WON BY 6 WICKETS

1899
AUSTRALIA WON SERIES 1-0

1st Test at Trent Bridge
Nottingham June 1,2,3
AUSTRALIA 252 (C Hill 52 SE Gregory 48 J Darling 47 MA Noble 41 W Rhodes 4-58 JT Hearne 4-71) and 230-8 dec (C Hill 80 MA Noble 45)
ENGLAND 193 (CB Fry 50 KS Ranjitsinhji 42 E Jones 5-88) and 155-7 (KS Ranjitsinhji 93*)

MATCH DRAWN

2nd Test at Lord's
June 15,16,17
ENGLAND 206 (FS Jackson 73 GL Jessop 51 E Jones 7-88) and 240 (AC MacLaren 88* TW Hayward 77)
AUSTRALIA 421 (C Hill 135 VT Trumper 135* MA Noble 54) and 28-0

AUSTRALIA WON BY 10 WICKETS

3rd Test at Headingley
Leeds June 29, 30 July 1 (no play)
AUSTRALIA 172 (J Worrall 76 HI Young 4-30) and 224 (H Trumble 56 F Laver 45 JT Hearne 4-50)
ENGLAND 220 (AFA Lilley 55 TW Hayward 40* H Trumble 5-60) and 19-0

MATCH DRAWN

4th Test at Old Trafford
July 17,18,19
ENGLAND 372 (TW Hayward 130 AFA Lilley 58 FS Jackson 44 HI Young 43) and 94-3 (KS Ranjitsinhji 49*)
AUSTRALIA 196 (MA Noble 60* H Trumble 44 WM Bradley 5-67 HI Young 4-79) and 346-7 dec (MA Noble 89 VT Trumper 63 J Worrall 53)

MATCH DRAWN

5th Test at The Oval
August 14,15,16
ENGLAND 576 (TW Hayward 137 FS Jackson 18 CB Fry 60 KS Ranjitsinhji 54 AC MacLaren 49 E Jones 4-164)
AUSTRALIA 352 (SE Gregory 117 J Darling 71 J Worrall 55 WH Lockwood 7-71) and 254-5 (CE McLeod 77 J Worrall 75 MA Noble 69*)

MATCH DRAWN

THE GOLDEN YEARS

1901-02

The English tour led by Archie MacLaren was the fifteenth and last under private management. A number of leading players were not available but the inclusion of Sydney Barnes, plucked out of league cricket with very little first-class experience and plunged straight into the turmoil of an Australian tour, was a surprise. Like the previous series in Australia in 1897-98, the Australians lost the first Test, but won the next four.

MacLaren scored a century in the first Test, making him the first batsman to score four Test centuries. It was the last by an England captain for nearly 60 years! Sydney Barnes took 5 for 65 on his debut in Australia's first innings whilst Len Braund, another England debutant in Sydney, scored a half-century and took seven wickets as the visitors won by an innings and 124 runs.

A record 25 wickets fell on the first day of the second Test in Melbourne on a rain-affected pitch, with England dismissed for 61 in just 68 minutes in their first innings. The first of Clem Hill's string of missed hundreds during the series came in the second innings, when he became the first Test batsman to be out for 99. Victorian Hugh Trumble, who had been a key player for over a decade, completed Australia's victory by 229 runs by taking a hat-trick.

500 RUNS IN A SERIES

Barnes, who had taken 19 wickets in the first two Tests, twisted his knee after just seven overs and his loss was critical to the balance of the match and the series. Clem Hill scored 98 and 97 to complete a bizarre sequence and he went on to become the first player to score 500 runs in a series without a century as Australia triumphed by four wickets.

In the fourth Test at Sydney, Victorian left-arm John Saunders made his Test debut, taking nine wickets, including 5 for 43 in England's second innings as they were bowled out for 99. It proved to be his only appearance in the series as he missed the final Test with a fractured collarbone. Australian wicket-keeper James Kelly took eight catches – the first

BEST FOOT FORWARD: ENGLAND'S SYDNEY BARNES SHOWS HOW IT SHOULD BE DONE

GREAT PLAYERS

Sydney Barnes

(England) 1901-14

Test Average *16.43*
Test Best *9-103 v. South Africa, Old Wanderers 1913*
Ashes Average *21.58*
Ashes Best *7-60, Sydney Cricket Ground 1908*

Sydney Barnes always seemed to be at loggerheads with officials and he missed at least five years during his peak (1902-07) because Test selectors found him so difficult to handle. But when he was bowling for England and he had it in his mind to get wickets, he was almost unplayable. Indeed many believe Barnes may have been the finest bowler of any era. In his first game for England on his first tour of Australia he took five wickets against South Australia, followed by 12 for 99 against Victoria, 5 for 65 in the first innings of the first Test and 13 for 163 in the second. Sadly, he broke down with a knee injury after seven overs of the third Test. In 1911-12 he took 34 wickets in the series. Recovering from flu at Melbourne, he took 5 for 44, though at one stage he had 5 for 6 including bowling Clem Hill with a ball that changed direction twice! In 27 Tests he took an amazing 189 wickets at 16.43 and in just seven Tests against South Africa he took 83 wickets including 34 in three matches of the 1912 Triangular series.

Test wicket-keeper to do so, and a record for more than 50 years until Gil Langley made nine dismissals at Lord's in 1956.

Australia, who won the toss for the first time in the series in the final meeting at Melbourne, failed on a pitch which several times changed character as showers occurred during the four days. England didn't fare much better and Australia through Clem Hill, who was missed twice during his stylish innings of 87, set about building a new lead. Needing 211 to win, England struggled against Noble and Trumble on a lifting pitch and lost by 32 runs.

1902

The Australians having dominated the home series a few months earlier travelled to England where they won yet again. Whilst the 2-1 result meant Australia had won four successive rubbers, the traumatic events of Old Trafford, linked for all time with the name of Fred Tate, and the exhilarating victory at The Oval,

inspired by Gilbert Jessop, have long tortured English cricket followers with what might have been.

This series began with the first Test to be staged at Edgbaston where after England had amassed a substantial total, Australia were shot out for just 36 after heavy rain – their lowest on record. Wilfred Rhodes was the pick of the English bowlers, taking 7 for 17. But the rain that had treated the tourists so unkindly returned to save them.

The second Test at Lord's was spoilt by constant rain, play being limited to a total of just 105 minutes on the first day. However, the opening overs were certainly not without sensation as Hopkins dismissed Fry and Ranjitsinhji without a run on the board. Jackson (55 not out) had made just one when he was dropped at slip, but he and MacLaren who made 47, were still there when the match was abandoned.

The third match was the only Test ever played at Bramall Lane, the home of Sheffield United Football Club. Played against a drab background in appalling light, Australia gained a first innings lead of 49 before Trumper and Hill decided the issue by aggressive batting, sweeping aside the combined efforts of Barnes, Hirst, Braund, Jackson and Rhodes. The 339 target left for England to win proved too much. ▶

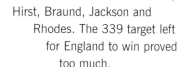

GILBERT JESSOP OF GLOUCESTERSHIRE AND ENGLAND

Victor Trumper
(Australia) 1938-48

Test Average *39.05*
Test Best *214 v. South Africa, Adelaide Oval 1911*
Ashes Average *32.8*
Ashes Best *185 v. England, Sydney Cricket Ground 1903*

Victor Trumper was not prolific like Don Bradman, he was simply the best batsman of his time. Indeed, there are some who believe him to have been better than Bradman! A batsman capable of destroying any attack under any conditions, he had every stroke in the book and a few others of his own invention. In the wet English summer of 1902, Trumper was a sensation, scoring 2,570 runs, including 11 centuries. At Old Trafford in the fourth Test he became the first player to make a century before lunch. It was the pinnacle of his career. Against England in 1903-04 he made 185 not out in the first Test, 74 out of a team total of 122 on a difficult pitch in the second, 113 and 59 in the third and 88 in the fifth. At Sydney in 1907-08 he made 166 against England whilst in 191-12 in his last series, also against England he scored his final Test century in the first Test and 50 in his last innings. Trumper's death from Bright's Disease in 1915 at the age of 37 was universally mourned and forced even the War news off the front pages.

THE RESULTS

ENGLAND v AUSTRALIA
Played at The Oval, August 11-13 1902

AUSTRALIA

VT Trumper	b Hirst	42	run out	2
RA Duff	c Lilley b Hirst	23	b Lockwood	6
C Hill	b Hirst	11	c MacLaren b Hirst	34
J Darling	c Lilley b Hirst	3	c MacLaren b Lockwood	15
MA Noble	c and b Jackson	52	b Braund	13
SE Gregory	b Hirst	23	b Braund	9
WW Armstrong	b Jackson	17	b Lockwood	21
A Hopkins	c MacLaren b Lockwood	40	c Lilley b Lockwood	3
H Trumble	not out	64	not out	7
JJ Kelly	c Rhodes b Braund	39	lbw b Lockwood	0
JV Saunders	lbw b Braund	0	c Tyldesley b Rhodes	2
Extras		10		9
Total		**324**		**121**

Fall of wickets 1-47 2-63 3-69 4-82 5-126 6-174 7-175 8-256 9-324 10-324
Second Innings 1-6 2-9 3-31 4-71 5-75 6-91 7-99 8-114 9-115 10-121

England Bowling (4-ball overs)

	O	M	R	W	O	M	R	W
Lockwood	24	2	85	1	20	6	45	5
Rhodes	28	9	46	0	22	7	38	1
Hirst	29	5	77	5	5	1	7	1
Braund	16.5	5	29	2	9	1	15	2
Jackson	20	4	66	2	4	3	7	0
Jessop	6	2	11	0				

ENGLAND

AC MacLaren	c Armstrong b Trumble	10	b Saunders	2
LCH Palairet	b Trumble	20	b Saunders	6
JT Tyldesley	b Trumble	33	b Saunders	0
TW Hayward	b Trumble	0	c Kelly b Saunders	7
Hon FS Jackson	c Armstrong b Saunders	2	c and b Trumble	49
LC Braund	c Hill b Trumble	22	c Kelly b Trumble	2
GL Jessop	b Trumble	13	c Noble b Armstrong	104
GH Hirst	c and b Trumble	43	not out	58
WH Lockwood	c Noble b Saunders	25	lbw b Trumble	2
AA Lilley	c Trumper b Trumble	0	c Darling b Trumble	16
W Rhodes	not out	0	not out	6
Extras		15		11
Total		**183**		**263-9**

Fall of wickets 1-31 2-36 3-62 4-67 5-67 6-83 6-137 8-179 9-183 10-183
Second Innings 1-5 2-5 3-10 4-31 5-48 6-157 7-187 8-214 9-248

Australia Bowling

	O	M	R	W	O	M	R	W
Trumble	31	13	65	8	33.5	4	108	4
Saunders	23	7	79	2	24	3	105	4
Noble	7	3	24	0	5	0	11	0
Armstrong	-	-	-	-	4	0	28	1

ENGLAND WON BY 1 WICKET

A CHANCE THROWN AWAY

At Old Trafford in the fourth Test, Victor Trumper, who made 104, became the first player to score a century before lunch on the first day of a Test. He and Duff posted 135 for the first wicket – a record for Australia – in 78 minutes. The Australian captain Joe Darling, who hit Test cricket's first six in Adelaide four years earlier, hit another two sixes in his half-century – they were the first sixes in Tests in England. Australia, 37 ahead on first innings, were struggling at 10 for 3 in their second innings. Then Darling was dropped on the square leg boundary by the debutant Tate and the score was advanced to 64 before another wicket fell. Then Australian wickets tumbled quickly and England were left needing 124 for victory. With Trumble and Saunders bowling extremely well, four runs were needed as last man Tate joined Rhodes. Here was the perfect chance for him to redeem himself but he was bowled by a quicker ball from Saunders and never played Test cricket again, although his son Maurice would go on to become an outstanding Test bowler.

JESSOP'S MATCH

Known as 'Jessop's match', the final Test at The Oval was altered by England's success in avoiding the follow-on on a wet pitch which was worsening under a warm sun. England looked hopelessly placed in the fourth innings at 48 for 5 with 263 wanted but Jessop arrived to complete an astonishing hundred in 75 minutes – then the fastest on record in Test cricket. With his departure, caught at short leg off Armstrong, much responsibility fell on Hirst. When Rhodes joined his fellow Yorkshireman for England's last wicket, 15 runs were needed for victory. The runs were not obtained in singles, as legend has it, but the last wicket partnership did take England to victory, despite Hugh Trumble's 8 for 65 and 4 for 108, the first Australian to score a 50 and take 10 wickets in the same Test.

1903-04

The England side for this series was the first to be selected and managed by the Marylebone Cricket Club. Pelham 'Plum' Warner, who was to become a central figure in the 'Bodyline' series almost 30 years later, was the England captain. Australia, after winning four consecutive series, were overthrown by the extraordinary variety of the English attack in which Bernard Bosanquet's googlies were the decisive factor.

THE HIGHEST SCORE ON DEBUT

The first Test was remarkable for two of the greatest innings ever played. 'Tip' Foster scored 287 on debut for England, setting a string of records. It was the record Test score until 1929-30 when Sandham scored 325. It remains the highest by a player in his first Test, the highest for England in Australia and the record for any Test in Sydney. He was also the first batsman to share in three century partnerships in the same Test innings, and his 10th wicket stand of 130 with Wilfred Rhodes is still the record in Ashes Tests. His knock gave England a big first innings lead before Victor Trumper helped set England a size-able fourth innings task with an unbeaten 185. England proved equal to the challenge, and won by five wickets. A section of the crowd demonstrated against the umpire when Hill was run out and only a personal appeal by Australian captain Noble dissuaded 'Plum' Warner from withdrawing his team.

RHODES' RECORD

England won the second Test at Melbourne through getting in their first innings before the rain came, with Lancashire's John Tyldesley falling three runs short of a century. Wilfred Rhodes then took an England record 15 wickets – this despite having eight catches dropped from his bowling!

▶

THE RESULTS

AUSTRALIA v ENGLAND
Played at Sydney, December 11-17 1903

AUSTRALIA

RA Duff	c Lilley b Arnold	3	c Relf b Rhodes	84
VT Trumper	c Foster b Arnold	1	not out	185
C Hill	c Lilley b Hirst	5	run out	51
MA Noble	c Foster b Arnold	133	st Lilley b Bosanquet	22
WW Armstrong	b Bosanquet	48	c Bosanquet b Rhodes	27
AJ Hopkins	b Hirst	39	c Arnold b Rhodes	20
WP Howell	c Relf b Arnold	5	c Lilley b Arnold	4
SE Gregory	b Bosanquet	23	c Lilley b Rhodes	43
F Laver	lbw b Rhodes	4	c Relf b Rhodes	6
JJ Kelly	c Braund b Rhodes	10	b Arnold	13
JV Saunders	not out	11	run out	2
Extras		3		28
Total		**285**		**485**

Fall of wickets	1-2 2-9 3-12 4-118 5-200 6-207 7-259 8-263 9-266 10-285
2nd Innings	1-36 2-108 3-191 4-254 5-334 6-393 7-441 8-468 9-473 10-485

England Bowling (4-ball overs)

	O	M	R	W	O	M	R	W
Hirst	24	8	47	2	29	1	79	0
Arnold	32	7	76	4	28	3	93	2
Braund	26	9	39	0	12	2	56	0
Bosanquet	13	0	52	2	24	1	100	1
Rhodes	17.2	3	41	2	40.2	10	94	5
Relf	6	1	27	0	13	5	35	0

ENGLAND

PF Warner	c Kelly b Laver	0	b Howell	8
TW Hayward	b Howell	15	st Kelly b Saunders	91
JT Tyldesley	b Noble	53	c Noble b Saunders	9
EG Arnold	c Laver b Armstrong	27		
RE Foster	c Noble b Saunders	287	st Kelly b Armstrong	19
LC Braund	b Howell	102	c Noble b Howell	0
GH Hirst	b Howell	0	not out	60
BJT Bosanquet	c Howell b Noble	2	not out	1
AA Lilley	c Hill b Noble	4		
AE Relf	c Armstrong b Saunders	31		
W Rhodes	not out	40		
Extras		16		6
Total		**577**		**194 for 5**

Fall of wickets	1-0 2-49 3-73 4-117 5-309 6-311 7-318 8-332 9-447 10-577
2nd Innings	1-21 2-39 3-81 4-82 5-181

Australia Bowling

	O	M	R	W	O	M	R	W
Saunders	36.2	8	126	2	18.5	3	51	2
Laver	37	12	116	1	16	4	37	0
Howell	31	7	113	3	31	18	35	2
Noble	34	8	99	3	12	2	37	0
Armstrong	23	3	47	1	18	6	28	1
Hopkins	11	1	40	0	-	-	-	-
Trumper	7	1	12	0	-	-	-	-
Gregory	2	0	8	0	-	-	-	-

ENGLAND WON BY 5 WICKETS

Wilfred Rhodes (England)1899-1930

Test Average *26.97*
Test Best 8-68 *v. Australia, Melbourne Cricket Ground 1904*
Ashes Average *24.00*
Ashes Best *(see above)*

Wilfred Rhodes took more first-class wickets than anyone ever has. He alone has a total of over 4000 wickets and he alone has taken a hundred wickets in a season 23 times. His career lasted 30 years and in that time he transformed himself from a bowler who batted at 10 or 11 to the regular opening partner of Jack Hobbs. The Yorkshireman was already in relative decline when he visited Australia in 1903-04 – he took 15 for 124 on a sticky at Melbourne, a game in which he also had eight chances missed off him. Then at Sydney he bowled 40.2 overs to take 5 for 94 as Trumper went on a rampage against the other England bowlers. He ended the series with 31 wickets at 15.74 runs apiece. In 1911-12, Rhodes didn't take a single wicket but averaged 57.87 with the bat and at Melbourne he and Hobbs put

on the English first-wicket partnership of 323. In 1926 at the age of 48, Rhodes did the 'double' for the 16th and final record-setting time. He was recalled for the Oval Test against Australia – his 45 overs brought him 6 for 79 and the Ashes!

In the third Test at Adelaide, Trumper and Syd Gregory became the first players to score four centuries against England whilst Clem Hill, who struggled throughout the series despite hitting 88 in the first innings, became the first batsman to reach 2,000 Test runs. Needing 494 to win, England's opening batsmen Warner and Hayward started well and put on 148 for the first wicket but then an unaccountable batting collapse saw Australia win by 216 runs.

Winning the toss in the vital fourth Test, England again faltered, but a fine defensive innings by Albert Knight dominated a recovery. The Australians, handicapped by rain that quickened the wicket and mesmerised by Bosanquet, who took 6 for 51 in Australia's second innings, never got into the game. Again there were crowd demonstrations, provoked this time by the stoppages.

In the fifth Test, England had the same wretched luck with the weather as the Australians had had in the second and were easily beaten. Albert 'Tibby' Cotter,

ENGLAND IN AUSTRALIA 1903-04: (BACK ROW, L-R) ARTHUR LILLEY, ALBERT KNIGHT, ARTHUR FIELDER, TED ARNOLD, ALBERT RELF, LEN BRAUND; (MIDDLE ROW, L-R) JOHNNY TYLDESLEY, RE FOSTER, PELHAM WARNER, GEORGE HIRST, BERNARD BOSANQUET, THOMAS HAYWARD; (FRONT ROW, L-R) BERT STRUDWICK, WILFRED RHODES

appearing in his second Test at 19, had batsmen taking evasive action and finished with eight wickets. Hugh Trumble's career came to an end with 7 for 28 in the second innings, including the second hat-trick of his Test career. The final Test was also a milestone for Monty Noble, who reached the Test double of 1,000 runs and 100 wickets, as George Giffen had done seven years earlier

1905

This became known as 'Jackson's Year' with FS (Stanley) Jackson leading England to victory over an Australian side that again looked a strong one, but with the bowling weakened by the decline of Noble, was below their usual Test match standard. Jackson won the toss in each of the five Tests, headed the batting averages with 70.28 and the bowling averages with 15.46.

Some fast bumpers from 'Tibby' Cotter gave Australia an encouraging start at Trent Bridge but Jessop replied in kind and the bumpers were withheld from then on. England amassed 426 for 5 declared in their second innings, before Bosanquet struck with his googly, taking 8 for 107 to give England victory by 213 runs. Bosanquet played in only seven Tests, and this was his finest performance. Also in this match former England captain Archie MacLaren scored a record fifth Test century – the first at the Nottingham ground.

The second Test at Lord's, though drawn, went very much in England's favour. Ten days of wet weather plus thunderstorms on each night of the match, left the pitch helpful to bowlers. Fry spent almost four hours over his 73 but when Australia batted, Trumper and Duff hit a swift 57 before the pitch dried to an awkward state. Following a sudden flurry of quick wickets, Darling and Armstrong managed to avoid the follow-on. MacLaren played a fine attacking innings of 79, ▶

1905 BECAME KNOWN AS 'JACKSON'S YEAR', AFTER ENGLAND CAPTAIN STANLEY JACKSON

leaving England 252 ahead, but the final day was washed out.

Another drawn Test at Headingley saw Stanley Jackson score the first Test century at the famous Yorkshire ground. Arnold Warren playing in his only Test, bagged the wicket of Victor Trumper cheaply twice. John Tyldesley scored 100 in England's second innings, which Jackson declared at 295 for 5, 401 ahead. Many critics felt he should have declared sooner but Blythe took three early wickets and only his dropping of a catch from Noble scuppered England's drive for victory.

PLAY STOPPED, RAIN

At Old Trafford, Stanley Jackson got his second Test century in successive matches as England totalled 446. By lunch on the second day, Australia were 27 for 3, Brearley having bowled with exceptional speed, but a fine innings by Darling, whose hits regularly scattered the inhabitants of the press box, took Australia to 197. Following-on, Australia were 118 for 1 at the end of the second day but wickets were lost with such abandon that the match was all over by lunch on the third and final day. When minutes later rain began to fall, cricket fans everywhere wondered why Australia had not fought harder for a draw.

The Hon. FS Jackson, born the same day as Darling the Australian captain, won his fifth successive toss and for the fifth time in the series, England batted first. Fry at last showed the visitors how he won his great reputation with an innings of 144. The Oval Test was to be the last appearance for Australian opener Reggie Duff, whose 146 gave him the distinction of being the first player to score a century in both his first and last Tests between Australia and England. Another century by Tyldesley enabled Jackson to declare at 261 for 6 but Australia played out time without much trouble.

1907-08

The extraordinary depth and resilience of the Australian batting finally mastered an England attack that relied chiefly on pace. England were also unsettled in this series by captaincy problems, with appointed captain Arthur Jones of Notts missing the first three Tests after falling ill in Brisbane. In his absence, opening batsman Frederick Fane took over the leadership, becoming the first Essex player to captain England.

Due to Jones' illness, another Nottinghamshire batsman, George

THE SECOND TEST AT MELBOURNE SAW THE DEBUT OF ONE OF ENGLAND'S GREATEST PLAYERS, JACK HOBBS

Gunn, made an unexpected debut in the first Test at Sydney. Although not an official member of the touring party, Gunn made the most of his opportunity, top-scoring with 119 and 74. Set 275 to win, Australia slumped to 219 for 8 before 'Tibby' Cotter and 19-year-old debutant Gerry Hazlitt, added the 56 runs required for a two-wicket victory. Charlie Macartney, known as the 'Governor General', made the first of his 35 appearances – he was to play in all five Tests occupying six different batting positions during the series.

HOBBS' DEBUT

The second Test marked the debut of one of England's greatest players, Jack Hobbs, who went on to play in 41 Tests against Australia. He scored 83

and with Ken Hutchings hitting a fine 126, England made 382. Australia's second innings saw five of their batsmen score half-centuries, leaving England 282 to win. Though acting captain Frederick Fane made 50, it was the English tail that wagged, the last pair putting on 39 runs for victory.

In the third Test, England, after outplaying Australia for more than three days, were demoralised in the hosts' second innings by an eighth wicket stand of 243 between Clem Hill and Roger Hartigan. Hill, who dropped down the batting order in the second innings because of influenza, made 160, the highest score for anyone batting at No.9 in a Test. Hartigan, who made 116, became the fourth Australian to score a century on debut. Needing 428 for victory, England were bowled out for 183 with Saunders and O'Connor taking five wickets apiece.

England's hopes of retaining the Ashes were washed away with a rain-affected wicket on day two of the fourth Test at Melbourne, leaving the visitors 105 all out in their first innings in reply to Australia's 214. But they hit back so well that the Australians slumped to 77 for 5. However, Warwick Armstrong with 133 not out helped the Australian total reach 385. England, chasing 495 to win, were bowled out for 186 to give Australia the Ashes.

With Sydney Barnes taking 7 for 60, Australia were bowled out for just 137 on the first day of the final Test and with England ending the day on 116 for 1, Arthur Jones' decision to put Australia in could be said to be successful. But then rain interruptions on the second and third days meant that England had to be satisfied with a lead of 144 on the first innings. But again the Australian batting, led by Trumper who made 166 came back to ensure victory as England, chasing 279 for victory, were bowled out for 229.

1909

Australia began their tour badly and were beaten in the first Test. They had, however, brought a side of considerable all-round strength, and of players new to England. Vernon Ransford nearly always made runs and Warren Bardsley and Charles Macartney did well. Brilliant fielding and the astute leadership of Noble finally saw them to victory.

England won the first Test by 10 wickets but as the scores reflect, rain beforehand dictated the course of the match. Australia found the swerve of Hirst and the spin of Blythe too much and were bowled out for 74. A fourth wicket stand of 48 between Tyldesley and Jones was the major stand of England's innings in a total of 121. In Australia's second innings, England's two left-arm bowlers again had their way and the hosts were left with 105 to make for victory. Hobbs and Fry, who both went first ball to Macartney in the first innings, were unbeaten as England gained a surprisingly resounding victory by 10 wickets.

ARMSTRONG 6 FOR 35

The turning point in the series came in the second Test at Lord's, when Australia won comfortably by 9 wickets. England did well to total 269 after being put in to bat with John King, a 38-year-old left-hand batsman from Leicestershire, top-scoring with 60. England though had no fast bowler in their side and Australia, helped by dropped catches, gained a lead of 81 after Ransford made an unbeaten 143. Operating from the Nursery end with the slope helping his leg-breaks, Warwick Armstrong produced his best-ever Test figures of 6 for 35 as England were dismissed for 121.

England made six changes for the third Test at Headingley and this proved the decisive game. The wicket gave the bowlers a chance and England began confidently getting Australia out for 188

and then reaching 137 for 2 in reply. Then Macartney with 7 for 58 ran through the side. The struggle proved completely absorbing as Australia fought to set England a formidable fourth innings target and it was Macartney who provided the stability when Australia were in trouble at 127 for 7. Set 214 to win, England reached 56 for 2 overnight but then collapsed at the hands of Cotter and Macartney.

One up, Australia concentrated on avoiding defeat at Old Trafford after Barnes and Blythe had taken five wickets apiece in their first innings total of 147. At the age of 39, Victorian medium-pacer Frank Laver – chosen on the tour as player/manager – took 8 for 31 in 18.2 overs in England's first innings total of 119. Rain restricted play on the ▶

THE 'GOVERNOR-GENERAL:
CHARLES MACARTNEY OF AUSTRALIA
KEEPS HIS EYE ON THE BALL

AS ENGLAND REACHED 137 FOR 2 IN THE THIRD TEST AT HEADINGLEY MACARTNEY STRUCK, TAKING 7 FOR 58

Jack Hobbs
(England) 1908-30

Test Average 56.95
Test Best 211 v. South Africa, Lord's 1924
Ashes Average 54.27
Ashes Best 187 v. Australia, Adelaide Oval 1912

Jack Hobbs was one of the finest batsmen ever to play the game – he scored over 61,000 runs and 197 first-class hundreds, despite losing five years to World War One. It is a tribute to his skill that he made 98 of them after he had turned 40, when most batsmen were ready to retire! The partnership of Hobbs and Sutcliffe was remarkable for their understanding of each other's running and their joint mastery of difficult pitches, such as that at The Oval in 1926 when England won back the Ashes. On a drying pitch they made 172 together, Hobbs' 100 coming through the worst of difficulties and steering England to victory. In the 1920s, he stood supreme on all pitches against all types of bowling and when he was taken ill with appendicitis during the 1921 series against Australia, it was akin to a national disaster. It was almost incidental that he was the first man to score 5000 Test runs. His skill allied to his unfailingly gentlemanly conduct on and off the pitch makes him a true cricketing great. He was knighted in 1953.

second day and then Noble allowed Australia's second innings to continue until England were left with only two-and-a-half hours to make 308 for victory.

Noble won the toss for Australia for the fifth time in the series, as Jackson had done for England in 1905. Bardsley, who went on to become the first batsman ever to make two centuries in a Test, made 136 in Australia's total of 325, whilst a grossly overbowled Carr, still in his first season of county cricket, took 5 for 146. On a final day lacking in urgency, Australia batted until hardly more than two hours' play remained with Bardsley and Gregory posting 180 for the first wicket – a record for Australia until 1964.

1911-12

Engand's appointed captain, 'Plum' Warner, fell ill early in the tour and JWHT 'Johnny Won't Hit Today' Douglas led the side throughout the five-match series including in his debut first Test in Sydney. Three years after he won an Olympic Games gold medal as a middleweight boxer! The series, which England won 4-1 to regain the Ashes, will always be remembered for the great bowling of Frank Foster and Sydney Barnes, but a decisive battle had to be fought by the England batsmen before these two bowlers could triumph.

There was barely a clue in the first Test in Sydney that England were to run away with the series as Australia ended the first day on 317 for 5. Trumper went on to score 113 – it was his eighth Test century and his sixth against England – more than any other player to that time. Leg spinner Herbert 'Ranji' Hordern, who toured England with an American side known as 'The Gentlemen of Philadelphia' in 1907 was the first Australian to develop the googly and bowling with uncanny accuracy for a bowler of his kind he took 12 wickets as Australia won by 146 runs.

A famous opening spell by Syd Barnes gave England a grip on the match which they never relinquished. Unwell before the match and forced to rest after nine overs, Barnes at one time had figures of 11-7-6-5 – his victims being Bardsley, Kellaway, Hill and Minnett. From 38 for 6 Australia fought back and Barnes was booed for taking his time in placing his field and for a time he refused to bowl. For England, Jack Hearne was the only England batsman to play Hordern with any assurance and he made 114 of their total of 265. Armstrong batted forcibly in Australia's second innings but with Hobbs making an unbeaten 126, the first of his 12 centuries against Australia, England won by 8 wickets.

In the third Test at Adelaide, England were ahead on first innings before losing a wicket after Foster and Barnes had bowled the home side out for 133 on a fast pitch. Hobbs and Rhodes took the score to 147 before the latter departed whilst Hobbs went on to make 187, the highest of his centuries against Australia. Australia fought back magnificently to

ENGLAND IN AUSTRALIA: (BACK ROW, L-R) BERT STRUDWICK, SEP KINNEIR, TIGER SMITH, FRANK WOOLLEY, JIM IREMONGER, PHIL MEAD, 'YOUNG' JACK HEARNE, BILL HITCH, JOSEPH VINE; (FRONT ROW, L-R) SYDNEY BARNES, WILFRED RHODES, JOHNNY DOUGLAS, PELHAM WARNER, FRANK FOSTER, JACK HOBBS, GEORGE GUNN

total 476 in their second innings with nightwatchman Carter making 72. England's target of 112 might have been more demanding had Trumper not been forced to bat at No.11 after taking a fierce drive by Woolley on the leg.

At Melbourne, venue of the fourth Test, Douglas put Australia in and the Foster-Barnes combination had done its work by late afternoon. England's openers Hobbs and Rhodes scored 178 and 179 respectively – their partnership of 323 remains England's best for any wicket in Australia. Rain during the third night freshened the wicket and Douglas rammed home his decision to field first by taking half the wickets, the final one bringing the Ashes back home to England.

The final Test at Sydney, although interrupted by rain, proved the most even contest. Hordern worried all

the England batsmen but a century by Frank Woolley ensured a final total of 324. His unbeaten 133 was the first century by an England left-hander in Australia. Though the Australian batting again failed, Hordern's googlies gave them a chance and with 363 wanted for victory, they reached 193 for 3 on the fifth day. Then came more rain and England won by 70 runs.

1912

The experiment of running a triangular tournament between England, Australia and South Africa proved a failure, partly because of a disastrously wet summer. The overall result of the tournament hinged on the third Test – match nine of the tournament at The Oval. And to ensure a result the encounter was

declared a 'timeless Test' – the first to be staged in England. England won the match and the tournament.

Rain ruined the drawn first Test at Lord's, although Jack Hobbs managed to add another century to his record book in England's total of 310 for 7 declared. For Australia Charles Macartney missed out on another Test hundred by just one run as Australia replied with 282 for 7.

Rain also hit the second Test at Old Trafford, with a total of just 300 minutes play on the first two days and not a ball bowled on the third. Wilfred Rhodes was the pick of the English batsmen with an innings of 92 in their total of 203

In this play-to-a-finish Test, England set up their victory with a 134-run lead on the first innings. Australia were bowled out for 111 – thanks to Barnes' 5 for 30 and Woolley's 5 for 29 – with the last eight wickets falling for just 21 runs. Fry, who trod on his stumps without actually dislodging the bails, made 79 in England's second innings but with Gerry Hazlitt taking 7 for 25, including the last five wickets for one run, England were bowled out for 175 leaving Australia 310 to win. In an inglorious second innings, Australia was dismissed for 65 with Woolley taking 5 for 20 and Dean 4 for 19.

ENGLAND SET UP THEIR VICTORY IN THE PLAY-TO-A-FINISH TEST WITH A 134-RUN LEAD ON THE FIRST INNNINGS

1901-02

AUSTRALIA WON SERIES 4-1

1st Test at Sydney

December 13,14,16

ENGLAND 464 (AC MacLaren 116 AFA Lilley 84 TW Hayward 69 LC Braund 58 CE McLeod 4-84)

AUSTRALIA 168 (SE Gregory 48 C Hill 46 SF Barnes 5-65) and 172 (SE Gregory 43 LC Braund 5-61 C Blythe 4-30)

ENGLAND WON BY AN INNINGS AND 124 RUNS

2nd Test at Melbourne

January 1,2,3,4

AUSTRALIA 112 (SF Barnes 6-42 C Blythe 4-64) and 353 (RA Duff 104 C Hill 99 WW Armstrong 45* SF Barnes 7-121)

ENGLAND 61 (MA Noble 7-17) and 175 (JT Tyldesley 66, MA Noble 6-60 H Trumble 4-49)

AUSTRALIA WON BY 229 RUNS

3rd Test at Adelaide Oval

January 17,18,20,21,22,23

ENGLAND 388 (LC Brand 103* TW Hayward 90 WG Quaife 68 AC MacLaren 67) and 247(TW Hayward 47 AC MacLaren 44 WG Quaife 44 H Trumble 6-74)

AUSTRALIA 321 (C Hill 98 VT Trumper 65 SE Gregory 55 RA Duff 43 JR Gunn 5-76) and 315-6 (C Hill 97 J Darling 69 H Trumble 62*)

AUSTRALIA WON BY 4 WICKETS

4th Test at Sydney

February 14,15,17,18

ENGLAND 317 (AC MacLaren 92 JT Tyldesley 79 TW Hayward 41 AFA Lilley 40 JV Saunders 4-119) and 99 (MA Noble 5-54 JV Saunders 5-43)

AUSTRALIA 299 (MA Noble 56 WW Armstrong 55 AJY Hopkins 43 LC Braund 4-118) GL Jessop 4-68) and 121-3 (RA Duff 51*)

AUSTRALIA WON BY 7 WICKETS

5th Test at Melbourne

February 28 March 1,3,4

AUSTRALIA 144 (TW Hayward 4-22 JR Gunn 4-38) and 255 (C Hill 87 SE Gregory 41LC Braund 5-95)

ENGLAND 189 (AFA Lilley 41 H Trumble 5-62) and 178 (AC MacLaren 49 MA Noble 6-98)

AUSTRALIA WON BY 32 RUNS

1902

AUSTRALIA WON SERIES 2-1

1st Test at Edgbaston

May 29, 30,31

ENGLAND 376-9 dec (JT Tyldesley 138 Hon FS Jackson 53 WH Lockwood 52* GH Hirst 48)

AUSTRALIA36 (W Rhodes 7-17) and 46-2

MATCH DRAWN

2nd Test at Lord's

June 12, 13(no play), 14 (no play)

ENGLAND 102-2 (Hon FS Jackson 55* AC MacLaren 47*)

AUSTRALIA did not bat

MATCH DRAWN

3rd Test at Bramall Lane, Sheffield

July 3,4,5

AUSTRALIA 194 (MA Noble 47 SF Barnes 6-49) and 289 (C Hill 119, VT Trumper 62AJY Hopkins 40* W Rhodes 5-63)

ENGLAND 145 (JV Saunders 5-50 MA Noble 5-51) and 195 (AC MacLaren 63 GL Jessop 55 MA Noble 6-52 H Trumble 4-49)

AUSTRALIA WON BY 143 RUNS

4th Test at Old Trafford

July 24,25,26

AUSTRALIA 299 (VT Trumper 104 C Hill 65 RA Duff 54 J Darling 51 WH Lockwood 6-48 W.Rhodes 4-104) and 86 (WH Lockwood 5-28)

ENGLAND 262 (Hon FS Jackson 128 LC Braund 65 H Trumble 4-75) and 120 (H Trumble 6-53 JV Saunders 4-52)

AUSTRALIA WON BY 3 RUNS

5th Test at The Oval

August 11,12,13

AUSTRALIA 324 (H Trumble 64* MA Noble 52 VT Trumper 42 AJY Hopkins 40 GH Hirst 5-77) and 121 (WH Lockwood 5-45)

ENGLAND 183 (GH Hirst 43 H Trumble 8-65) and 263-9 (GL Jessop 104 GH Hirst 58 Hon FS Jackson 49 H Trumble 4-108 JV Saunders 4-105)

ENGLAND WON BY 1 WICKET

1903-04

ENGLAND WON SERIES 3-2

1st Test at Sydney

December 11, 12, 14, 15, 16, 17

AUSTRALIA 285 (MA Noble 133, WW Armstrong 48, EG Arnold 4-76) and 485 (VT Trumper 185* RA Duff 84 C Hill 51 SE Gregory 43 W Rhodes 5-94)

ENGLAND 577 (RE Foster 287 LC Braund 102 JT Tyldesley 53 W Rhodes 40*) and 194-5 (TW Hayward 91 GH Hirst 60*)

ENGLAND WON BY 5 WICKETS

2nd Test at Melbourne

January 1, 2, 4,5

ENGLAND 315 (JT Tyldesley 97 PF Warner 68 TW Hayward 58 RE Foster 49 ret ill H Trumble 4-107 WP Howell 4-43) and 103 (JT Tyldesley 62 H Trumble 5-34)

AUSTRALIA 122 (VT Trumper 74 W Rhodes 7-56) and 111 (W Rhodes 8-68)

ENGLAND WON BY 185 RUNS

3rd Test at Adelaide Oval

January 15, 16, 18, 19, 20

AUSTRALIA 388 (VT Trumper 113 C Hill 88 RA Duff 79 MA Noble 59) and 351(SE Gregory 112 MA Noble 65 VT Trumper 59 BJT Bosanquet 4-73)

ENGLAND 245 (GH Hirst 58 PF Warner 48) and 278 (PF Warner 79 TW Hayward 67 GH Hirst 44 AJY Hopkins 4-81)

AUSTRALIA WON BY 216 RUNS

4th Test at Sydney

February 26, 27,29 (no play) March 1, 2, 3

ENGLAND 249 (AE Knight 70* M Noble 7-100) and 210 (TW Hayward 52)

AUSTRALIA 131 (RA Duff 47 W Rhodes 4-33 EG Arnold 4-28) and 171 (MA Noble 53* BJT Bosanquet 6-51)

ENGLAND WON BY 157 RUNS

5th Test at Melbourne

March 5, 7, 8

AUSTRALIA 247 (VT Trumper 88 LC Braund 8-81) and 133 (GH Hirst 5-48)

ENGLAND 61 (A Cotter 6-40 MA Noble 4-19) and 101 (H Trumble 7-28)

AUSTRALIA WON BY 218 RUNS

1905

ENGLAND WON SERIES

1st Test at Trent Bridge

May 29, 30, 31

ENGLAND 196 (JT Tyldesley 56 F Laver 7-64) and 426-5 dec (AC MacLaren 140 Hon FS Jackson 82* JT Tyldesley 61 TW Hayward 47)

AUSTRALIA 221 (C Hill 54 MA Noble 50 A Cotter 45 Hon FS Jackson 5-52) and 188 (SE Gregory 51 J Darling 40 BJT Bosanquet 8-107)

ENGLAND WON BY 213 RUNS

2nd Test at Lord's

June 15,16,17 (no play)

ENGLAND 282 (CB Fry 73 AC MacLaren 56 JT Tyldesley 43) and 151-5 (AC MacLaren 79)

AUSTRALIA 181 (J Darling 41 Hon FS Jackson 4-50)

MATCH DRAWN

3rd Test at Headingley, Leeds

July 3, 4, 5

ENGLAND 301 (Hon FS Jackson 144*) and 295-5 dec (JT Tyldesley 100 TW Hayward 60 GH Hirst 40* WW Armstrong 5-122)

AUSTRALIA 195 (WW Armstrong 66 RA Duff 48 AR Warren 5-57) and 224-7 (MA Noble 62)

MATCH DRAWN

4th Test at Old Trafford

July 24,25, 26

ENGLAND 446 (Hon FS Jackson 113 TW Hayward 82 RH Spooner 52 C McLeod 5-125)

AUSTRALIA 197 (J Darling 73 W Brearley 4-72) and 169 (RA Duff 60 W Brearley 4-54)

ENGLAND WON BY AN INNINGS AND 80 RUNS

5th Test at The Oval

August 14,15, 16

ENGLAND 430 (CB Fry 144 Hon FS Jackson 76 TW Hayward 59 EG Arnold 40 A Cotter 7-148 and 261-6 dec (JT Tyldesley 112* RH Spooner 79)

AUSTRALIA 363 (RA Duff 146 J Darling 57 JJ Kelly 42 W Brearley 5-110) and 124-4

MATCH DRAWN

1907-08
AUSTRALIA WON SERIES 4-1

1st Test at Sydney

December 13, 14, 16, 17, 18 (no play)
ENGLAND 273 (G Gunn 119 KL Hutchings 42 A Cotter 6-101) and 300 (G Gunn 74 J Hardstaff snr 63 JV Saunders 4-68)
AUSTRALIA 300 (C Hill 87 VT Trumper 43 A Fielder 6-82) and 275-8 (H Carter 61 WW Armstrong 44 P McAlister 41)

AUSTRALIA WON BY 2 WICKETS

2nd Test at Melbourne

January 1, 2, 3, 4, 6, 7
AUSTRALIA 266 (MA Noble 61 VT Trumper 49 JN Crawford 5-79) and 397(WW Armstrong 77 MA Noble 64 VT Trumper 63 CG Macartney 54)
ENGLAND 382 (KL Hutchings 126 JB Hobbs 83 LC Braund 49 A Cotter 5-142) and 282-9 (FL Fane 50)

ENGLAND WON BY 1 WICKET

3rd Test at Adelaide Oval

January 10, 11, 13, 14, 15, 16
AUSTRALIA 285 (CG Macartney 75 RJ Hartigan 48 VS Ransford 44 A Fielder 4-80) And 506 (C Hill 160 RJ Hartigan 116 MA Noble 65)
ENGLAND 363 (G Gunn 65 JN Crawford 62 J Hardstaff snr 61 FL Fane 48) and 183 (J Hardstaff snr 72 LC Braund 47 JV Saunders 5-65 JDA O'Connor 5-40)

AUSTRALIA WON BY 245 RUNS

4th Test at Melbourne

February 7, 8, 10, 11
AUSTRALIA 214 (VS Ransford 51 MA Noble 48 JN Crawford 5-48 A Fielder 4-54) And 385 (WW Armstrong 133* H Carter 66 VS Ransford 54 A Fielder 4-91)
ENGLAND 105 (JB Hobbs 57 JV Saunders 5-28) and 186 (G Gunn 43 JV Saunders) 4-76)

RESULT   AUSTRALIA WON BY 308 RUNS

5th Test at Sydney

February 21, 22, 24, 25, 26, 27
AUSTRALIA 137 (SE Gregory 44 SF Barnes 7-60) and 422 (VT Trumper 166 SE Gregory 56 C Hill 44 JN Crawford 5-141 W Rhodes 4-102)
ENGLAND 281 (G Gunn 122* JB Hobbs 72) and 229 (W Rhodes 69 FL Fane 46 JV Saunders 5-82)

AUSTRALIA WON BY 49 RUNS

1909
AUSTRALIA WON SERIES 2-1

1st Test at Edgbaston

May 27, 28, 29
AUSTRALIA 74 (C Blythe 6-44 GH Hirst 4-28) and 151 (SE Gregory 43 VS Ransford 43 C Blythe 5-58 GH Hirst 5-58)
ENGLAND 121 (WW Armstrong 5-27) and 105-0 (JB Hobbs 62*)

ENGLAND WON BY 10 WICKETS

2nd Test at Lord's

June 14, 15, 16
ENGLAND 269 (JH King 60 AFA Lilley 47 JT Tyldesley 46 A Cotter 4-80) and 121(WW Armstrong 6-35)
AUSTRALIA 350 (VS Ransford 143* W Bardsley 46 AE Relf 5-85) and 41-1

AUSTRALIA WON BY 9 WICKETS

3rd Test at Headingley

July 1, 2, 3
AUSTRALIA 188 (SE Gregory 46 VS Ransford 45 W Rhodes 4-38) and 207 (WW Armstrong 45 SF Barnes 6-63)
ENGLAND 182 (J Sharp 61 JT Tyldesley 55 CG Macartney 7-58) and 87 (A Cotter 5-38 CG Macartney 4-27)

AUSTRALIA WON BY 126 RUNS

4th Test at Old Trafford

July 26,27, 28
AUSTRALIA 147 (SF Barnes 5-56 C Blythe 5-63) and 279-9 dec (VS Ransford 54* CG Macartney 51* VT Trumper 48 W Rhodes 5-83)
ENGLAND 119 (F Laver 8-31) and 108-3 (RH Spooner 58)

MATCH DRAWN

5th Test at The Oval

August 9, 10, 11
AUSTRALIA 325 (W Bardsley 136 VT Trumper 73 CG Macartnet 50 DW Carr 5-146) And 339-5 dec (W Bardsley 130 SE Gregory 74 MA Noble 55)
ENGLAND 352 (J Sharp 105 W Rhodes 66 CB Fry 62 KL Hutchings 59 A Cotter 6-95) and 104-3 (W Rhodes 54)

MATCH DRAWN

1911-12
ENGLAND WON SERIES 4-1

1st Test at Sydney

December 15, 16, 18, 19,20 21
AUSTRALIA 447 (VS Trumper 113 RB Minnett 90 WW Armstrong 60 C Hill 46) and 308 (C Kellaway 70 C Hill 65 FR Foster 5-92 JWHT Douglas 4-50)
ENGLAND 318 (JW Hearne 76 JB Hobbs 63 FR Foster 56 W Rhodes 41 HV Hordern 5-85) and 291 (G Gunn 62 JW Hearne 43 HV Hordern 7-90)

AUSTRALIA WON BY 146 RUNS

2nd Test at Melbourne

December 30 January 1, 2, 3
AUSTRALIA 184 (HV Hordern 49* VS Ransford 43 SF Barnes 5-44) and 299 (WW Armstrong 90 A Cotter 41 FR Foster 6-91)
ENGLAND 265 (JW Hearne 114 W Rhodes 61 A Cotter 4-73 HV Hordern 4-66) and 219-2 (JB Hobbs 126* G Gunn 43)

ENGLAND WON BY 8 WICKETS

3rd Test at Adelaide

January 12, 13, 15, 16, 17
AUSTRALIA 133 (FR Foster 5-36) and 476 (C Hill 98 H Carter 72 W Bardsley 63 TJ Matthews 53 SF Barnes 5-105)
ENGLAND 501 (JB Hobbs 187 FR Foster 71 W Rhodes 59 CP Mead 46 A Cotter 4-125) And 112-3 (W Rhodes 57* G Gunn 45)

ENGLAND WON BY 7 WICKETS

4th Test at Melbourne

February 9, 10, 12, 13
AUSTRALIA 191 (RB Minnett 56 SF Barnes 5-74 FR Foster 4-77) and 173 (JWHTDouglas 5-46)
ENGLAND 589 (W Rhodes 179 JB Hobbs 178 G Gunn 75 FE Woolley 56 FR Foster 50)

ENGLAND WON BY AN INNINGS AND 225 RUNS

5th Test at Sydney

February 23, 24, 26 (no play), 27, 28, 29 (no play), March 1
ENGLAND 324 (FE Woolley 133* G Gunn 52 HV Hordern 5-95) and 214 (G Gunn 61 JB Hobbs 45 HV Hordern 5-66)
AUSTRALIA 176 and 292 (RB Minnett 61 VT Trumper 50 SE Gregory 40 FR Foster 4-43 SF Barnes 4-106)

ENGLAND WON BY 70 RUNS

1912
ENGLAND WON SERIES 1-0

1st Test at Lord's

June 24,25, 26
ENGLAND 310-7 dec (JB Hobbs 107 W Rhodes 59 CB Fry 42)
AUSTRALIA 282-7 (CG Macartney 99 C Kellaway 61)

MATCH DRAWN

2nd Test at Old Trafford

July 29, 30, 31 (no play)
ENGLAND 203 (W Rhodes 92 GR Hazlitt 4-77 WJ Whitty 4-43)
AUSTRALIA 14-0

MATCH DRAWN

3rd Test at The Oval

August 19, 20, 21, 22
ENGLAND 245 (JB Hobbs 66 FE Woolley 62 W Rhodes 49 WJ Whitty 4-69 RB Minnett 4-34) and 175 (CB Fry 79 GR Hazlitt 7-25)
AUSTRALIA 111 (C Kellaway 43 SF Barnes 5-30 FE Woolley 5-29) and 65 (FE Woolley 5-20 H Dean 4-19)

ENGLAND WON BY 244 RUNS

FAREWELL HOBBS WELCOME BRADMAN

ABE WADDINGTON OF ENGLAND

ARMSTRONG, PELLEW AND KELLAWAY ALL HIT CENTURIES: ARMSTRONG'S WAS THE 100TH IN THE ASHES SERIES

1920-21

Australia cleared the board, for the only time in a five-match series between the two countries, and were not flattered. Their victories were by 377 runs, an innings and 91 runs, 19 runs, eight wickets and nine wickets and only in the third match of the series did England get the merest glimpse of a win. This was the first time Australia and England had met since before the First World War and due to the long period between Tests, a total of 18 players – nine from each side – made their debuts during the five Tests.

AUSTRALIA WIN EIGHT IN A ROW

Australia's first Test victory provided the springboard for eight successive wins, with Warwick Armstrong scoring a century in his first match as captain. Herbie Collins, who had made 70 in Australia's first innings total of 267, scored 104 in the second and at 31 became the oldest Australian to score a century on debut. There were three run outs in Australia's first innings but then 'Jack' Russell played on to the first ball of England's innings and despite good knocks from Woolley and Hobbs they conceded a lead. Australia built massively on this and England, set 659 for victory, were never in a position to feel optimistic.

A seemingly modest Australian score was inflated by an 8th wicket stand of 173 on the second day by 'Nip' Pellew batting at No.7 and Jack Gregory at No.9. Left-hander Gregory's innings of

100 lasted only 137 minutes. Victorian batsman Roy Park was selected for this Test. The story goes that his wife was knitting as Roy went out to bat. She bent down to pick up her wool....Roy was bowled first ball...and she'd missed her husband's entire Test career! After heavy rain on the Sunday, the sun turned the pitch into a gluepot yet Hobbs and Hendren stretched their third wicket partnership to 142 before a collapse took place. Hearne was ill and unable to bat in either innings and in the follow-on, had Australia held all their catches, England's defeat would have been more pronounced.

The third Test in Adelaide was the highest-scoring of all Ashes Tests with a total of 1753 runs. Six centuries were scored – four by Australians and two by Englishmen. Howell bowled well for England but with wretched luck; one of several chances off him (Collins to Rhodes at square-leg) would have left Australia on 96 for 5 but they climbed to 354 with Collins making 162. Russell and Woolley batted well for England, helping them to a lead of 93. In reply, Armstrong, Pellew and Kellaway all hit centuries, Armstrong's the 100th in the Ashes series. Gregory's late order assault took Australia 489 ahead, a margin clearly beyond England once Hobbs's brave innings of 123 had ended.

There was life in the Melbourne pitch before lunch on the fourth Test and the English batsmen had to withstand some hostile bowling from McDonald and Gregory but the diminutive Makepeace went on to make 117 in England's first innings total of 284. Australia were in trouble after Collins and Bardsley had started with 117, but Armstrong, though suffering from malaria, put on 145 with Gregory for the sixth wicket. The captain, who went on to his third century of the series, was left unbeaten on 123. After Hobbs departed early, Rhodes and Makepeace cleared the arrears and at 305 for 5, England looked likely to save the Test. But Arthur Mailey confounded the tail and ended with Australia's all-time best analysis of 9 for 121.

England hampered by injuries – Hobbs played despite a thigh strain – again disappointed in the final Test. After a solid start, they collapsed to 204 all out. Australia too were in trouble at 22 for 3 but then Macartney, who missed the preceding three Tests through illness, put on 198 in just 133 minutes with Gregory (who averaged 73.66 in the series, took 23 wickets and held 15 catches). England were reduced to 91 for 6 at their second attempt before Johnny Douglas resisted for 68 runs as his ship sank for the fifth time. For Australia, Mailey finished with an Australian record of 36 wickets in the series.

1921

Australia, having won the previous series 5-0, extended their unbroken run of victories by winning the first three Tests and the margins were again nearer to routs – 10 wickets, 9 wickets and 219 runs. Few England batsmen could cope with the lifting ball as propelled by Gregory, while the pace and accuracy of Ted McDonald proved the perfect foil.

The series started at Trent Bridge in what was the 100th Test match between England and Australia. The match was dominated by Jack Gregory, who took eight wickets, including three wickets in four balls in England's first innings total of 112. During his first innings analysis of 6 for 58, the Nottingham crowd roared their disapproval of his continued use of the short-pitched delivery. Australia's total of 232, in which Warren Bardsley top-scored with 66, was almost enough for an innings victory. In England's second innings, Ernest Tyldesley was hit in the face by another Gregory bouncer, the ball then falling on his stumps.

For the second Test at Lord's, England ▶

THE AUSTRALIA TEAM THAT TOURED ENGLAND, 1921: (BACK ROW, L-R) WARREN BARDSLEY, JACK RYDER, STORK HENDRY, JACK GREGORY, EDGAR MAYNE, TOMMY ANDREWS, MANAGER S SMITH; (MIDDLE ROW, L-R) ARTHUR MAILEY, TED MCDONALD, HERBIE COLLINS, WARWICK ARMSTRONG, CHARLES MACARTNEY, SAMMY CARTER, JOHNNY TAYLOR; (FRONT ROW, L-R) NIP PELLEW, BERT OLDFIELD

made six changes and CB Fry, at 49, was also invited to play, but declined. Australia made just one change and that was forced, with Mailey coming in for Collins, whose thumb was broken in the first Test. Despite the valiant efforts of Frank Woolley, who scored 90s in both innings, England were well beaten, with Australia's first innings total of 342 coming off just 84.1 overs.

THIRD TEST: HEADINGLEY

At Headingley, England made seven changes, as well as transferring the captaincy to the Hon. Lionel Tennyson. Australia batted first and totalled 407 with Charles Macartney scoring 115. Despite their domination, this proved to be the only century of the series for the visitors and was the first hundred by an Australian in a Headingley Test. In reply, England collapsed to 67 for 5 before Brown helped Douglas add 97 and Tennyson, with an injured hand, batted heroically to save the follow-on. Andrews and Carter – one a monumental mason, the other an undertaker – led the way as Australia built a substantial lead. England were left four-and-a-half hours to survive but it was ample time for the tourists to go 3-0 up.

The first day of the fourth Test at Old Trafford was yet another washout

ANDREWS AND CARTER LED THE WAY FOR AUSTRALIA AS THEY BUILT UP A SUBSTANTIAL FIRST INNINGS LEAD AT HEADINGLEY

but the succession of England defeats was finally stemmed in a match remembered for Tennyson's illegal declaration. This was nullified after Carter, Armstrong's wicket-keeper, pointed out that after loss of the first day, it was a two-day match; no declaration could be made in such circumstances within 100 minutes of the end of play. Some of the crowd became unruly and Tennyson and the umpires had to explain matters to them – by which time 25 minutes were lost. Armstrong then proceeded to bowl the first over, despite having bowled the last before the break. England's top six batsmen scored freely enabling Tennyson to declare at 362 for 4. Even though England then bowled Australia out for 175, it was felt that Tennyson's declaration in a two-day game had come too late. In the 13 overs required for England to bat out the match, they continued the original batting order, opening with numbers 7 and 8, and with No.9 at the fall of the first wicket.

FIFTH TEST: THE OVAL

England's prospects were dim at the end of a rain-interrupted first day in the final Test at The Oval as they closed on 129 for 4. However, Hampshire's Phil Mead batted superbly on day two, scoring an unbeaten 182 as England declared at 403 for 8 – it was the highest score for England against Australia in England and gave him the freak average for the series of 229! Hitch removed Collins and Bardsley early on but Macartney, Andrews and Taylor all batted well to help Australia to 389. When England batted again, there was no prospect of a result and Warwick Armstrong drifted out to the boundary, once picking up a stray newspaper 'to see who we're playing'. It was the 'Big Ship's' way of protesting at Tests limited to three days !

1924-25

Since Test cricket's beginning, the number of balls per over had varied from four to five and then six in England, and from four to six in Australia. In this series, Australia's authorities switched to eight-ball overs.

Two Australian greats made their debuts in the first Test at Sydney: Bill Ponsford and Vic Richardson. Ponsford, batting at No.3, became the third Australian to score a century in his first Test innings and it was his second wicket partnership of 190 with skipper Herbie Collins that formed the basis of Australia's first innings total of 450. Although Hobbs and Sutcliffe replied with an opening stand of 157, England were all out for 298. Australia batted solidly, including a last wicket stand of 127 between Taylor and Mailey. Set 605, England began well with Hobbs and Sutcliffe sharing another century opening partnership and Woolley making 123 but despite these brave performances, England fell a long way short.

SECOND TEST: MELBOURNE

Following his 110 on debut, Bill Ponsford made 128 in the second Test at Melbourne, the first player to score hundreds in his first two Test matches. With Vic Richardson making 138, Australia scored a record-breaking 600. Hobbs and Sutcliffe then became the first pair to bat through an entire day of a Test. They put on 283 on the third day, but Hobbs was out without addition for 154 on day four. Sutcliffe, with 115 in the second innings of the first Test, followed up with 176 and 127 in this match, becoming the first England player to score hundreds in both innings against Australia and also the first player to score successive Test hundreds.

Maurice Tate took 6 for 99 as

AUSTRALIA'S BILL PONSFORD (R) IS CLEAN BOWLED FOR 12 BY MINOR COUNTIES' MICHAEL FALCON

Australia were dismissed for 250 but even Sutcliffe's second hundred could not save England from 81-run defeat.

SEVEN DAYS AT ADELAIDE, THIRD TEST

The third successive match to enter a seventh day ended thrillingly at Adelaide when Freeman was caught by Oldfield off Mailey to give Australia victory by 11 runs. Australia were in trouble at 119 for 6 in their first innings before Jack Ryder scored 201 not out to equal Syd Gregory's then record score against England in Australia and helping Australia to recover to 489. In England's first innings, Hobbs and Sutcliffe batted at No.5 and No.6 respectively and though Hobbs scored 119 and Hendren 92, they still fell 124 runs short of Australia's total. Australia were 211 for 3 at one stage in their first innings, but rain on the fifth morning meant that their last seven wickets fell for just 39 runs. In their second innings, England's batting order underwent a major reshuffle with every player switching positions. Hobbs and Sutcliffe put on 63 for the first wicket and Whysall, in his first Test, made 75 but rain cut short the sixth day with England needing 27 to win and with two wickets left. Over 25,000 came to see the last few overs and after Gregory had England captain Gilligan caught, Mailey induced a fatal snick from Freeman.

England at last secured a victory. Their fourth Test win in Melbourne was their first over Australia in 12 years, Australia having won 11 of the previous 13. For two days England occupied the crease, with Hobbs and Sutcliffe putting up another century opening stand, and Sutcliffe batted through a day for the third time in the series for his fourth century. Light showers then put some life in the pitch and though Taylor twice batted well, Maurice Tate was back at his best and with the usual strong rearguard action of the Australian lower order not occurring in this Test, England won by an innings and 29 runs.

In the final Test, England were confounded in both innings by 33-year-old New Zealand-born leg spinner Clarrie Grimmett. After Australia had scored 295 in their first innings, Grimmett swept through the England lower order after Woolley and Hearne had taken the score to 96 for 4 and they were all out for 167. The crucial second innings stand for Australia was that between Kellaway and Collins and with Oldfield making an unbeaten 65 in putting on 116 with Kellaway – the highest stand of the match – England needed 453 to win. Grimmett's accuracy and variation – he took 6 for 37 – then put a seal on the game.

GREAT PLAYERS

Herbert Sutcliffe
(England) 1924-35

Test Average 60.73
Test Best 194 v. Australia, Sydney 1932
Ashes Average 66.85
Ashes Best (as above)

One of the game's immortals, Herbert Sutcliffe was a batsman of immense concentration, unflinching courage, imperturbable temperament and consistent success. Alongside Jack Hobbs, the Yorkshire batsman formed a well-nigh waterproof opening partnership. In the first Test against Australia at Sydney in 1924-25 they put on 157 and 110 together, followed by 283 in the second at Melbourne where Sutcliffe made 176 and 127. And against at Melbourne in the fourth Test, he scored 143 in another century opening partnership. He headed the Test averages with 734 runs at 81.55. In 1930 he headed the England batting averages with 436 runs at 87.20 and against Australia in 1932-33 and 1934 (with a variety of opening partners) he still averaged over 50 per series and at Sydney in 1932-33 he made his Test highest score of 194. For Yorkshire his stand of 555 with Percy Holmes against Essex at Leyton in 1932 stood as the world record for 45 years, his score of 313 not out remaining his highest.

1926

After the heavy run-scoring and seven-day Tests of the previous tour in Australia, this series got under way with rain – and plenty of it with just 50 minutes play on the first day and none thereafter at Trent Bridge. The four drawn matches were remarkable for the aggressive batting of Macartney, who made hundreds in the three middle Tests and the consistency of opening pair Hobbs and Sutcliffe. This meant that in the final 'timeless' Test at The Oval there was all to play for.

TRENT BRIDGE: WOODFULL'S DEBUT

In the rain-ruined first Test at Trent Bridge, Bill Woodfull, who would be captain when Australia next toured England, made his debut...in the field for just 17.2 overs. So too did England spinner Fred Root, although with Hobbs and Sutcliffe batting and Australia failing to take a wicket, he spent his entire maiden test as a spectator!

Warren Bardsley, by now 43 and on his fourth tour of England, scored an unbeaten 193 in the second Test at Lord's to become the oldest Australian to score a century against England and the oldest to carry his bat through a Test innings.

Nottinghamshire fast bowler Harold Larwood made his Test debut at 21 in this match, taking three wickets and giving no clue of the impact he was to have on the 1932-33 tour of Australia. When England batted, Hobbs and Sutcliffe continued to dominate, putting on 182 for the first wicket. Hobbs, on his way to 119, became the first player to pass 4,000 Test runs. However, England's top scorer was Patsy Hendren with 127 not out: at 37, he was the youngest of the four centurions! In Australia's second innings, Macartney made 133 not out with deft and sometimes brutal strokeplay.

Bardsley assumed the Australian captaincy for the third Test when Collins fell ill but made an inglorious start when Tate dismissed him with the first ball of the match. Macartney scored a century before lunch on the first day – 112 in 116 minutes – before he was finally out for 151. With Bill Woodful making 141 and Arthur Richardson 100, Australia totalled 494. England's batsmen struggled, and only a ninth wicket partnership of 108 between Geary

and Macaulay helped them reach 294. Hobbs and Sutcliffe put on 156 for the first wicket in the follow-on to see England to safety.

Only ten balls were possible on the first day of the fourth Test at Old Trafford and on the Monday, Carr was down with tonsilitis, so Hobbs took over the captaincy – the first professional to lead England since the 1880s. Once more Macartney (making his third consecutive Test century) and Woodfull (his second) made a large second wicket stand: 192. Wickets then fell steadily thereafter to Root's leg-theory and Steven's leg spin. For England, Tyldesley's was a chancy but attractive innings while Woolley hit Grimmett over the sightscreen and Mailey into the pavilion.

THE 'TIMELESS' TEST

For the 'timeless' Test, England dropped their captain Arthur Carr for Percy Chapman. They also restored Harold Larwood and the 48-year-old Wilfred Rhodes. They won the toss but frittered away the advantage by being bowled out for 280 on the first day and Australia led on the first innings by 22 runs. The story of how Hobbs and Sutcliffe defied the Australian spinners on a 'sticky dog' has become legendary. The bowlers best suited to the conditions were Arthur Richardson, off-spin round the wicket and Charlie Macartney, left-arm over and they spun and kicked viciously from an impeccable length. But somehow Hobbs and Sutcliffe came through. Hobbs made 100 out of 172, by which time the match was virtually won; Sutcliffe went on to make 161 as England set their opponents a target of 415 for victory. Rhodes spun the ball off the worn area and midst noisy jubilation the innings fell apart – England had regained the Ashes.

JACK HOBBS AND HERBERT SUTCLIFFE GOING IN TO BAT, 3RD TEST HEADINGLEY, 1926

Wally Hammond
(England) 1927-47

Test Average 58.46
Test Best 336 New Zealand, Eden Park 1933
Ashes Average 51.85
Ashes Best 251, Sydney 1928

Wally Hammond became the greatest English batsman of the inter-war years and one of the very greatest in the history of the game. In 1928-29 he made 905 runs, an aggregate exceeded only by Don Bradman's 974 in 1930. Twice he passed 200 and in the fourth Test at Adelaide, which England won by 12 runs, he made 119 not out and 177. His feats in the next ten years were sometimes overshadowed by those of his contemporary Bradman, but they nevertheless included many superb innings. His 33 not out at Auckland in 318 minutes in 1932-33 remained the highest innings in Test cricket until Len Hutton's 364 in 1938. In 1938 he was appointed captain of England for that summer's series against Australia. He made 240 in the Lord's Test and led England to the victory that squared the series at The Oval. After the War, he like many of his team, was not fit enough and he was a shadow of the great player he had once been, with only Hobbs and Hendren having scored more first-class centuries.

ENGLAND 1928-9: (BACK ROW, L-R) GEORGE DUCKWORTH, LES AMES, PHIL MEAD, MAURICE TATE, PATSY HENDREN, GEORGE GEARY; (MIDDLE ROW, L-R) MORRIS LEYLAND, SAM STAPLES, WALLY HAMMOND, MANAGER SIR FREDERICK TOONE, HERBERT SUTCLIFFE, HAROLD LARWOOD, TICH FREEMAN; (FRONT ROW, L-R) DICK TYLDESLEY, JACK WHITE, PERCY CHAPMAN, DOUGLAS JARDINE, JACK HOBBS

1928-29

Little did the people of Brisbane realise just how significant a place in history their first Test staged at the Exhibition Ground would be. It marked the debut of the greatest batsman of all-time, Don Bradman, whilst his rivals included one Douglas Jardine and Harold Larwood ...the trio pivotal to the 1932-33 'Bodyline' series. However, the series was dominated by the monolithic batting of Wally Hammond. After a moderate first Test, he made 251 in the second, 200 in the third and 119 not out and 177 in the fourth. A disappointing final match left him 95 runs short of a thousand for the series.

England's strong all-round side began a successful series with an overwhelming victory, made so by the advisability of not enforcing a follow-on in a 'timeless' Test. In their first innings total of 521, there was but one century partnership, the record 124 for the eighth wicketof Hendren, who went on to make 169, and Larwood. Bradman's maiden Test appearance was unspectacular, scoring as he did 18 and 1, but he did run out Hobbs in England's first innings. Larwood was the pick of the English bowlers, taking 6 for 32 as Australia were bowled out for 122. When England batted a second time, they declared their innings closed at 342 for 8 – the first declaration of an innings in a Test in Australia. Having been set 742 for victory, Australia had Jack Gregory (serious knee injury) and Charlie Kellaway (food poisoning) unavailable to bat and were bowled out for just 66 giving England victory by the huge margin of 675 runs.

WALLY HAMMOND'S DOUBLE

In the second Test at Sydney, after Australia had been bowled out for 253, Wally Hammond began an extraordinary run of scores with the second double-century ever made for England against Australia. On the second afternoon, the eve of Jack Hobbs's 46th birthday, 'The ▶

Master' was presented out in the middle by Monty Noble with a shilling-fund collection, the result of a newspaper appeal. He was then escorted around the outfield to the acclaim of a record 58,456 crowd. In Australia's second innings both 'Stork' Hendry and Bill Woodfull made centuries, but England were left with just 15 to make for victory, which they achieved for just two wickets.

England's victories, like Australia's in 1924-25 were by ever-decreasing margins. Australia batted first at Melbourne, and were struggling at 57 for 3 when Kippax and Ryder, who both went on to record hundreds, put on 161 prior to the young Bradman making a patient 79. Hammond then made history with his second double-century running whilst 46-year-old off-spinner Don Blackie took 6 for 94 in England's first innings total of 417. When Australia batted for a second time, Woodfull made 107 whilst Bradman made 112, the first of his 19 centuries against England. Requiring 332 to win, Hobbs and Sutcliffe negotiated a famously sticky wicket to post 105 for the first wicket, with the Yorkshire opener going on to make 135 as England won a remarkable game by three wickets.

FOURTH TEST: ADELAIDE

An unbeaten 119 by Wally Hammond helped England to a total of 334 in their first innings of the fourth Test at Adelaide. Archie Jackson, aged 19 and rated by some to be in the Bradman class, had been included in the Australian side and he scored 164 in his maiden Test innings, as Australia led by 35 runs on the first innings. He was, and remains the youngest to score an Ashes Test century. He played just seven Tests before he died of tuberculosis at 23. In England's second innings, Hammond batted masterfully until exhaustion

defeated him. His stand of 262 with Jardine is a third-wicket record for England against Australia. The home side were left to make 349 for victory and as the seventh day dawned they were 260 for 6, needing a further 89 runs. The score had reached 308 when Chapman caught Oxenham but the decisive moment came shortly afterwards when Hobbs ran out Bradman. The match was still poised at lunch but Jack White took his seventh and eight wickets and England went 4-0 up.

Jack Hobbs crowned his last appearance in Melbourne in the fifth Test with yet another century – and at 46 years 82 days, he was the oldest player to score a Test century and on his way to 142 also became the first player to reach 5000 Test runs. Other major scorers for England in their first innings total of 519 were Leyland with 137 and Hendren with 95.

The core of Australia's determined reply was a stand of 183 for the fifth wicket between Bradman and Fairfax but their total of 491 was made at less than two runs an over. Bowled out for 257 in their second innings, with Hobbs again top-scoring with 65, England set the hosts 287 to win. There were useful contributions from Oldfield and Jackson before Ryder with an unbeaten 57 and Bradman saw their side home by five wickets.

JACK HOBBS CROWNED HIS FINAL APPEARANCE AT MELBOURNE WITH ANOTHER CENTURY

1930

If the 1928-29 series was dominated by Hammond, still more will that of 1930 be remembered for England's first sight of Don Bradman. Eight and 131; 254 and 1; 334; 14; and 232 – those were his scores in the five Tests, totalling 974 runs and averaging 139. It was an avalanche that would have overwhelmed most sides and England did well to go into the final Test all square.

FIRST OF ELEVEN FOR BRADMAN

Jack Hobbs at the age of 47 began the series well at Trent Bridge and was England's top scorer in a first innings total of 270, whilst the only other batsman to set about the bowling with any success was Chapman. Tate's opening burst reduced Australia to 16 for 3 and with Robins mopping up the lower order, they were all out for 144. Hobbs and Sutcliffe put on 125 for England's first wicket in their second innings, but the latter had to retire hurt after taking a blow on the thumb. It was left to Hendren to sustain England's command. Set 429, Australia were 229 for 3 when a superb diving catch by a comparatively unknown substitute fielder, Syd Copley of the Nottinghamshire groundstaff, broke a threatening stand between Bradman and McCabe. Though Australia eventually fell 93 runs short of their victory target, Bradman's century, in his first Test in England, was the first of 11 in that country.

Winning the toss again at Lord's, England, with Duleepsinhji emulating his illustrious uncle Ranji by scoring a century in his first Test, made enough runs to have ensured a draw in normal circumstances; but they reckoned without the astonishing speed and certainty of Bradman's run-getting and Australia replied to England's first innings 425 with 729 for 6 declared. Bradman made 254 and Woodfull 155 in what remains the highest team score in any Ashes Test at the home of cricket. In England's second innings, Percy Chapman scored a century – the first time rival skippers had both scored centuries in the same Ashes Test. With the help of Australian-born Gubby Allen, he saw the innings defeat staved off before his dismissal and though Australia lost three early wickets, they still had time and little trouble in making the required runs.

BRADMAN: 334 NOT OUT

The Headingley Test, in which a cloud-burst saved England, will always be remembered for Bradman's 334, of which 309 came on the first day (105 before lunch, 115 in the afternoon and 89 after tea). Along the way, in his 13th Test innings, he passed the 1,000-run milestone – all still at the age of 21. Bradman's strokeplay, footwork and placement were marvelled at and if his overall innings fell a trifle short of the perfection of his Lord's double century, his skills were now comprehensively appreciated by players, press and public. Wally Hammond scored 113 in England's first innings, matching Bradman's 1000 runs against Australia alone, but in his 14th Test. Rain and bad light came to England's salvation despite the follow-on and though the series remained alive, much depended on whether Bradman could be held in check.

FOURTH TEST: OLD TRAFFORD

The fourth Test at Old Trafford was spoiled by rain. After Ponsford and Woodfull's tedious opening stand of 106, Fairfax and Grimmett took Australia to a respectable total. Sutcliffe dominated a first wicket stand of 108 with Hobbs – their last of three figures against Australia – before being breathtakingly caught by Bradman at long leg, and ▶

THE RESULTS

ENGLAND v AUSTRALIA
Played at Lord's June 27-1 July 1930

ENGLAND

JB Hobbs	c Oldfield b Fairfax	1	b Grimmett	19
FE Woolley	c Wall b Fairfax	41	hit wkt b Grimmett	28
WR Hammond	b Grimmett	38	c Fairfax b Grimmett	32
KS Duleepsinhji	c Bradman b Grimmett	173	c Oldfield b Hornibrook	48
EH Hendren	c McCabe b Fairfax	48	c Richardson b Grimmett	9
APF Chapman	c Oldfield b Wall	11	c Oldfield b Fairfax	121
GO Allen	b Fairfax	3	lbw b Grimmett	57
MW Tate	c McCabe b Wall	54	c Ponsford b Grimmett	10
RWV Robins	c Oldfield b Hornibrook	5	not out	11
JC White	not out	23	run out	10
G Duckworth	c Oldfield b Wall	18	lbw b Fairfax	0
Extras		10		30
Total		**425**		**375**

Fall of wickets 1-13 2-53 3-105 4-209 5-236 6-239 7-337 8-363 9-387 10-425
Second Innings 1-45 2-58 3-129 4-141 5-147 6-272 7-329 8-354 9-372 10-375

Australia Bowling

	O	M	R	W	O	M	R	W
Wall	29.4	2	118	3	25	2	80	0
Fairfax	31	3	101	4	12.4	2	37	2
Grimmett	33	4	105	2	53	13	167	6
Hornibrook	26	6	62	1	22	6	49	1
McCabe	9	1	29	0	3	1	11	0
Bradman	-	-	-	-	1	0	1	0

AUSTRALIA

WM Woodfull	st Duckworth b Robins	155	not out	26
WH Ponsford	c Hammond b White	81	b Robins	14
DG Bradman	c Chapman b White	254	c Chapman b Tate	1
AF Kippax	b White	83	c Duckworth b Robins	3
SJ McCabe	c Woolley b Hammond	44	not out	25
VY Richardson	c Hobbs b Tate	30		
WA Oldfield	not out	43		
AG Fairfax	not out	20		
CV Grimmett	did not bat			
PM Hornibrook	did not bat			
TM Wall	did not bat			
Extras		19		3
Total		**729-6 dec**		**72-3**

Fall of wickets 1-162 2-393 3-585 4-588 5-643 6-672
Second Innings 1-16 2-17 3-22

England Bowling

	O	M	R	W	O	M	R	W
Allen	34	7	115	0	-	-	-	-
Tate	64	16	148	1	13	6	21	1
White	51	7	158	3	2	0	8	0
Robins	42	1	172	1	9	1	34	2
Hammond	35	6	82	1	4.2	1	6	0

AUSTRALIA WON BY 7 WICKETS

Clarrie Grimmett
(Australia) 1925-36

Test Average *24.22*
Test Best *7-40 v. South Africa, Old Wanderers 1936*
Ashes Average *32.44*
Ashes Best *6-37, Sydney 1925*

Clarrie Grimmett was a match-winner with the ball as Bradman was with the bat. But he was no overnight success – he had to emigrate from Dunedin in the South Island of New Zealand to Australia because the Plunkett Shield offered very little scope. When Australia first called on his services in 1924-25, he took 11 English wickets for 82 runs Soon he was half of Australia's attack and in the 1930 series in England, where he found the turf more responsive than at home, he had 29 wickets (in the game against Yorkshire he had an innings best of 10 for 37) and 25 more in 1934. With his jerky action, accuracy and deceptive flight, Grimmett would go on to become the first bowler ever to take 200 Test wickets. It is said that Bradman had it in for him but as late as 1939-40 when he was 49, the little man was taking 73 wickets for South Australia in the Sheffield Shield – another record.

ENGLAND'S JACK HOBBS FINDS THAT HE HAS BEEN CLEAN BOWLED BY AUSTRALIA'S CLARRIE GRIMMETT

after Duleep's fine innings, the wet weather put and end to England's reply.

Australia won the fifth Test – a 'time-less' Test – to regain the Ashes on captain Bill Woodfull's 33rd birthday. Bob Wyatt replaced Chapman as England captain and thanks largely to a sixth-wicket stand of 170 between Sutcliffe, who made a splendid 161 and his new captain, England totalled 405. In any normal series this would have ensured a fight; but Australia now demonstrated their batting superiority beyond all doubt and with Bradman scoring 232, they made 695. Hammond, with 60, was England's top scorer in their second innings, the seventh of left-arm bowler Hornibrook's wickets after a blank fifth day through rain.

1932-33

Faith in fast bowling as the only form of attack likely to subdue Bradman was triumphantly vindicated in this series. But the manner in which it was deployed was bitterly resented throughout Australia. Fast leg-theory as conceived by Jardine, or 'Bodyline' as it was dubbed by the Australians, took on a different connotation when projected by bowlers of the pace and accuracy of Harold Larwood and Bill Voce, and the batsmen felt themselves under continual physical attack. Nevertheless, Jardine persisted with his policy throughout an explosive series, which at one point seemed likely to be abandoned as forthright and bitter cables were exchanged between the respective governing bodies.

The 'Bodyline' tour got underway with

one of the most heroic innings in the game's history. With Larwood and Voce bowling short-pitched balls in the direction of the batsman with a cluster of short legs and a man or two out for the hook or top-edge, England's attack under the unrelenting direction of captain Douglas Jardine created unparalleled discomfort for batsmen and controversy which spread from onlookers through the sports pages into editorials and even into the music halls. Stan McCabe arrived at the wicket with Australia 82 for 3 and after hooking Larwood to the boundary off the first ball he faced, proceeded to score an unbeaten 187 in Australia's total of 360.

SUTCLIFFE'S LAST AND HIGHEST

Sutcliffe's eighth, last and highest century against Australia spanned century stands for England's first three wickets, whilst Hammond also reached three figures as England made 524. Larwood, with a strained side strapped up, bowled fast and accurately, seldom pitching short in Australia's second innings to take 5 for 28 as England won by 10 wickets.

Bradman, who missed the first Test due to illness, was out to the first ball he faced in the 'Bodyline' series – not to Larwood or Voce but to Yorkshireman Bill Bowes. Fingleton's was a dour and courageous innings and McCabe and Richardson also made valuable contributions in Australia's first innings total of 228. Wall's pace and O'Reilly's fast-medium spinners were too much for England who were dismissed for 169. In Australia's second innings, Bradman made a highly creditable century, ducking and stepping across his wicket to Larwood, who sometimes had no off-side fielder in front of point. England's concentration on speed and the leg-theory was such that no specialist slow bowler was included. The move backfired as O'Reilly took 10 wickets in the match to bowl Australia to victory.

THE RESULTS

AUSTRALIA v ENGLAND
Played at the Adelaide Oval, Jan 13-19 1933

ENGLAND

Batsman	Dismissal	Runs	Dismissal	Runs
H Sutcliffe	c Wall b O'Reilly	9	c sub b Wall	7
DR Jardine	b Wall	3	lbw b Ironmonger	56
WR Hammond	c Oldfield b Wall	2	b Bradman	85
LEG Ames	b Ironmonger	3	b O'Reilly	69
M Leyland	b O'Reilly	83	c Wall b Ironmonger	42
RES Wyatt	c Richardson b Grimmett	78	c Wall b O'Reilly	49
E Paynter	c Fingleton b Wall	77	not out	1
GO Allen	lbw b Grimmett	15	lbw b Grimmett	15
H Verity	c Richardson b Wall	45	lbw b O'Reilly	40
W Voce	b Wall	8	b O'Reilly	8
H Larwood	not out	3	c Bradman b Ironmonger	8
Extras		15		32
Total		**341**		**412**

Fall of wickets 1-4, 2-16, 3-16, 4-30, 5-186, 6-196, 7-228, 8-324, 9-336, 10-341
Second Innings 1-7, 2-91, 3-123, 4-154, 5-245, 6-296, 7-394, 8-395, 9-403, 10-412

Australia Bowling

	O	M	R	W	O	M	R	W
Wall	34.1	10	72	5	29	6	75	1
O'Reilly	50	19	82	2	50.3	21	79	4
Ironmonger	20	6	50	1	57	21	87	3
Grimmett	28	6	94	2	35	9	74	1
McCabe	14	3	28	0	16	0	42	0
Bradman					4	0	23	1

AUSTRALIA

Batsman	Dismissal	Runs	Dismissal	Runs
JH Fingleton	c Ames b Allen	0	b Larwood	0
WM Woodfull	b Allen	22	not out	73
DG Bradman	c Allen b Larwood	8	c and b Verity	66
SJ McCabe	c Jardine b Larwood	8	c Leyland b Allen	7
WH Ponsford	b Voce	85	c Jardine b Larwood	3
VY Richardson	b Allen	28	c Allen b Larwood	21
WA Oldfield	retired hurt	41	absent hurt	0
CV Grimmett	c Voce b Allen	10	b Allen	6
TW Wall	b Hammond	6	b Allen	0
WJ O'Reilly	b Larwood	0	b Larwood	5
H Ironmonger	not out	0	b Allen	0
Extras		14		12
Total		**222**		**193**

Fall of wickets 1-1, 2-18, 3-34, 4-51, 5-131, 6-194, 7-212, 8-222, 9-222
Second Innings 1-3, 2-12, 3-100, 4-116, 5-171, 6-183, 7-183, 8-192, 9-193

England Bowling

	O	M	R	W	O	M	R	W
Larwood	25	6	55	3	9	3	71	4
Allen	23	4	71	4	17.2	5	50	4
Hammond	17.4	4	30	1	9	3	27	0
Voce	14	5	21	1	4	1	7	0
Verity	16	7	31	0	20	12	26	1

ENGLAND WON BY 338 RUNS

Harold Larwood
(England) 1926-33

Test Average 28.36
Test Best 6-32 v. Australia –
Exhibition Ground 1928
Ashes Average 29.88
Ashes Best (as above)

Many people believe that Harold Larwood was the fastest and best fast bowler in cricket history. It was, therefore all the sadder that his career should have declined among the bitterness of the bodyline controversy in which he was one of the two central figures. Before that 1932-33 tour he had taken only 45 Test wickets with a best of 6 for 32 against Australia at Brisbane in 1928-29. In Australia on that unhappy tour, he bowled superbly to his orders. Though it was the short ball, fast and accurate that undermined the batsmen, he could put in a devastating yorker at will. In addition he was helped by the fast that there were other fine fast bowlers in the side. In the first Test, Larwood took five wickets in each innings and thereafter he was the spearhead of England's attack, taking 33 wickets in all. And in the last test at Sydney, which was to be the last of his career, he went in as nightwatchman and made 98. After the War, he, his wife and five daughters emigrated to Australia. His part in the series had been forgotten and forgiven and he became a much respected Australian citizen.

BILL WOODFULL OF AUSTRALIA DUCKS TO AVOID A RISING BALL FROM HAROLD LARWOOD

'THE MOST UNPLEASANT TEST OF ALL'

The series erupted at Adelaide where Woodfull, hit sickeningly over the heart by Larwood, who then reverted to his leg-side attack, told 'Plum' Warner, the MCC manager, that only one of the sides was playing cricket. Oldfield suffered a cracked skull as he mishooked at Larwood. Mounted police lined up in readiness as the crowd's fury reached fever pitch. The Australian Board sent a cable of protest to Lord's; the MCC responded that they had full confidence in their team management. The Battle of Adelaide began with an England collapse but Leyland, Wyatt and Paynter shored up the innings. Larwood and Allen then demolished Australia with Ponsford, reinstated, bravely taking much fast stuff on the back. England built a lead laboriously and on the fifth afternoon after an animated innings from Bradman, the back of Australia's innings was broken, Woodfull going on valiantly to carry his bat for the second time against England.

Richardson and Woodfull began Woolloongabba's first Test with a stand of 133 but apart from Bradman, who was bowled leg stump by Larwood as he tried to cut, no-one else made an impression. Jardine and Sutcliffe too began with a century stand, but a minor collapse was stemmed only when Paynter, the Lancashire left-hander, left hospital, where he had been confined with acute tonsilitis, to make 24 before returning for another night under observation. Next day he put on a crucial 92 with Verity for the ninth wicket. For England, all but debutant No.11 Tommy Mitchell reached double figures in their first innings total of 356. Larwood, Allen and Verity then found ways of getting rid of the home batsmen in Australia's second innings and with Leyland making 86, England won by four wickets. Woodfull won his fourth toss of the series but after electing to bat, saw Vic Richardson dismissed before a run was scored —as he was in the second innings. Australia's overnight 296 for 5 was extended to 435 thanks in part to a combination of dropped catches and near misses and England were 159 for 2 that night after Sutcliffe and Hammond had put on 122 for the second wicket. Though Hammond went on to record his second century of the series, the most emotive innings was Larwood's. Sent in as nightwatchman, he surprised everyone in making 98. Australia's second innings owed almost everything to a stand of 115 between the defiant Woodfull and Bradman. Verity used the worn patches to take 5 for 33 but Ironmonger was not so devastating as England set about getting 164 to win. Hammond, who made an unbeaten 75, ended the game with a six to give England a 4-1 victory.

1934

With feelings still running high after the 'Bodyline' series, Woodfull's Australians journeyed to England for a five-Test series. But the England side were without Jardine, Larwood and Voce and injuries to other key players crucially weakened the team.

Australia's Arthur Chipperfield had played only three first-class innings before being chosen to make this tour. Although he may have been unknown beforehand, he soon captured the headlines, batting at No.7 in the first Test at Trent Bridge and becoming the first player to score 99 on debut. Australia totalled 374. Leg-spinners Grimmett and O'Reilly bowled well in tandem to dismiss the home side for 268, whilst for England Ken Farnes, also making his debut, took five wickets in each innings to have match figures of 10 for 179. Stan McCabe, who batted soundly in the first innings, made a quickfire 88 in the second as Australia declared their innings closed at 273 for 8. Needing 380 to win, England again struggled against the spin of Grimmett and O'Reilly, with the latter returning figures of 7 for 54 as Australia won a thrilling victory with only 10 minutes to spare.

The second Test belonged to Hedley Verity and was the first to be won by England against Australia at Lord's since 1896 and the last to the time of writing. Wicket-keeper Les Ames scored 120 for England – the first time a keeper had scored a century in Ashes Tests. Maurice Leyland also reached three figures in an England total of 440. Queenslander Bill Brown, playing in his second Test at the age of 21, scored his maiden Test century as Australia ended the second day at 192 for 2. Heavy rain over the weekend meant that Hedley Verity dominated the third day's play. He took 7 for 61 as Australia failed by just seven runs to avoid the follow-on and then produced even better figures, 8 for 43 as England won by an innings and 38 runs. His match figures of 15 for 104 included 14 for 80 on the third day – no-one has taken more wickets in a day's play in Ashes Tests.

In the third Test at Old Trafford, England scored a massive 627 for 9 declared, with seven batsmen passing 50. The two century-makers were Maurice Leyland and Patsy Hendren. The match though is remembered as much ▶

Bill O'Reilly
(Australia) 1932-46

Test Average *22.60*
Test Best *7-54 v. England – Trent Bridge 1934*
Ashes Average *25.36*
Ashes Best *(as above)*

Bill 'Tiger' O'Reilly was one of cricket's greatest bowlers. His use of the leg break was devastating, a fact recognised by his teammate and occasional sparring partner, Don Bradman, who called him the best he had ever faced or seen. Like nobody else, O'Reilly took 20 wickets or more in four consecutive Ashes series from 1932-33 to 1938. In 19 Tests against England he claimed 102 wickets and he did it all in an idiosyncratic way for he was as much his own man in leg-spin as he was in other walks of life. O'Reilly's first series against England was renowned for 'Bodyline' the fact that he took 10 for 129 from 59 overs to send England to their one defeat has been forgotten. He did get to within a whisker of a Test hat-trick. In 1934 at Old Trafford, he had Cyril Walters caught, bowled Wyatt next ball and conceded four to a thin inside edge by a bewildered Hammond before bowling him with the fourth ball!

DON BRADMAN SKIES THE BALL TO LOSE HIS WICKET IN THE SECOND INNINGS, WATCHED BY ENGLAND'S HERBERT SUTCLIFFE, WICKETKEEPER LES AMES AND WALLY HAMMOND

for anything else for O'Reilly's sensational spell on the first morning. With successive balls he had Walters caught at short leg, bowled Wyatt, elicited a not entirely voluntary leg glance for four by Hammond and then bowled him. Wyatt declared at 4pm on the second day. Thanks to Stan McCabe's fighting knock of 137, Australia found safe waters but might have done so with greater comfort had both Bradman and Chipperfield not been laid low with throat infections. England declared their second innings at 123 for 0, but Australia's victory target of 260 was never a realistic one.

HEADINGLEY: DON BRADMAN'S TEST

The fourth Test was remarkable for the feat of one man – Don Bradman. For the second time in successive Ashes Tests at Headingley, he scored a triple century – 304 – and shared a 388-run partnership with Ponsford (181) that remains a fourth wicket record in Ashes Tests. England, who had collapsed in their first innings to Australia's spinners, faced arrears of 384 and were 188 for 5 on the third evening, but rain resulted in a draw.

At The Oval, where Australia won the toss, Bradman (244) and Ponsford (266) broke their own record with a second wicket partnership of 451 in 316 minutes on the first day. Australia's first innings total of 701 was daunting, but England through Sutcliffe and Walters began with 104. Wickets then clattered until Leyland was supported by Ames and Allen. The Yorkshire left-hander's third century helped England to 321 but Woodfull decided to bat again and England were eventually set 708 to win. Australia's victory margin of 562 runs is still in the record books as their biggest in terms of runs and for the second time on successive England tours, the Ashes were secured on skipper Woodfull's birthday.

ENGLAND AND MIDDLESEX BOWLER GEORGE 'GUBBY' ALLEN IN ACTION. HE WAS KNIGHTED IN 1986

1936-37

Don Bradman's career took on a further dimension when he was appointed Australia's captain. This was his first series in charge and though his suffered big defeats in the first two Tests (when Bradman himself was dismissed for two successive ducks), Australia recovered to win the series with Bradman's score's including 270, 212 and 169 in the last three Tests. It was also the first time a country had won a series after losing the first two Tests.

A fiery spell of bowling by Ernie McCormick, which saw Stan Worthington dismissed by the first ball of the match, reduced England to 20 for 3, but with the ever-reliable Leyland making 126, they eventually totalled 358. Australia replied with 234 with Jack Fingleton's 100 making him the first player to score centuries in four successive Test innings. Leg-spinner Ward was England's problem until Allen, the captain, put bat to ball in making a fine 68. Faced with scoring 381 for victory, Australia lost Fingleton to the first ball of the innings in poor light, and after overnight rain were bowled out for just 58 in 12.3 overs to give

England victory by 322 runs – Bradman's Test captaincy initiation was one he would have been happy to forget!

Wally Hammond who had had so much success on Australian wickets on the previous two tours, started this series with a duck, but made amends in the second Test at Sydney with 231 not out. His sequence of Test scores at Sydney was now 251, 112, 101, 75 not out and 231 not out. After England had declared at 426 for 6, a thunderstorm on the third morning left Australia with uneasy prospects. The first three wickets fell with just one run on the board, Bradman amongst them for his second successive duck. Voce took 4 for 10 as Australia were dismissed for 80. Allen enforced the follow-on and though they reached the close of play on 145 for 1, once Bradman had gone, only McCabe offered any resistance and England won by an innings and 22 runs.

THIRD TEST: MELBOURNE

Having won the first two Tests and with Australia 130 for 6 in their first innings on a good wicket at Melbourne, England must have thought the Ashes were theirs. Soon afterwards came the rain and Bradman declared at 200 for 9. Worthington once again went without a run on the board on a gluepot of a wicket, and only Hammond with 32 batted with any conviction as Sievers and O'Reilly made the ball leap off a length – England declared at 76 for 9. Bradman decided to open Australia's second innings with his tailenders O'Reilly and Fleetwood-Smith. The move, late on the second day, was successful because, despite Australia losing both makeshift openers with only 3 runs on the board, it meant that the recognised batsmen had better conditions the next day. Fingleton at No. 6 scored 136 and Bradman at No.7, 270. They put on 346 for the

sixth wicket to help Australia recover from 97 for 5 to 564 all out. Set 689 to win, England set about their task and though Leyland made his sixth century against Australia, the home side won by 365 runs.

England bowled and fielded well in the fourth Test at Adelaide to dismiss Australia for 288 on a good pitch with Stan McCabe batting with his customary skill and sparkle. For England, Charlie Barnett made 129 in a total of 330 but if his innings was of great value, Bradman's saved the series. Batting all through the fourth day, he went on to make 212 – the second time he had scored double-centuries in back-to-back Tests. It was his 17th Test century, passing the 16 hundreds held by Sutcliffe and Hammond. Chasing a total of 392, England were 148 for 3 at the end of the fifth day but with Fleetwood-Smith, who was known to make birdcalls as he ran in to bowl, taking 6 for 110 (10 wickets in the match), Australia won by 148 runs.

THREE AUSTRALIAN CENTURIES

After Bradman had won the vital toss in the final Test at Melbourne, three Australians scored centuries in a first innings total of 604 – Bradman 169, McCabe 112 and Tasmanian-born Jack Badcock 118. For Bradman his 12th century against England took his aggregate for the series to 810 at an average of 90, which is a record for a Test captain. For England, Ken Farnes recorded the best performance of his England career, taking 6 for 96. After a solid start, England had reached 236 for 5 but the last five wickets fell for just three runs and they were forced to follow-on. Hammond and Barnett both batted well but with Fleetwood-Smith and O'Reilly taking three wickets apiece, the Ashes were soon safe in Australia's keeping – a longish-odds prospect at Christmas! ▶

Don Bradman
(Australia) 1928-48

Test Average 99.94
Test Best 334 v. England, Headingley 1930
Ashes Average 89.79
Ashes Best (as above)

There has been no greater batsman in world cricket than Don Bradman nor has there been a more successful captain in Test cricket. At Headingley in 1930, he made 309 not out on the first day of the third Test, increasing it to 334 the next day. In a single day, Bradman had beaten a Test record that had stood since 1903. He was to hit another triple century at Headingley in 1934 and at The Oval he scored 244, sharing a record stand of 451 in 316 minutes with Ponsford for the second wicket. Named as captain of Australia for England's visit in 1936-37, he had an inauspicious beginning. After losing the first two Tests, his side came back to win the remaining three – his innings of 270, 212 and 169 in those three games played a major part in the result. The unbeaten record of the 1948 Australians was a suitable climax, though his own Test career finished at The Oval on a note of anti-climax. Playing his last Test innings, he was bowled second ball by Eric Hollies. He had needed only four runs from that innings to average exactly 100 in Test matches.

Len Hutton
(England) 1937-55

Test Average *56.67*
Test Best *364 v. Australia, Oval 1938*
Ashes Average *56.47*
Ashes Best *(as above)*

Len Hutton won recognition as one of the greatest batsmen in cricket history through many prodigious feats, one of the earliest being his 364 in The Oval test in 1938. It was at 13 hours 17 minutes, the longest innings and highest Test total to that time and remains the highest innings played in an Ashes series. Many of Hutton's most important innings were played sustaining an uncertain England batting side. Once at Lord's in 1948 he batted so unimpressively that he was dropped for the next Test – a strange decision in retrospect, for he played Lindwall and Miller at their fastest supremely well. This was especially marked in 1950-51 when he averaged 88.83. At Lord's in 1953 he made 145 against Australia and that winter became the first professional to take an MCC side overseas. In 1954-55, his form in the tour matches was as impeccable as ever – he made over 1000 runs in Australia – but after two Tests in New Zealand, he announced his retirement from the game.

BILL O'REILLY IS CLEAN BOWLED, BUT BY A NO-BALL. ENGLAND WICKET-KEEPER LES AMES LOOKS ON

1938

This five-Test series was reduced to four matches with the Manchester rain striking again – the third Test at Old Trafford was abandoned without a ball being bowled. In a contest between two talented teams, led by two of the all-time batting greats, it was ironic that a dusty pitch at Headingley should decide the fate of the Ashes in a drawn series.

At Trent Bridge, for the first time in Tests, four batsmen scored centuries in the same innings in England's 658 for 6 declared – Barnett 126, Hutton 100, Paynter 216 not out and Compton 102. Compton was only 20 years and 19 days – still the youngest to score a century for England. Yet the innings of the match was played by Stan McCabe. With Australia facing impending danger at 194 for 6, McCabe put on 69 with Ben Barnett, then dominated the strike so successfully that he made 127 out of the last 148 in 80 minutes after Barnett was out. He made 232 out of a total of 411. Australia followed-on but Brown with 133 and Bradman with an unbeaten 144 saved the match. It was Bradman's 13th hundred against England, setting a new record in Ashes Tests.

England, reduced to 31 for 3 by McCormick on a lively Lord's pitch in the second Test, were rescued by a fourth wicket stand of 222 by Paynter and Hammond. The little Lancastrian was dismissed one run short his hundred whilst Hammond made 240 – the highest score against Australia at Lord's and the biggest score by an England captain in Ashes Tests. In reply to England's 494, Bill Brown carried his bat through Australia's first innings with 206, his highest score and Australia's 100th century against England. McCormick was again a problem to England on a damp pitch but on the fourth day, Compton and Wellard saw to it that Australia's target was too distant. Bradman was unbeaten on 102 – it was the 200th century in Ashes Tests and Bradman passed Hobbs as the highest scorer in the history of this fixture.

The third Test at Old Trafford having been abandoned because of rain without a ball being bowled, meant that the fourth Test at Headingley took on great importance. Only Hammond was unaffected by the pace of McCormick and the spin of O'Reilly and Fleetwood-Smith and he top-scored with 76 in England's first innings score of 223. Bradman then scored 103 – the sixth Test in a row in which he'd scored a century; it was also his third hundred in successive Tests at Headingley. Bill O'Reilly in England's second innings took another five wickets and in doing so passed the 100-wicket mark in Ashes Tests. Let to make 105 for victory, Australia suffered early setbacks but Lindsay Hassett batted confidently for 33 after being missed at slip second ball and the match was won before the rain came.

HUTTON AT THE OVAL

The course of the final Test at The Oval was virtually determined when Hammond won the toss and elected to bat. At the end of the first day, England were 347 for 1 with Hutton 160 and Leyland 156 – Hutton's century was the 100th for England against Australia. Hutton went on to score a Test record 364 in England's all-Test record of 903 for 7 declared, while Leyland scored a career-high 187 and Hardstaff 169 not out. This was Leyland's last Test, making him the first Englishman to score centuries in his first and last innings against Australia. Australia's cause wasn't helped by injuries to key batsmen Bradman and Fingleton, who were both hurt while in the field. Neither batted in either innings as the visitors were bowled out for 201 and then 123. Despite England's huge win, Australia retained the Ashes.●

THE RESULTS

ENGLAND V AUSTRALIA
Played at The Oval, August 20-24 1938

ENGLAND

L Hutton	c Hassett b O'Reilly	364
WJ Edrich	c Hassett b O'Reilly	12
M Leyland	run out	187
WR Hammond	lbw b Fleetwood-Smith	59
E Paynter	lbw b O'Reilly	0
D Compton	b Waite	1
J Hardstaff	not out	169
A Wood	c and b Barnes	53
H Verity	not out	8
K Farnes	did not bat	
WE Bowes	did not bat	
Extras		50
Total	**903-7 dec**	

Fall of wickets 1-29 2-411 3-546 4-547 5-555 6-770 7-876

Australia Bowling

	O	M	R	W	O	M	R	W
Waite	72	16	150	1				
McCabe	38	8	85	0				
O'Reilly	85	26	178	3				
Fleetwood-Smith	87	11	298	1				
Barnes	38	3	84	1				
Hassett	13	2	52	0				
Bradman	3	2	6	0				

AUSTRALIA

CL Badcock	c Hardstaff b Bowes	0	b Bowes	9
WA Brown	c Hammond b Leyland	69	c Edrich b Farnes	15
SJ McCabe	c Edrich b Farnes	14	c Wood b Farnes	2
AL Hassett	c Compton b Edrich	42	lbw b Bowes	10
S Barnes	b Bowes	41	lbw b Verity	33
BA Barnett	c Wood b Bowes	2	b Farnes	46
MG Waite	b Bowes	8	c Edrich b Verity	0
WJ O'Reilly	c Wood b Bowes	0	not out	7
LO'B Fleetwood-Smith	not out	16	c Leyland b Farnes	0
DG Bradman	absent hurt	0	absent hurt	0
JHW Fingleton	absent hurt	0	absent hurt	0
Extras		9		1
Total		**201**		**123**

Fall of wickets 1-0 2-19 3-70 4-145 5-147 6-160 7-160 8-201
Second Innings 1-15 2-18 3-35 4-41 5-115 6-115 7-117 8-123

England Bowling

	O	M	R	W	O	M	R	W
Farnes	13	2	54	1	12.1	1	63	4
Bowes	19	3	49	5	10	3	25	2
Edrich	10	2	55	1	-	-	-	-
Verity	5	1	15	0	7	3	15	2
Leyland	3.1	0	11	1	5	0	19	0
Hammond	2	0	8	0	-	-	-	-

ENGLAND WON BY AN INNINGS AND 579 RUNS

1920

AUSTRALIA WON SERIES 5-0

1st Test at Sydney

December 17, 18, 20, 21, 22
AUSTRALIA 267 (HL Collins 70) and 581 (WW Armstrong 158 HL Collins 104 C Kellaway 78 CG Macartney 69 W Bardsley 57 JM Taylor 51)
ENGLAND 190 (FE Woolley 52 JB Hobbs 49) and 281 (JB Hobbs 59 JW Hearne 57 EH Hendren 56 W Rhodes 45)

AUSTRALIA WON BY 377 RUNS

2nd Test at Melbourne

December 31 January 1, 3, 4
AUSTRALIA 499 (CE Pellew 116 JM Gregory 100 JM Taylor 68 HL Collins 64 W Bardsley 51)
ENGLAND 251 (JB Hobbs 122 EH Hendren 67 JM Gregory 7-69) and 157 (FE Woolley 50 WW Armstrong 4-26)

AUSTRALIA WON BY AN INNINGS AND 91 RUNS

3rd Test at Adelaide

January 14, 15, 17, 18, 19, 20
AUSTRALIA 354 (HL Collins 162 WAS Oldfield 50 J Ryder 44 CH Parkin 5-60) and 582 (C Kellaway 147 WW Armstrong 121 CE Pellew 104 JM Gregory 78* H Howell 4-15)
ENGLAND 447 (CAG Russell 135* FE Woolley 79 JWH Makepeace 60 JWHT Douglas 60 AA Mailey 5-160) and 370 (JB Hobbs 123 CAG Russell 59 EH Hendren 51 PGH Fender 42 AA Mailey 5-142)

AUSTRALIA WON BY 119 RUNS

4th Test at Melbourne

February 11, 12, 14, 15, 16
ENGLAND 284 (JWH Makepeace 117 JWHT Douglas 50 AA Mailey 4-115) and 315 (W Rhodes 73 JWHT Douglas 60 PGH Fender 59 JWH Makepeace 54 AA Mailey 9-121)
AUSTRALIA 389 (WW Armstrong 123* JM Gregory 77 HL Collins 59 W Bardsley 56 PGH Fender 5-122) and 211-2 (JM Gregory 76* J Ryder 52*)

AUSTRALIA WON BY 8 WICKETS

5th Test at Sydney

February 25, 26, 28, March 1
ENGLAND 204 (FE Woolley 53 JB Hobbs 40 C Kellaway 4-27) and 280 (JWHTDouglas 68 PGH Fender 40 AA Mailey 5-119)
AUSTRALIA 392 (CG Macartney 170 JM Gregory 93 PGH Fender 5-90) and 93-1(W Bardsley 50*)

AUSTRALIA WON BY 9 WICKETS

1921

AUSTRALIA WON SERIES 3-0

1st Test at Trent Bridge

May 28, 30
ENGLAND 112 (JM Gregory 6-58) and 147 (EA McDonald 5-32)
AUSTRALIA 232 (W Bardsley 66) and 30-0

AUSTRALIA WON BY 10 WICKETS

2nd Test at Lord's

June 1,13,14
ENGLAND 187 (FE Woolley 95 EA McDonald 4-58 AA Mailey 4-55) and 283 (FE Woolley 93 Hon LH Tennyson 74* AE Dipper 40 JM Gregory 4-76 EA McDonald 4-89)
AUSTRALIA 342 (W Bardsley 88 JM Gregory 52 H Carter 46 CE Pellew 43 FJ Durston 4-102) and 131-2 (W Bardsley 63* THE Andrews 49)

AUSTRALIA WON BY 8 WICKETS

3rd Test at Headingley

July 2, 4, 5
AUSTRALIA 407 (CG Macartney 15 WW Armstrong 77 CE Pellew 52 JM Taylor 50 CH Parkin 4-106) and 273-7 dec (TJ Andrews 92 H Carter 47)
ENGLAND 259 (JWHT Douglas 75 Hon LH Tennyson 63 G Brown 57 EA McDonald 4-105) and 202 (G Brown 46)

AUSTRALIA WON BY 219 RUNS

4th Test at Old Trafford

July 23 (no play) 25, 26
ENGLAND 362-4 dec (CAG Russell 101 GE Tyldesley 78* CP Mead 47, PGH Fender 44* FE Woolley 41) and 44-1
AUSTRALIA 175 (HL Collins 40 CH Parkin 5-38)

MATCH DRAWN

5th Test at The Oval

August 13, 15, 16
ENGLAND 403-8 dec (CP Mead 182* Hon LH Tennyson 51 EA McDonald 5-143) and 244-2 (CAG Russell 102* G Brown 84 JW Hitch 51*)
AUSTRALIA 389 (TJ Andrews 94 JM Taylor 75 CG Macartney 61)

MATCH DRAWN

1924-25

AUSTRALIA WON SERIES 4-1

1st Test at Sydney

December 19, 20, 22, 23, 24, 26, 27
AUSTRALIA 450 (HL Collins 114 WH Ponsford 110 JM Taylor 43 VY Richardson 42 MW Tate 6-130) and 452 (JM Taylor 108 AJ Richardson 98 HL Collins 60 AA Mailey 46* MW Tate 5-98)
ENGLAND 298 (JB Hobbs 115 EH Hendren 74* H Sutcliffe 59 JM Gregory 5-111 AA Mailey 4-129) and 411 (FE Woolley 123 H Sutcliffe 115 JB Hobbs 57 AP Freeman 50* APF Chapman 44)

AUSTRALIA WON BY 193 RUNS

2nd Test at Melbourne

January 1,2, 3, 5, 6, 7, 8
AUSTRALIA 600 (VY Richardson 138 WH Ponsford 128 AEV Hartkopf 80 JM Taylor 72 JM Gregory 44) and 250 (JM Taylor 90 MW Tate 6-99)
ENGLAND 479 (H Sutcliffe 176 JB Hobbs 154) and 290 (H Sutcliffe 127 FE Woolley 50 AA Mailey 5-92 JM Gregory 4-87)

AUSTRALIA WON BY 81 RUNS

3rd Test at Adelaide

January 16, 17, 19, 20, 21, 22, 23
AUSTRALIA 489 (J Ryder 201* TJ Andrews 72 AJ Richardson 69 WAS Oldfield 47 R Kilner 4-127) and 250 (J Ryder 88 WH Ponsford 43 FE Woolley 4-77 R Kilner 4-51)
ENGLAND 365 (JB Hobbs 119 EH Hendren 92) and 363 (WW Whysall 75 H Sutcliffe 59 APF Chapman 58)

AUSTRALIA WON BY 11 RUNS

4th Test at Melbourne

February 13, 14, 16, 17, 18
ENGLAND 548 (H Sutcliffe 143 WW Whysall 76 R Kilner 74 JB Hobbs 66 EH Hendren 65 JW Hearne 44 FE Woolley 40 AA Mailey 4-186)
AUSTRALIA 269 (JM Taylor 86) and 250 (JM Taylor 68 JM Gregory 45 C Kellaway 42 MW Tate 5-75)

ENGLAND WON BY AN INNINGS AND 29 RUNS

5th Test at Sydney

February 27, 28 March 2,3, 4
AUSTRALIA 295 (WH Ponsford 80 AF Kippax 42 MW Tate 4-92 R Kilner 4-97) and 325 (TJ Andrews 80 C Kellaway 73 WAS Oldfield 65* MW Tate 5-115)
ENGLAND 167 (FE Woolley 47 CV Grimmett 5-45) and 146 (CV Grimmett 6-37)

AUSTRALIA WON BY 307 RUNS

1926

ENGLAND WON SERIES 1-0

1st Test at Trent Bridge

June 12, 14 (no play) 15 (no play)
ENGLAND 32-0
AUSTRALIA did not bat

MATCH DRAWN

2nd Test at Lord's

June 26, 28, 29
AUSTRALIA 383 (W Bardsley 193 R Kilner 4-70) and 194-5 (CG Macartney 133*)
ENGLAND 475-3 dec (EH Hendren 127* JB Hobbs 119 FE Woolley 87 H Sutcliffe 82 APF Chapman 50*)

MATCH DRAWN

3rd Test at Headingley

July 10, 12, 13
AUSTRALIA 494 (CG Macartney 151 WM Woodfull 141 AJ Richardson 100 J Ryder 42 MW Tate 4-99)
ENGLAND 294 (CG Macaulay 76 JB Hobbs 49 CV Grimmett 5-88) and 254-3 (H Sutcliffe 94 JB Hobbs 88 APF Chapman 42*)

MATCH DRAWN

4th Test at Old Trafford

July 24, 26, 27
AUSTRALIA 335 (WM Woodfull 117 CG Macartney 109 CF Root 4-84)
ENGLAND 305-5 (GE Tyldesley 81 JB Hobbs 74 FE Woolley 58)

MATCH DRAWN

5th Test at The Oval

August 14, 16, 17, 18
ENGLAND 280 (H Sutcliffe 76 APF Chapman 49 AA Mailey 6-138) and 436 (H Sutcliffe 161 JB Hobbs 100)
AUSTRALIA 302 (JM Gregory 73 HL Collins 61) and 125 (W Rhodes 4-44)
Captains APF Chapman (E) HL Collins (A)

ENGLAND WON BY 289 RUNS

1928-29

ENGLAND WON SERIES 4-1

1st Test at Brisbane

November 30, December 1, 3, 4, 5
ENGLAND 521 (EH Hendren 169 H Larwood 70 APF Chapman 50 JB Hobbs 49 WR Hammond 44) and 342-8 dec (CP Mead 73 DR Jardine 65 EH Hendren 45 CV Grimmett 6-131)
AUSTRALIA 122 (H Larwood 6-32) and 66 (JC White 4-7)

ENGLAND WON BY 675 RUNS

2nd Test at Sydney

December 14, 15, 17, 18, 19, 20
AUSTRALIA 253 (WM Woodfull 68 WAS Oldfield 41* G Geary 5-35) and 397 (HSTL Hendry 112 WM Woodfull 111 J Ryder 79 OE Nothling 44 MW Tate 4-99)
ENGLAND 636 (WR Hammond 251 EH Hendren 74 G Geary 66 H Larwood 43 JB Hobbs 40 DD Blackie 4-148) and 16-2

ENGLAND WON BY 8 WICKETS

3rd Test at Melbourne

December 29, 31 January 1, 2, 3, 4, 5
AUSTRALIA 397 (J Ryder 112 AF Kippax 100 DG Bradman 79 EL a Beckett 41) and 351 (DG Bradman 112 WM Woodfull 107 AF Kippax 41 JC White 5-107)
ENGLAND 417 (WR Hammond 200 DR Jardine 62 H Sutcliffe 58 DD Blackie 6-94) and 332-7 (H Sutcliffe 135 JB Hobbs 49 EH Hendren 45)

ENGLAND WON BY 3 WICKETS

4th Test at Adelaide

February 1, 2, 4, 5, 6, 7, 8
ENGLAND 334 (WR Hammond 119* JB Hobbs 74 H Sutcliffe 64 CV Grimmett 5-102) and 383 (WR Hammond 177 DR Jardine 98 MW Tate 47 RK Oxenham 4-67)
AUSTRALIA 369 (AA Jackson 164 J Ryder 63 DG Bradman 40 JC White 5-130 MW Tate 4-77) and 336 (J Ryder 87 DG Bradman 58 AF Kippax 51 JC White 8-126)

ENGLAND WON BY 12 RUNS

5th Test at Melbourne

March 8, 9, 11, 12, 13, 14, 15, 16
ENGLAND 519 (JB Hobbs 142 M Leyland 137 EH Hendren 95) and 257 (JB Hobbs 65 MW Tate 54 M Leyland 53* TW Wall 5-66)
AUSTRALIA 491 (DG Bradman 123 WM Woodfull 102 AG Fairfax 65 G Geary 5-105) and 287-5 (J Ryder 57* WAS Oldfield 48 AA Jackson 46)

AUSTRALIA WON BY 5 WICKETS

1930
AUSTRALIA WON SERIES 2-1

1st Test at Trent Bridge
June 13, 14,,16,17
ENGLAND 270 (JB Hobbs 78 APF Chapman 52 RWV Robins 50 CV Grimmett 5-107) and 302 (JB Hobbs 74 EH Hendren 72 H Sutcliffe 58 ret hurt CV Grimmett 5-94)
AUSTRALIA 144 (AF Kippax 64* RWV Robins 4-51) and 335 (DG Bradman 131 SJ McCabe 49)

ENGLAND WON BY 93 RUNS

2nd Test at Lord's
June 27, 28, 30 July 1
ENGLAND 425 (KS Duleepsinhji 173 MW Tate 54 EH Hendren 48 FE Woolley 41 AG Fairfax 4-101) and 375 (APF Chapman 121 GOB Allen 57 KS Duleepsinhji 48 CV Grimmett 6-167)
AUSTRALIA 729-6 dec (DG Bradman 254 WM Woodfull 155 AF Kippax 83 WH Ponsford 81 SJ McCabe 44 WAS Oldfield 43*) and 72-3

AUSTRALIA WON BY 7 WICKETS

3rd Test at Headingley
July 1, 12, 14, 15
AUSTRALIA 566 (DG Bradman 334 AF Kippax 77 WM Woodfull 50 MW Tate 5-124)
ENGLAND 391 (WR Hammond 113 APF Chapman 45 M Leyland 44 CV Grimmett 5-135) and 95-3

MATCH DRAWN

4th Test at Old Trafford
July 25, 26, 28, 29 (no play)
AUSTRALIA 345 (WH Ponsford 83 WM Woodfull 54 AF Kippax 51 CV Grimmett 50 AG Fairfax 49)
ENGLAND 251-8 (H Sutcliffe 74 KS Duleepsinhji 54 SJ McCabe 4-41)

MATCH DRAWN

5th Test at The Oval
August 16, 18, 19, 20, 21 (no play), 22
ENGLAND 405 (H Sutcliffe 161 RES Wyatt 64 KS Duleepsinhji 50 JB Hobbs 47 CV Grimmett 4-135) and 251 (PM Hornibrook 7-92)
AUSTRALIA 695 (DG Bradman 232 WH Ponsford 110 AA Jackson 73 WM Woodfull 54 SJ McCabe 54 AG Fairfax 53* IAR Peebles 6-204)

AUSTRALIA WON BY AN INNINGS AND 39 RUNS

1932-33
ENGLAND WON SERIES 4-1

1st Test at Sydney
December 2, 3, 5, 6, 7
AUSTRAL!A 360 (SJ McCabe 187* VY Richardson 49 H Larwood 5-96 W Voce 4-110) and 164 (JWH Fingleton 40 H Larwood 5-28)
ENGLAND 524 (H Sutcliffe 194 WR Hammond 112 Nawab of Pataudi Sr 102) and 1-0

ENGLAND WON BY 10 WICKETS

2nd Test at Melbourne
December 30, 31 January 2, 3
AUSTRALIA 228 (JHW Fingleton 83) and 191 (DG Bradman 103*)
ENGLAND 169 (H Sutcliffe 52 WJ O'Reilly 5-63 TW Wall 4-52) and 139 (WJ O'Reilly 5-66 H Ironmonger 4-26)

AUSTRALIA WON BY 111 RUNS

3rd Test at Adelaide
January 13, 14, 16, 17, 18, 19
ENGLAND 341 (M Leyland 83 RES Wyatt 78 E Paynter 77 H Verity 45 TW Wall 5-72) and 412 (WR Hammond 85 LEG Ames 69 DR Jardine 56 RES Wyatt 49 M Leyland 42 H Verity 40 WJ O'Reilly 4-79)
AUSTRALIA 222 (WH Ponsford 85 WAS Oldfield 41 retired hurt GO Allen 4-71) and 193 (WM Woodfull 73* DG Bradman 66 H Larwood 4-71 GO Allen 4-50)

ENGLAND WON BY 338 RUNS

4th Test at Woolloongabba, Brisbane
February 10, 11, 13, 14, 15, 16
AUSTRALIA 340 (VY Richardson 83 DG Bradman 76 WM Woodfull 67 H Larwood 4-101) and 175
ENGLAND 356 (H Sutcliffe 86 E Paynter 83 DR Jardine 46 WJ O'Reilly 4-120) and 162-4 (M Leyland 86)

ENGLAND WON BY 6 WICKETS

5th Test at Sydney
February 23, 24, 25, 27, 28
AUSTRALIA 435 (LS Darling 85 SJ McCabe 73 LPJ O'Brien 61 WAS Oldfield 52 DG Bradman 48 PK Lee 42 H Larwood 4-98) and 182 (DG Bradman 71 WM Woodfull 67 H Verity 5-33)
ENGLAND 454 (WR Hammond 101 H Larwood 98 H Sutcliffe 56 RES Wyatt 51 GO Allen 48 M Leyland 42 PK Lee 4-111) and 168-2 (WR Hammond 75* RES Wyatt 61*)

ENGLAND WON BY 8 WICKETS

1934
AUSTRALIA WON SERIES 2-1

1st Test at Trent Bridge
June 8, 9, 11, 12
AUSTRALIA 374 (AG Chipperfield 99 SJ McCabe 65 WH Ponsford 53 K Farnes 5-102) and 273-8 dec (SJ McCabe 88 WA Brown 73 K Farnes 5-77)
ENGLAND 268 (EH Hendren 79 H Sutcliffe 62 G Geary 53 CV Grimmett 5-81) and 141 (CF Walters 46 WJ O'Reilly 7-54)

AUSTRALIA WON BY 238 RUNS

2nd Test at Lord's
June 22, 23, 25
ENGLAND 440 (LEG Ames 120 M Leyland 109 CF Walters 82 TM Wall 4-108)
AUSTRALIA 284 (WA Brown 105 H Verity 7-61) and 118 (WM Woodfull 43 H Verity 8-43)

ENGLAND WON BY AN INNINGS AND 38 RUNS

3rd Test at Old Trafford
July 6, 7, 9, 10
ENGLAND 627-9 dec (M Leyland 153 EH Hendren 132 LEG Ames 72 H Sutcliffe 63 GO Allen 61 H Verity 60* CF Walters 52 WJ O'Reilly 7-189) and 123-0 dec (H Sutcliffe 69* CF Walters 50*)
AUSTRALIA 491 (SJ McCabe 137 WM Woodfull 73 WA Brown 72 H Verity 4-78) and 66-1

MATCH DRAWN

4th Test at Headingley
July 20, 21, 23, 24
ENGLAND 200 (CF Walters 44 CV Grimmett 4-57) and 229-6 (M Leyland 49* CF Walters 45 RES Wyatt 44 EH Hendren 42)
AUSTRALIA 584 (DG Bradman 304 WH Ponsford 181 WE Bowes 6-142) Captains RES Wyatt (E) WM Woodfull (A)

MATCH DRAWN

5th Test at The Oval
August 18, 20, 21, 22
AUSTRALIA 701 (WH Ponsford 266 DG Bradman 244 WM Woodfull 49 WAS Oldfield 42* WE Bowes 4-164 GO Allen 4-170) and 327 (DG Bradman 77 SJ McCabe 70 HI Ebeling 41 WE Bowes 5-55 EW Clark 5-98)
ENGLAND 321 (M Leyland 110 CF Walters 64) and 145 (WR Hammond 43 CV Grimmett 5-64)

AUSTRALIA WON BY 562 RUNS

1936-37
AUSTRALIA WON SERIES 3-2

1st Test at Brisbane
December 4, 5, 7, 8, 9
ENGLAND 358 (M Leyland 126 CJ Barnett 69 J Hardstaff jnr 43 WJ O'Reilly 5-102) and 256 (GO Allen 68 FA ward 6-102)
AUSTRALIA 234 (JHW Fingleton 100 SJ McCabe 51 W Voce 6-41) and 58 (GO Allen 5-36 W Voce 4-16)

ENGLAND WON BY 322 RUNS

2nd Test at Sydney
December 18, 19, 21, 22
ENGLAND 426-6 dec (WR Hammond 231* CJ Barnett 57 M Leyland 42)
AUSTRALIA 80 (W Voce 4-10) and 324 (SJ McCabe 93 DG Bradman 82 JHW Fingleton 73)

ENGLAND WON BY AN INNINGS AND 22 RUNS

3rd Test at Melbourne
January 1, 2, 4, 5, 6, 7
AUSTRALIA 200-9 dec (SJ McCabe 63) and 564 (DG Bradman 270 JHW Fingleton 136 KE Rigg 47)
ENGLAND 76-9 dec (MW Sievers 5-21) and 323 (M Leyland 11* RWV Robins 61 WR Hammond 51 LO'B Fleetwood-Smith 5-124)

AUSTRALIA WON BY 365 RUNS

4th Test at Adelaide
January 29, 30 February 1, 2, 3, 4
AUSTRALIA 288 (SJ McCabe 88 AG Chipperfield 57* WA Brown 42) and 433 (DG Bradman 212 SJ McCabe 55 RG Gregory 50 WR Hammond 5-57)
ENGLAND 330 (CJ Barnett 129 LEG Ames 52 M Leyland 45 LO'B Fleetwood-Smith 4-129 WJ O'Reilly 4-51) and 243 (RES Wyatt 50 J Hardstaff jnr 43 LO'B Fleetwood-Smith 6-110)

AUSTRALIA WON BY 148 RUNS

5th Test at Melbourne
February 26, 27 March 1, 2, 3
AUSTRALIA 604 (DG Bradman 169 CL Badcock 118 SJ McCabe 112 RG Gregory 80 K Farnes 6-96)
ENGLAND 239 (J Hardstaff jnr 83 TS Worthington 44 WJ O'Reilly 5-51 LJ Nash 4-70) and 165 (WR Hammond 56 CJ Barnett 41)

AUSTRALIA WON BY AN INNINGS AND 200 RUNS

1938
SERIES DRAWN 1-1

1st Test at Trent Bridge
June 10, 11, 13, 14
ENGLAND 658-8 dec (E Paynter 216* CJ Barnett 126 DCS Compton 102, L Hutton 100 LEG Ames 46 LO'B Fleetwood-Smith 4-153)
AUSTRALIA 411 (SJ McCabe 232 DG Bradman 51 WA Brown 48 K Farnes 4-106 DVP Wright 4-153) and 427-6 dec (DG Bradman 144* WA Brown 133 JHW Fingleton 40)

MATCH DRAWN

2nd Test at Lord's
June 24, 25, 27, 28
ENGLAND 494 (WR Hammond 240 E Paynter 99 LEG Ames 83 EL McCormick 4-101 WJ O'Reilly 4-93) and 242-8 dec (DCS Compton 76* E Paynter 43)
AUSTRALIA 422 (WA Brown 206 AL Hassett 56 WJ O'Reilly 42) and 204-6 (DG Bradman 102* AL Hassett 42)

MATCH DRAWN

■ The 3rd Test at Old Trafford was abandoned without a ball being bowled

4th Test at Headingley
July 22, 23, 25
ENGLAND 223 (WR Hammond 76 WJ O'Reilly 5-66) and 123 (WJ O'Reilly 5-56 LO'B Fleetwood-Smith 4-34)
AUSTRALIA 242 (DG Bradman 103 BA Barnett 57 K Farnes 4-77) and 107-5

AUSTRALIA WON BY 5 WICKETS

5th Test at The Oval
August 20, 22, 23, 24
ENGLAND 903-7 dec (L Hutton 364 M Leyland 187 J Hardstaff jnr 169* WR Hammond 59 A Wood 53)
AUSTRALIA 201 (WA Brown 69 AL Hassett 42 SG Barnes 41 WE Bowes 5-49) and 123 (BA Barnett 46 K Farnes 4-63)

ENGLAND WON BY AN INNINGS AND 579 RUNS

THE ASHES COMPLETES A CENTURY

1946-47

The last pre-war Test had ended in England's biggest-ever victory; the first post-war Test brought a record victory for Australia. Yet England might have come much closer to recovering the Ashes but for Bradman. And even Bradman needed a slice of luck to re-establish himself in Test cricket at the age of 38.

After an uncertain beginning in the first Test at Brisbane, Bradman had made 28 when he gave what seemed a perfectly clean catch to Ikin in the gully, only to be given not out. He went on to make 187 and his newly-appointed deputy Hassett 128 as they added 276 for the third wicket. All-rounder Colin McCool, playing in his first Test against England, missed a century by just five runs as Australia scored 645. By the time a demoralised England had started to bat on the third day, the light had deteriorated and there were frequent rain showers. Keith Miller was unplayable and took 7 for 60 as England were bowled out for 141. After a torrential storm, accompanied by hail and winds of up to 80 mph, during which the ground was submerged and the covers and stumps floated away, play was miraculously resumed on the fifth morning. After Hutton had been dis-missed by the first ball of the second innings, Ernie Toshack finished off a match won almost as much by the ele-ments as by the Australian team.

Though England had cruel luck with the weather at Brisbane, they could offer no such excuse at Sydney, where Johnson's off-spin had them in all sorts of trouble and they were all out for 255. Australia's total of 659 for 8 declared was due mainly to a record fifth-wicket partnership of 405 between Barnes and Bradman, who both scored 234. For England, the extrovert Godfrey Evans was making his Test debut behind the stumps and he demonstrated why he would go on to play in 91 Tests by not conceding a single bye during Australia's big total. Edrich, who had top scored in England's first innings with 71 made a splendid 119 in the second and though at one stage it looked as if England might hold out for a draw, the leg-spin of Colin McCool demolished the tail and Australia won by mid-afternoon on the final day.

COOL HAND McCOOL

At Melbourne, England, hampered as they were by injuries to Edrich and Voce, did well to have Australia 192 for 6 but McCool, having narrowly missed a debut century, reached a timely hundred as the hosts scored 365. England's total of 351 owed everything to two stands: 147 by Washbrook and Edrich and 113 for the sixth wicket by Ikin and Yardley. With little in it on first innings, Arthur Morris batted for over six hours in the second for 155 whilst Ray Lindwall, coming in at No.9, made a whirlwind 100. Set an out-of-reach 551, England made a good start with openers Washbrook and Hutton putting on 138, but wickets fell steadily thereafter until Yardley and Bedser, assisted by a delay for rain, saw

COLIN McCOOL OF AUSTRALIA ON HIS WAY TO A MAIDEN CENTURY AT MELBOURNE, SECOND TEST 1947

RAY LINDWALL, COMING IN AT NUMBER NINE, MADE A WHIRLWIND 100 IN THE MELBOURNE TEST

the crisis through. It was the first drawn Test in Australia for 65 years.

Compton and Morris provided an unusual double in the fourth Test at Adelaide in each making two hundreds in the match, though Compton's second was of greatest value, coming as it did when England needed time as well as runs. Hutton and Washbrook gave England a start of 137 and with Hardstaff and Compton adding 118, they were certain of a considerable total. England were disappointed that their total of 460 was passed, especially after Bedser bowled Bradman for 0, but a brilliant fourth morning innings by Miller, who made 141 not out gave Australia the edge. Hutton and Washbrook again gave England a century opening partnership but then wickets began to tumble until Compton farmed the strike and this eventually enabled England to declare. There wasn't enough time for Australia to make the 314 for victory but Morris made his third consecutive century against England.

LINDWALL STRIKES AT SYDNEY

In the final Test at Sydney, Hutton and Edrich resisted some hostile early bowling on a moist pitch to add 150 for the second wicket as England ended the first day on 237 for 6. After Saturday was washed out, Hutton was stricken by tonsilitis and could not resume on Monday as Lindwall demolished the tail. Barnes and Morris gave Australia a start of 126 but Bedser dismissed them both before Doug Wright, with 7 for 105 off 29 eight-ball overs, helped England gain a lead of 27 on the first innings. With Hutton unable to bat in England's second innings, however, only Compton got to grips with McCool's leg-spin, hitting 76 in a total of 186. Australia needed 214 to win and although they lost a couple of early wickets, fine knocks by Bradman and Hassett and Miller's bold strokeplay saw them home by five wickets.

1948

With Lindwall and Miller reaching their peak, ably backed up by Bill Johnston, with Arthur Morris emerging as a left-hander in the great Australian tradition, and with Bradman, Barnes and Lindsay Hassett as effective as ever, this was a great Australian side, lacking only a top-class spinner. Australia had four big victory margins in five Tests and it was only at Old Trafford that Australia was unable to force victory.

In the opening Test at Trent Bridge, England were unlucky to bat first on a wicket enlivened by rain and struggled to 74 for 8 when Bedser linked with Laker to add 89. This was Bradman's farewell tour and he and Hassett both made centuries as Australia gained a first innings lead of 344 runs. England fought back well with Denis Compton making 184, his highest score against Australia. Compton and Hutton weathered bad light, occasional drizzle and a lot of short-pitched bowling to take England to 441. Bradman then failed to score for only the fifth time against England, but ▶

ENGLAND WICKET-KEEPER GODFREY EVANS IN ACTION

Arthur Morris
(Australia) 1946-55

Test Average *46.49*
Test Best *206 v. England, Adelaide Oval 1951*
Ashes Average *50.73*
Ashes Best *(as above)*

Left-handed Arthur Morris was one of Australia's finest opening batsmen. So successful were his methods that in 24 matches against England, he scored 2,080 runs, including eight centuries and averaged just over 50. His consistency meant that England, in the early days of Morris at least, rarely managed the good start that usually gives a side encouragement. In 1946-47 he scored 155 in the second innings at Melbourne and this was followed by 122 and 124 not out at Adelaide – the first time an Australian had hit a century in each innings of a Test in his own country. He did even better on his first tour of England in 1948. He headed the Test averages above Bradman at 87.00. He hit 196 at The Oval, 182 at Headingley and 105 at Lord's. At Headingley he and Bradman put on 301 for the second wicket and helped Australia to a remarkable victory by 7 wickets when set to get 404 in 345 minutes on the last day.

14 AUGUST 1948: DON BRADMAN IS BOWLED FOR A DUCK BY A GOOGLY FROM ERIC HOLLIES

an in-form Barnes led the visitors to an eight-wicket victory.

The 150th Test match between England and Australia at Lord's bore the hallmark of Australia's all-round competence. England did well have Australia 258 for 7 at the end of the first day but the tail held on and they reached 350. Lindwall then ripped the heart out of the England batting in a fiery spell, giving Australia a first innings lead of 135 runs. Barnes and Morris extended that lead with an opening stand of 122, then Barnes and Bradman put on 174. Though Bradman missed a century, his innings of 89 made it 14 successive Ashes Tests in which he had scored at least half a century. After Miller's quick-fire 74, the declaration came and so did rain. England, facing an absurd victory target of 596 on a lively pitch, offered no resistance once Compton had been superbly caught by Miller and Australia won by 409 runs.

Compton was again the hero at Old Trafford, scoring 145 not out in England's total of 363, this after retiring hurt on four while attempting to hook Lindwall. During the course of England's

first innings, Barnes at silly mid-on was seriously injured when hit by a pull-drive by Pollard and Australia, disrupted by his absence at the start of the innings began badly and never recovered. Bedser and Pollard did the damage as Australia were dismissed for 221. Washbrook and Edrich extended England's lead before declaring at 174 for 3. Needing 317 for victory, Australia were 92 for 1 when the rain came.

Australia's seven-wicket win in the fourth Test at Headingley ranks as one of the most famous of all time. At one point 423 for 2, England had cause to feel disappointment at being all out for 496, with Washbrook and Edrich both making centuries. For Australia, 19-year-old Neil Harvey, playing in his first Test against England scored 112 – he was the first Australian left-hander to score a century in his maiden Ashes Test. Loxton and Lindwall then saw to it that Australia came close to England's considerable total. Yardley's team then made steady progress towards a big lead and when England declared on the last morning, Australia wanted 404 in 344 minutes to win. Fittingly, Bradman played a major role with his last Test century. He scored 173 not out and with Arthur Morris making 182, put on 301 for the second wicket in only 217 minutes. Bradman's century was his fourth in six innings at Headingley, and for the first time in Ashes history, a team won against a third innings declaration.

Australia then hammered home their superiority in the final Test at The Oval, with Ray Lindwall taking 6 for 20 as they bowled England out for just 52, a score which remains England's lowest in a home Test. By the end of the first day, Australia were already 101 ahead for the loss of two wickets, one of which was Bradman. Needing just four runs for a Test average of 100, he was out second ball to an Eric Hollies googly. Morris went on to make 196, his third century of the series, taking his five-Test aggregate to 696 runs at an average of 87. Hutton, top-scorer with 30 in England's first innings, again stood alone, batting over four hours with a variety of partners for a top-score of 64 as Australia won by an innings and 149 runs. ▶

DENIS COMPTON PLAYS A BOUNCER FROM AUSTRALIAN FAST BOWLER RAY LINDWALL

THE RESULTS

ENGLAND v AUSTRALIA
Played at Headingley, July 22-27 1948

ENGLAND

Batsman	Dismissal	R	Dismissal	R
L Hutton	b Lindwall	81	c Bradman b Johnson	57
C Washbrook	c Lindwall b Johnston	143	c Harvey b Johnston	65
WJ Edrich	c Morris b Johnston	111	lbw b Lindwall	54
AV Bedser	c and b Johnson	79	c Hassett b Miller	17
DCS Compton	c Saggers b Lindwall	23	c Miller b Johnston	66
JF Crapp	b Toshack	5	b Lindwall	18
NWD Yardley	b Miller	25	c Harvey b Johnston	7
K Cranston	b Loxton	10	c Saggers b Johnston	0
TG Evans	c Hassett b Loxton	3	not out	47
JC Laker	c Saggers b Loxton	4	not out	15
R Pollard	not out	0		
Extras		12		19
Total		**496**		**365-8 dec**

Fall of wickets 1-168 2-268 3-423 4-426 5-447 6-473 7-486 8-490 9-496 10-496
Second Innings 1-129 2-129 3-232 4-260 5-277 6-278 7-293 8-330

Australia Bowling (4-ball overs)

	O	M	R	W	O	M	R	W
Lindwall	38	10	79	2	26	6	84	2
Miller	17.1	2	43	1	21	5	53	1
Johnston	38	13	86	1	29	5	95	4
Toshack	35	6	112	1	-	-	-	-
Loxton	26	4	55	3	10	2	29	0
Johnson	33	9	89	2	21	2	85	1
Morris	5	0	20	0	-	-	-	-

AUSTRALIA

Batsman	Dismissal	R	Dismissal	R
AR Morris	c Cranston b Bedser	6	c Pollard b Yardley	182
AL Hassett	c Crapp b Pollard	13	c and b Compton	17
DG Bradman	b Pollard	33	not out	173
KR Miller	c Edrich b Yardley	58	lbw b Cranston	12
RN Harvey	b Laker	112	not out	4
SJE Loxton	b Yardley	93		
IW Johnson	c Cranston b Laker	10		
RR Lindwall	c Crapp b Bedser	77		
RA Saggers	st Evans b Laker	5		
WA Johnston	c Edrich b Bedser	13		
ERH Toshack	not out	12		
Extras		26		16
Total		**458**		**404-3**

Fall of wickets 1-13 2-65 3-68 4-189 5-294 6-329 7-344 8-355 9-403 10-458
Second Innings 1-57 2-358 3-396

England Bowling

	O	M	R	W	O	M	R	W
Bedser	31.2	4	92	3	21	2	56	0
Pollard	38	6	104	2	22	6	55	0
Cranston	14	1	51	0	7.1	0	28	1
Edrich	3	0	19	0	-	-	-	-
Laker	30	8	113	3	32	11	93	0
Yardley	17	6	38	2	13	1	44	1
Compton	3	0	15	0	15	3	82	1
Hutton	-	-	-	-	4	1	30	0

AUSTRALIA WON BY 7 WICKETS

ARTHUR MORRIS (SECOND L, HALF HIDDEN) IS CAUGHT BY ENGLAND'S TREVOR BAILEY (DIVING) OFF THE BOWLING OF ALEC BEDSER (SECOND L), WATCHED BY ENGLAND WICKETKEEPER GODFREY EVANS

1950-51

After twenty years of trying to counter Australia's batting genius Don Bradman, England were now taking on a team without him. But with Morris, Harvey, Miller, Lindwall and new captain Lindsay Hassett, this was still a formidable Australian side, which won the first four Tests before England struck in the fifth.

Australia were bowled out on a good pitch on the first day for 228 before England were caught on a rain-affected wicket. Freddie Brown was now the England captain and he declared at 68 for 7 as his side had no answer in the impossible conditions to Johnston and Miller. The move paid dividends as Australia lost their first three wickets without a run on the board and after being overwhelmed by medium-pacers Bedser and Bailey, Australia too declared, this time at 32 for 7! Needing 193 to win, England slumped to 30 for 6, and even a great last day great innings of 62 not out by Len Hutton, coming in at number 8, could not save them.

England showed again with a smaller margin of defeat at Melbourne that there wasn't a great deal between the sides. Bedser and Bailey dismissed Australia for 194 on the first day. However, England were struggling at 61 for 6 before skipper Brown, with Bailey's help, more than doubled the score and Evans hit a rapid 49. A two-day break for Sunday and Christmas Day was followed by an England fightback. Bedser and Bailey again bowled admirably and Brown took four middle-order wickets leaving England in need of 179. Hutton batted well but the combination of Johnston, Lindwall and Iverson proved just too much for the tourists.

In making 290 in their first innings of the third Test at Sydney, England suffered injuries to Bailey (thumb broken by a ball from Lindwall) and Wright (torn tendon as he was run out). This left them with three main bowlers, and Miller with an unbeaten 145 took full advantage to help Australia make 426. The Australian all-rounder had thus exerted a huge influence on the match so far, having taken three key wickets in his 4 for 37 and a dazzling slip catch to dismiss Washbrook. Now Iverson the spinner took over and with his mixture of off and top-spin took 6 for 27 as England collapsed to lose by an innings.

Arthur Morris, who had struggled in the first three Tests with just 45 runs including two ducks, struck form with his career-best 206 in Australia's first innings of the fourth Test at Adelaide. England's innings owed everything to Hutton. Scoring an unbeaten 156, he became the first English batsman since the turn of the century to twice carry his bat through an innings. Burke, only 20 and playing in his first Test, proceeded to his hundred but Miller fell one run short before Hassett declared, leaving England to make 503 to win. Hutton and Washbrook started with 74 but Compton's run of cheap dismissals continued and after top-scorer Simpson became Johnston's fourth victim, the tail collapsed against Miller and Johnson. England skipper Freddie Brown didn't bat in the second innings, having been involved in a car accident during the match.

FIFTH TEST: THE OVAL

England's eight-wicket victory in the fifth Test represented their first win over Australia in more than two decades, dating back to the record innings and 579-run margin at The Oval in 1938. With Bedser and Brown taking five wickets apiece, Australia were bowled out for 217. This time England followed up, though their lead was not as large as at one time seemed likely. Reg Simpson was eight runs short of his century when last man Roy Tattersall joined him. The Lancashire bowler stayed with him while 74 precious runs were made. Simpson who went on to make 156 – his only century against Australia, reached his hundred on his 31st birthday. Australia then lost four wickets in erasing the deficit and with Bedser claiming another five wickets to take his tally for the series to 30, England were left with just 95 to make for victory. Fittingly, Hutton was at the crease when the winning runs were scored and although he scored only one century, he averaged 88.83 for the series.

1953

After almost twenty years of domination by Australia, England regained the Ashes. Four draws and victory at The Oval to England was history repeating itself. But there the comparisons ended, for the four drawn games were packed with drama. The England captain by now was Hutton and the Ashes triumph came despite his rival Hassett winning the toss in each of the five Tests.

In a first Test noted for batting collapses, Lindsay Hassett made a staunch century as Australia lost their last seven wickets for just 12 runs in making 249. Bedser took 7 for 55 and he and Bailey took the last six wickets for five runs. Lindwall had England 17 for 3 before Hutton and Graveney added 59 but then wickets fell steadily and they trailed by 105 runs. Bedser routed Australia on the third day to finish with match figures of 14 for 99 – they remain a record for a Trent Bridge Test. But then a washed-out fourth and a delayed final day meant England could only play out time.

The Lord's Test was remarkable for the great match-saving stand between Willie Watson and Trevor Bailey after England had begun the final day facing almost certain defeat. Hassett's second successive Test match hundred and Davidson's attacking 76 saw Australia to a total of 346. England replied with 372 with Hutton making 145, his fifth hundred against Australia. Morris and Miller set up Australia's second innings, adding 165 for the second wicket – Miller taking five hours to make his 109. Needing 343 to win, England were 73 for 4 – 270 runs from victory and with nearly five hours remaining – when Watson and Bailey came together. They withstood the Australian bowling until late in the day when Watson, in his first Test, was out for 109. Bailey soon followed as England ended on 282 for 7.

A little less rain in the third Test at Old Trafford could have made this match a thriller. As it was, too much time – including the whole of Monday – was lost. Neil Harvey, who was dropped by Evans after making just four runs, went on to score 122 as he and Hole added 173 for the fourth wicket in an Australian total of 318. England's main resistance came in a 94-run stand by Hutton and Compton and it was left to Simpson and Bailey in a seventh-wicket stand of 60 to avoid the follow-on. ▶

ENGLAND CAPTAIN LEN HUTTON TOSSES THE COIN TO START THE FOURTH TEST AT THE OVAL, 23 AUGUST 1953. AUSTRALIA CAPTAIN LINDSAY HASSETT LOOKS ON

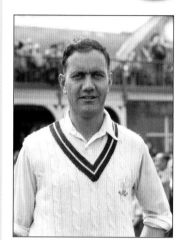

RAY LINDWALL OF AUSTRALIA IN ACTION DURING THE SECOND DAY OF THE FINAL ASHES TEST MATCH AT THE OVAL, AUGUST 1953

Yorkshire wrist-spinner Johnny Wardle claimed 4 for 7 off five overs as Australia collapsed to 35 for 8 – just 77 runs ahead – when time ran out.

Another half-hour's play was lost for rain on the opening day of the Headingley Test, where England laboured to 142 for 7. Hutton on his home ground was bowled second ball by Lindwall. Australia in the shape of Harvey and Hole fought hard and despite good bowling by Bedser ended their first innings with a lead of 99 runs. Trevor Bailey then held up the Australian bid for victory, batting 262 minutes for just 38 runs and after England had wiped off the arrears, Jim Laker batting at No.9 made a quickfire 48. Wanting 177 to win in 115 minutes, Australia made a bold bid for victory. But that man Bailey, bowling down the leg-side to a negative field between time-consuming field adjustments, frustrated the tourists who finished on 147 for 4.

England won back the Ashes at The Oval after Fred Trueman, in his maiden Australian Test, found life in a rain-freshened pitch to remove Harvey, de Courcy and Hole and only a hard-hitting innings from Lindwall helped the tourists reach 275. Hutton, wearing his 1938 cap – which fell inches from the stumps as he avoided a short ball from Lindwall – top-scored with 82 but the middle of the innings fell away and it was only Bailey and Bedser's last wicket stand of 44 that enabled England to pass Australia's total.

A sensational afternoon followed as Lock and Laker on a responsive pitch had Australia reeling from 59 for 1 to 85 for 6. Archer and Davidson tried to hit their way out of trouble, but Lock snapped them both up, and England were left to make 132 to set the seal on an emotional victory. Hutton was run out for 17 but May stayed with Edrich for 64 runs before Compton swept Morris for four to win the match.

1954-55

England, with the Ashes safely in their grasp, took with them to Australia two secret weapons in the form of speed twins Frank 'Typhoon' Tyson and Brian Statham. In a series in which the Australian batting was vulnerable, they took 46 wickets, ensuring that England held on to the Ashes with a 3-1 margin.

For the first time in Australia, the first Test pitch was completely covered and as a result, England captain Len Hutton made one of cricket's biggest blunders, misreading the pitch and sending Australia in to bat. Although chances were missed in the field, Australia always seemed certain to compile a massive score. Both Harvey and Morris made big centuries as Australia declared their first innings closed at 601 for 8. To make matters worse for England, Compton broke a finger on the boundary fence and had to bat last. England started disastrously, losing their first four wickets for 25 runs before debutant Colin Cowdrey joined the ever-dependable Bailey in a productive stand. Even so, England had to follow-on and with only May and Edrich offering any prolonged resistance, Lindwall and Miller demonstrated that they were still great bowlers, taking Australia to victory by an innings and 154 runs.

In the second Test at Sydney, England themselves were put in and Lindwall, Archer, Davidson and Johnston had them at 111 for 9 before Wardle and Statham smashed 43 in the biggest stand of the innings. Bailey had some early successes in Australia's innings and Tyson's yorkers and short-pitched deliveries did the rest but Australia still had a lead of 74 runs. In their second innings, England were 55 for 3 and in an apparently hopeless position when May and Cowdrey put on 116, the former going on to make 104. Once more there was a useful last-wicket stand, this time of 46 between Statham and Appleyard. The Tyson onslaught began in Australia's second innings, with assistance from Tyson's rival Lindwall. When batting in England's second innings, the Northamptonshire fast bowler was struck by a Lindwall bouncer and knocked unconscious. He responded with six wickets as Australia needing 223 to win, were bowled out for 184.

THIRD TEST: MELBOURNE

Early life in the wicket at Melbourne had England in trouble but Colin Cowdrey, on the first of his six tours to Australia, became the 50th Englishman to score a century against Australia. He scored 102 out of England's first innings total of 191. England then had their opponents on 92 for 5 on an improved pitch – which was apparently illegally watered on the rest day – but their grip was relaxed and Australia moved into the lead. May held England's second innings together with a powerfully struck 91, setting Australia 240 to win. The hosts faced the final day in a similar position to that at Sydney: needing 165 to win with eight wickets in hand. Tyson then demolished the innings on a pitch of uneven bounce, taking 6 for 16 in 51 balls, bowling at frightening speed, with Statham probing from the other end. The collapse began when Evans took a superb diving leg-side catch from Harvey – the first of the eight wickets to fall for 34 runs.

At Adelaide, the wicket was more suited to spin but with Australia struggling at 229 for 8 on the second day, Maddocks and Johnson put on 92 so that the home side reached 323 before the last wicket fell. England replied with 341, Hutton and Cowdrey adding 99 in high heat and there was solid batting from all the middle-order. When Morris, Burke and Harvey fell to Appleyard's medium pace off-spin on the fourth evening, it looked ominous for Australia, yet it was Tyson and Statham who did the damage the next day and for the second Test running, 'Nelson' struck with the hosts being bowled out for 111. Set only 94 to retain the Ashes, England were dazed by Miller, who had them 18 for 3 in a fiery spell of new ball bowling until resolute batting from Compton and Bailey, with support from Peter May, saw them win by five wickets.

Play in the final Test at Sydney didn't get underway until well into the fourth day due to continuous heavy rain in the city. When it did, England's Tom Graveney became the 100th player to score a century in Ashes contests and Ray Lindwall claimed his 100th wicket in Ashes Tests when he bowled Bailey. England declared at 371 for 7: Australia were 82 for 2 at the close of the penultimate day and a draw seemed certain. However, the Australian batsmen then became bemused by Wardle's flighted leg-spin and with one run needed to avoid the follow-on, Johnson was run out. In the two hours play that remained, some inept Australian batting and some more fine bowling by Wardle left the home side on 118 for 6 when stumps were drawn. ▶

BRIAN STATHAM TRAPS HIS OLD ADVERSARY IAN CHAPPELL ON A 1960s MCC TOUR OF AUSTRALIA

Jim Laker
(England) 1948-59

Test Average *21.25*
Test Best *10-53 v. Australia, Old Trafford 1956*
Ashes Average *18.28*
Ashes Best *(as above)*

Jim Laker will always be remembered for one of the most extraordinary feats in cricket history – his 19 wickets for 90 runs against Australia at Old Trafford in 1956. No one else in the history of the first-class game had ever taken more than 17 wickets in a match. Laker first burst into the record books in the Test trial at Bradford in 1950, when on a drying pitch, he took eight 'Rest' wickets for two runs, completely ruining the match as a trial. Laker's greatest triumphs were to come in 1956 when he took 46 wickets in the series against Australia at an average of 9.60. In addition to his overall bag of 19 wickets at Old Trafford, he became the first player to take 10 wickets in an innings more than once; he had accomplished the feat earlier in the season with 10 for 88 for Surrey, also against the Australians ! Laker later maintained his association with the game, becoming a successful television commentator and writer.

JIM LAKER TRAPS KEITH MILLER FOR A DUCK ON HIS WAY TO HIS STILL RECORD-BREAKING 19 FOR 90 AT OLD TRAFFORD

1956

After Australia had won the second Test at Lord's, England found themselves having to come from behind to win the series. They need not have worried as Jim Laker and Tony Lock took 38 of the 40 Australian wickets to fall in the third and fourth Tests and then another 10 in the final Test at the Oval to ensure that the Ashes stayed in England.

Australia were handicapped in the first Test by injuries to Lindwall and Davidson. Yet England were missing the now retired Hutton, as well as Compton, Tyson, Trueman and Statham, who were all injured. After a shortened first day and the second day rained off, Peter Richardson in his first Test batted well, as did Peter May, allowing an England declaration at 217 for 8. Australia who were 19 for 2 at the end of the third day were bowled out for 148 on a drying wicket by mid-afternoon of the following day. Richardson and Cowdrey made 129 that evening and carried their opening stand to 151 on the final day. The declaration left Australia 258 to win in four hours but after they lost three early wick-

ets, Burke and Burge decided to play out the last two hours.

The Lord's Test saw the return of Trueman and Statham but a good team performance by Australia brought a well-earned victory. McDonald and Burke began with 137 in the solid old-fashioned tradition as the tourists scored 285 in their first innings. Keith Miller, now 36 years old, bowled well to take 5 for 72, including the wicket of Colin Cowdrey, spectacularly caught by Benaud in the gully. Benaud then put Australia in command with a hard-hit audacious innings of 97, and though Trueman took five wickets for England, the home side were chasing 362 to win. Keith Miller took 5 for 80 and so achieved the only 10-wicket haul of his career. In Australia's 185-run victory, wicket-keeper Gil Langley created a long-standing world record with nine dismissals – eight catches and one stumping.

THIRD TEST: HEADINGLEY

Only Peter May had made runs for England at Lord's and the selectors recalled 41-year-old Lancashire batsman Cyril Washbrook for the third Test at Headingley. He and May took their side from the plight of 17 for 3, after Archer had used the seam alarmingly well, to 204 before May fell to a fine leg-side catch by Lindwall. Washbrook was leg-before to Benaud two runs short of his century but Bailey and Evans took the score to 325. After Trueman had removed McDonald, the Headingley wicket provided the Australians with their first nightmares of spin-twins Laker and Lock, who took the remaining nine wickets to dismiss the tourists for 143. Following-on, Trueman again dismissed McDonald before Laker and Lock repeated the feat of the first innings, with the former having match figures of 11 for 113 in a victory by an innings and 42 runs for England.

OLD TRAFFORD: 'LAKER'S MATCH'

The fourth Test at Old Trafford will always be known simply as 'Laker's Match'. The 34-year-old Surrey off-spinner Jim Laker was handed the ball at the Stretford End and promptly took 9 for 37 in Australia's first innings, whilst in the second he took all 10 wickets for the amazing match analysis of 68-27-90-19. Yet the greatest bowling feat of all-time in a Test match was not without controversy! Pitch preparation was never easy in this wet summer and patches were apparent during England's first innings. The home side, all the same, proceeded steadily to their large total with Richardson, who made his maiden Test century, and Cowdrey leading off with 174. David Sheppard, brought back to Test cricket after just four first-class innings, chipped in with a well-earned 113. Wicket-keeper Godfrey Evans also made a breezy 47 as England were eventually all out for 459. Laker and Lock were soon on when Australia batted, but by tea they had only lost two wickets while making 62 runs. Then the bowlers changed ends and with the first ball after the break, Lock took his only wicket of the match. The ball was now turning sharply and the fieldsmen crowded in. Laker took 7 for 8 off 22 ▶

THE RESULTS

ENGLAND v AUSTRALIA
Played at Old Trafford, July 26, 27, 28, 30, 31 1956

ENGLAND

PE Richardson	c Maddocks b Benaud	104
MC Cowdrey	c Maddocks b Lindwall	80
Rev D Sheppard	b Archer	113
PBH May	c Archer b Benaud	43
TE Bailey	b Johnson	20
C Washbrook	lbw b Johnson	6
ASM Oakman	c Archer b Johnson	10
TG Evans	st Maddocks b Johnson	47
JC Laker	run out	3
GAR Lock	not out	25
JB Statham	c Maddocks b Lindwall	0
Extras		8
Total		**459**

Fall of wickets   1-174 2-195 3-288 4-321 5-327 6-339 7-401 8-417 9-458 10-459

Australia Bowling

	O	M	R	W	O	M	R	W
Lindwall	21.3	6	63	2				
Miller	21	6	41	0				
Archer	22	6	73	1				
Johnson	47	10	151	4				
Benaud	47	17	123	2				

AUSTRALIA

CC McDonald	c Lock b Laker	32	c Oakman b Laker	89
W Burke	c Cowdrey b Lock	22	c Lock b Laker	33
RN Harvey	b Laker	0	c Cowdrey b Laker	0
ID Craig	lbw b Laker	8	lbw b Laker	38
KR Miller	c Oakman b Laker	6	b Laker	0
K Mackay	c Oakman b Laker	0	c Oakman b Laker	0
RG Archer	st Evans b Laker	6	c Oakman b Laker	0
R Benaud	c Statham b Laker	0	b Laker	18
RR Lindwall	not out	6	c Lock b Laker	8
L Maddocks	b Laker	4	lbw b Laker	2
IW Johnson	b Laker	0	not out	1
Extras		0		16
Total		**84**		**205**

Fall of wickets   1-48 2-48 3-62 4-62 5-62 6-73 7-73 8-78 9-84 10-84
Second Innings 1-28* 2-55 3-114 4-124 5-130 6-130 7-181 8-198 9-203 10-205

England Bowling

	O	M	R	W	O	M	R	W
Statham	6	3	6	0	16	9	15	0
Bailey	4	3	4	0	20	8	31	0
Laker	16.4	4	37	9	51.2	23	53	10
Lock	14	3	37	1	55	30	69	0
Oakman	-	-	-	-	8	3	21	0

*At 28 McDonald left the field with an injured knee, being replaced by Harvey who was out to Laker's first ball. Craig joined Burke, the latter falling at 55, when McDonald continued his innings.

ENGLAND WON BY AN INNINGS AND 170 RUNS

1958-59

This was the first series to be tele-vised and though the occasion may have been momentous, the cricket most certainly was not, with England's Trevor Bailey batting for almost six hours in reaching what was the slow-est half-century the game had ever seen! Ironically, in this first televised series, Australia were captained by Richie Benaud – for so long the face of Australian cricket – and his team regained the Ashes with a 4-0 victory.

The opening contest at Brisbane featured some pitiful cricket as slow over rates and negative cricket evoked widespread protests. The pitch, green-ish on the first day when England were bowled out for 134, did not deteriorate as half-expected and Colin McDonald, top scorer with 42, gave Australia the lead on first innings. In England's second innings, Trevor Bailey gave the most outrageous dis-play, batting seven-and-a-half hours for 68, whilst Benaud, who took 4 for 66, bowled 51.7 eight-ball overs. It was only in Australia's second innings that bat was put to ball with 21-year-old Norman O'Neill making his debut for the home side, scoring an unbeaten 71 as Australia won by eight wickets.

CAPTAIN'S CENTURY

England made a disastrous start to the second Test, losing three wickets in five balls to Alan Davidson to crash to 7 for 3 before Peter May scored the first century by an England captain in Australia for more than 50 years. He was ably supported by Bailey and Cowdrey before the innings fell away – Davidson claiming 6 for 64 in England's total of 259. For Australia, Neil Harvey made a magnificent 167 in 370 minutes without giving a chance and he was joined in big

ENGLAND TEAM GROUP, 1956 ASHES SERIES: (BACK ROW, L-R) FRED TRUEMAN, JOHNNY WARDLE, TOM GRAVENEY, BRIAN STATHAM, COLIN COWDREY, PETER RICHARDSON; (FRONT ROW, L-R) WILLIE WATSON, TREVOR BAILEY, PETER MAY, JIM LAKER, GODFREY EVANS

balls and Australia were all out for 84! Rain allowed only short periods of play on the next two days but it dead-ened the wicket and Australia put up a terrific fight. Colin McDonald and Ian Craig were together for more than four hours but then the sun came out and the pitch stirred. Bowling again from the Stretford End, Laker began taking wickets and at one stage Johnson appealed to the umpires at sawdust blowing in his eyes – a mark of Australia's despair. Laker bowled perfectly and relentlessly on, and with an hour still to play, he had Maddocks leg-before to complete his great feat of taking all 10 wickets and 19 in the match to put England one up, so retaining the Ashes. The result also broke a sequence of draws at Old Trafford dating back over half a century to 1905.

In the final Test, Denis Compton became the third inspired comeback selection for England in the series, making 94 despite the recent loss of his right kneecap. He went in at 66 for 3 and helped May take the score to 222. Three wickets then fell at that score and the innings subsided the next day. Rain made the wicket inter-esting and Laker and Lock reduced Australia to 47 for 5. Harvey and Miller saved the follow-on, however, and with Benaud's quickfire 32, there was little in it after all. England then batted confidently either side of rain interruptions and May left the tourists only two hours in which to make 228 for victory. Far from being a chance to level the series, it was time enough for further humiliations – Australia 27 for 5 with Laker taking his tally of wickets for the series to a record 46 at 9.60.

stands by McDonald and O'Neill. Lancashire fast bowler Brian Statham on one of four tours to Australia took his career-best figures of 7 for 57. When England batted a second time, they collapsed to the erratic bowling of Ian Meckiff who took 6 for 38 as Australia went on to win, as at Brisbane, by eight wickets.

THIRD TEST: SYDNEY

In the Third Test at Sydney, England, after their now-customary bad start, rallied through the efforts of May and Swetman, who had replaced the injured Evans behind the stumps. Even so, Benaud bowled well to take 5 for 83 and England were dismissed for 219. Though Laker and Lock bowled well on an unresponsive pitch, O'Neill and Favell added 110 for the fourth wicket and Mackay and Davidson a precious 115 for the seventh to give Australia a lead of 138 runs on the first innings. England were tottering at 64 for 3 – still 74 behind – when Cowdrey joined May. The two carried the score to 246 before Burke got a ball through May's defences. Benaud had now gone on the defensive but Cowdrey reached 100 not out before May declared with the match saved.

QUESTIONS OF THE UMPIRE

Having won three tosses and failed to make a substantial first innings total, England captain Peter May this time put Australia in; but no wicket fell until there were 171 runs on the board. Australia were 200 for 1 by the close of the first day. Next day, Brian Statham took three quick wickets and umpire McInnes appeared to err on occasions. Mackay 'walked' after being given 'not out' to a catch behind by Evans, and when McDonald was given 'not out' as his runner raced for the crease behind the

umpire, the batsman took matters into his own hands by swinging wildly at the next delivery and being bowled by Trueman for 170. McDonald was the 50th Australian to score an Ashes century. Meckiff, whose action was generally conceded to constitute a throw, missed the match through injury and the man who caught the eye was the giant Rorke, whose drag was unprecedented. He ripped through England's middle order and with Benaud clearing up the tail, England were all out for 240. Australia enforced the follow-on but after Richardson and Watson had gone, wickets began to tumble with regularity. That the match extended well into the sixth day was thanks to Graveney's disciplined innings but Australia won by 10 wickets to claim back the Ashes.

FINAL TEST

Put in to bat in the final Test, England were bowled out for 205 with Richardson making 68 and John Mortimore 44 not out – the Gloucestershire all-rounder having been flown out to reinforce the touring party. The dependable Colin McDonald made yet another century for Australia but they too were struggling at 209 for 6 when Wally Grout and Richie Benaud took their side to 324 for 7. When England batted a second time, they began 146 runs behind. They were dealt a cruel blow, when Cowdrey, who had made 46, was the victim of a disputed run out. Struggling to 214 all out, England surrendered the final Test to Benaud's men by 9 wickets, as Australia knocked off the 69 runs required to complete their 4-0 series win. Ray Lindwall, playing his last Test against England, became Australia's leading Test wicket-taker by passing Clarrie Grimmett's record of 216 wickets. ▶

Richie Benaud
(Australia) 1952-64

Test Average *27.03*
Test Best *7-72 v. India, Corporation Stadium 1956*
Ashes Average *31.82*
Ashes Best *6-70, Old Trafford 1961*

Richie Benaud was one of Australia's finest captains as well as being a magnificent all-rounder. He was the most successful leg-spinner since the Second World War, a hard-hitting batsman and brilliant fieldsman close to the wicket. He was appointed captain for the 1958-59 Ashes series. Most had favoured Neil Harvey for the job but Benaud emerged with a 4-0 victory over what was thought to be one of England's strongest ever teams. His most memorable bowling feat occurred at Old Trafford in July 1961 when England needed 256 runs to win. Benaud, troubled with a persistent shoulder condition since the initial first-class match of the tour, had bowled himself sparingly. But with England 150 for 1, he bowled round the wicket into the rough and Australia won the match by 54 runs and kept the Ashes – in 32 overs, Benaud had taken 6 for 70 including a spell of 5 for 12 in just 25 balls. The first Australian to score 2000 runs and take 200 wickets in Test cricket, he now commands the greatest respect as a cricket commentator.

1961

This Ashes series came just a few months after the famous rubber between Australia and the West Indies, featuring the first-ever tied Test at the Gabba. Under the captaincy of Richie Benaud, Australian cricket was on a high...the Ashes won back in 1958-59 and now on English soil, the success continued with a 2-1 victory.

BACK AT EDGBASTON

Ashes cricket returned to Edgbaston for the first time in more than 50 years for the first Test. Mackay, with deceptively innocuous-looking medium-pacers, stole four good England wickets either side of lunch as the home side were bowled out for 195. Harvey and O'Neill mastered the bowling of Trueman, Statham, Allen and Illingworth in a stand of 146 in 17 minutes. Harvey, on his fourth and final tour of England, scored his 20th Test century and the first by an Australian at Edgbaston. After rain had cut the third and fourth day's play, England began the final day at 106 for 1, still 215 behind, but Dexter and Subba Row, in his first Ashes Test, took their stand to 109. After Cowdrey's dismissal at 239, Barrington stayed with Dexter while 161 further matchsaving runs were made. Dexter went on to make 180, his highest score against Australia while Subba Row's 112 made him the twelfth England batsman to score a hundred in his first Ashes Test.

On a responsive pitch ideal for seam bowling at Lord's, Australia, in the shape of Alan Davidson, soon disposed of an England side for whom only Subba Row made any worthwhile contribution. With Benaud injured, Neil Harvey captained the Australian side but it was the tall left-hander Bill Lawry, playing in only his second Test,

ENGLAND'S KEN BARRINGTON SWEEPS THE AUSTRALIAN BOWLING IN THE FINAL DAY OF THE DRAWN FIRST TEST MATCH AT EDGBASTON

who caught the eye with a courageous innings of 130. Mackay stretched the tourists' lead with stands of 53 with McKenzie for the ninth wicket and 49 for the tenth with Misson. McKenzie, making his Australian debut, found the wicket still helpful and took 5 for 37 as England were routed for 202 in their second knock. Queensland wicket-keeper Wally Grout took five catches in England's second innings (eight in the match), leaving his side just 69 runs to make for victory. After Statham and Trueman had reduced Australia to 19 for 4, Lock got his hands to a misjudged hook by Burge but could not hang on to it, and though Simpson went at 58, Burge saw his side home to their eighth victory at Lord's.

Two extraordinary breakthroughs by Fred Trueman on an unpredictable wicket at Headingley settled the third Test. After being 183 for 2 at tea on the opening day, Australia tumbled to 208 for 9 as Trueman took 5 for 16 in six overs, aided by good catches by Lock and Cowdrey. England owed much when batting to Colin Cowdrey, but after cutting his pace, McKenzie ran through the middle and late order. Tony Lock, though, did crack a useful 30, many off Benaud, who was troubled throughout the series by a damaged shoulder. Australia, 62 runs behind on first innings, had taken their second innings score to 102 for 4 when Trueman proceeded to take five wickets without conceding a run, and 6 for 4 in 45 balls all told. Australia's last eight wickets fell in 50 minutes and England made the necessary runs for victory that evening.

With the series level, the two teams

went to Old Trafford where the scene was set for one of the greatest of all Test matches. Australia won the toss, but thanks to fine bowling on his home ground by Brian Statham, they were dismissed for 190. With the wicket slightly easier, England made 367 with Peter May, Ken Barrington and Geoff Pullar all making half-centuries. Bobby Simpson, whose leg-spinners had brought him just two wickets in the first three Tests, had a spell of 4 for 2 to clean up the England tail. Then Bill Lawry and Bobby Simpson put on 113, with O'Neill making 67, but at 334 for 9, Australia were only 157 ahead. Soon afterwards, Davidson suddenly hit Allen for 20 in one over and 98 runs were made for the last wicket. With 256 wanted at 67 runs an hour, the game was brought to a thrilling climax by a magnificent 76 in 84 minutes by Ted Dexter. Then Benaud went round the wicket and aimed at the bowler's footmarks and in a spell of 5 for 12, he dismissed Dexter and May second ball. Australia won by 54 runs with 20 minutes to spare. Whatever happened at The Oval, Australia would retain the Ashes.

HANGING ON

After another poor start at The Oval – England were 20 for 3 – only a three-hour stand of 80 by May and Barrington held the innings together. Australia began unsteadily but O'Neill was in fine form and he and Burge put on 123. A delayed new ball allowed Booth to settle in, and with Burge hooking and sweeping powerfully, the score advanced to 396 before Booth fell to Lock. Burge batted solidly for seven hours in making 181 of Australia's total of 494. With Davidson injured, England managed to hang on for a draw with Subba Row finishing the series as he had started it, with a century.

1962-63

Ted Dexter had by now been appointed England captain and he took with him to Australia a team looking to regain the Ashes for the first time since 1956. But it was a big ask, with England not having won a Test on Australian soil since the fourth Test at Adelaide in February 1955.

FIRST TEST: BRISBANE

At Brisbane, Australia recovered from 194 for 6 to make 404 with Brian Booth making a controlled 112. He added 103 with the dour Mackay, who then stayed with Benaud while 91 were put on for the eighth wicket. England in turn were precariously placed at 169 for 4 but long defensive innings by Ken Barrington and Peter Parfitt helped them to 389. England could make no headway when Australia batted a second time. Lawry made 98 to set up a declaration on the fourth evening that invited England to make 378 in six hours. That an England win still looked possible in mid-afternoon was due to Dexter who fell one run short of what would have been a magnificent century. As it was, his bold innings was the 14th half-century of the match!

In the second Test at Melbourne, Australia again recovered from a moderate start to score 316, but England gained a narrow first innings lead thanks to a stand of 175 by Cowdrey (113) and Dexter (93). Inspired bowling by Fred Trueman had Australia at 69 for 4 in their second innings but Brian Booth hit his second century of the series to ensure that England were set a sizeable target for victory. The final day saw Sheppard, who had failed to score in the first innings and dropped two catches, steer England to a seven-wicket victory with a five-hour innings that included a stand ▶

of 124 with Dexter and one of 104 with Cowdrey. The scores were level when Sheppard was run out going for the winning run.

Without the accuracy of Richie Benaud, Bobby Simpson picked up five wickets in England's first innings with his mixture of leg-breaks and googlies, ably supported by Alan Davidson who took 4 for 54. When Colin Cowdrey, who was England's top-scorer with 85, was out, they were 201 for 4 but were dismissed for 279. In reply, Australia were 174 for 1 when Fred Titmus brought the match back to life with four wickets for five runs in 58 balls. The burly left-hander Shepherd hit Australia into the lead but it was thought not quite enough to compensate for the home side having to bat last. This soon ceased to be relevant as Davidson destroyed England's second innings with a fine spell of swing bowling. Australia made the runs for victory as rain fell and it was just as well because the fifth day was very wet.

DROPPED CATCHES

Australia were reeling at 16 for 2 when Neil Harvey was dropped off successive balls from Illingworth. Then, in oppressive heat, Harvey and Norman O'Neill added 194 runs in only 171 minutes – the strong stylish O'Neill getting out as much from exhaustion as to Dexter's bowling. Harvey's 154 in Australia's total of 393 was the last of his 21 Test hundreds. McKenzie led Australia's attack after Davidson had pulled up with a torn hamstring and he continually gained lift from the pitch to take 5 for 89 in England's total of 331. Dexter then set about containing, and though Simpson and Booth added 133 for the third wicket, Benaud decided to bat until lunch on the last day. England were 4 for 2 but Barrington, who reached his chanceless century

ENGLAND'S DAVID SHEPPARD (TOP R) DROPS A CATCH OFF THE BOWLING OF FRED TRUEMAN (BOTTOM L) TO HAND AUSTRALIA'S BILL LAWRY (C) A REPRIEVE

with a six off Simpson, ensured that England survived to draw.

With all to play for in the final Test at Sydney, neither side was prepared to take chances and England's first innings total of 321 in almost 10 hours set the pattern. Barrington again led the way for the tourists with 101 but there were only four boundaries in his innings. Australia were 74 for 3 at the end of the second day but O'Neill and Burge both batted well to give Australia a lead of 28 runs on the first innings. With Cowdrey indisposed, Barrington anchored England's second innings, falling just six runs short of scoring a century in each innings. Dexter declared at lunch on the last day, setting Australia 241 to win in four hours. After four wickets fell for 70, Lawry and Burge played out time to the echo of the crowd's dissatisfaction. For the first time, a five-match series in Australia had ended with an even scoreline.

1964

By now, the Richie Benaud era had ended for Australia and the new man in charge was Bobby Simpson. With Alan Davidson and Neil Harvey having also retired, England must have fancied their chances of regaining the Ashes. But unfortunately, rain affected the series with four matches being drawn. Australia's victory at Headingley in the third Test was sufficient to win the series.

Rain ruined the opening contest of a frustrating series with almost 15 hours' play being lost. In fact, it was the fourth morning before Dexter declared England's first innings closed, the first day having been heavily curtailed, the second partially and the third completely washed out. Geoff Boycott, making his debut, top-scored with 48. His opening partner in this match, Fred Titmus, was once stranded after colliding with the bowler but Australia's wicket-keeper Wally Grout won much admiration by refusing to break the wicket. Bobby Simpson saved his side from a serious deficit with 50 hard-earned runs. Dexter, opening England's second innings in place of Boycott, who had broken a finger, then hit 68 but the home side's run-rate fell back and the closure came too late for Australia to make a serious attempt at getting the 242 runs needed. The only remaining excitement came when O'Neill hooked the first four balls of Trueman's second over to the boundary.

RAIN-AFFECTED PLAY

The first two days of the Lord's Test were also lost to rain and then Dexter, on winning the toss, put Australia in to bat. Fred Trueman took early wickets and the tourists were struggling at 88 for 6, although with Tom Veivers making a half-century, they recovered to score 176. John Edrich, the cousin of Bill Edrich, had returned to the side and it was he, with a fine innings of 120, who was chiefly responsible for England's lead of 70. Australia batted more solidly at the second attempt with Burge particularly punishing England's pace attack. Gifford and Titmus were surprisingly not called upon until well into the morning and Australia were safe from defeat when the rain came again.

Wonderful fielding and accurate pace bowling by Hawke and McKenzie restricted England to 268 on a good batting track. Only a bright innings from Dexter, and valuable batting by wicket-keeper Parks, saved England's face. Australia were 187 for 7 in reply when Dexter opted to take the new ball, but Burge, who had been struggling against Titmus' off-spin, took 42 off seven overs of Trueman and Flavell. He went on to score 160 as Australia totalled 389. Needing 121

to avoid an innings defeat, England lost Parfitt with a broken knuckle early in their second knock and though Edrich and Barrington resisted grimly, Australia pressed home their advantage. With Redpath hitting an unbeaten 58, the tourists moved carefully to victory on the fourth evening.

OLD TRAFFORD: SIMPSON DIGS IN

Winning the toss and with a perfect Old Trafford wicket awaiting, Simpson set about making the Ashes safe. His innings, the longest ever played against England – 12 hours 42 minutes – was his first Test century. He was 109 at the end of the first day, when Australia were 253 for 2, and 265 at the end of the second when the tourists had moved on to 570 for 4. His opening stand of 201 with Lawry broke the 1909 record of Bardsley and Gregory and he added 219 with Booth for the fifth wicket, hitting uninhibitedly on the third morning with no serious regard for the individual Test record. Faced with avoiding the follow-on, England lost Edrich early and then Boycott at 126 before Dexter and Barrington settled

down for a partnership that realised 246 in 325 minutes. Dexter made 174 and Barrington 256. It was the Surrey player's highest Test score and though it was his 10th Test hundred, it was his first in England. It was a spirited reply that captured the imagination as they came within 45 runs of Australia's total, but the inevitable draw meant that the Ashes stayed with Australia.

A rained-off final day in the fifth Test at The Oval deprived England of the outside chance of squaring the series. Batting first in unfavourable conditions, England were bowled out for 182 with Neil Hawke taking 6 for 47. Australia's reply was sluggish with Lawry spending almost five-and-a-half hours on his 94, though Veivers with an unbeaten 67 later brought some vigour into the batting. Fred Trueman, in the twilight of his career, became the first player to reach 300 Test wickets when he had Hawke caught by Cowdrey at slip. Ahead on first innings by 197, England, through Boycott (113) and Cowdrey (93 not out) had more than restored the balance when rain stopped play. ▶

FRED TRUEMAN OF ENGLAND CELEBRATES TAKING HIS 300TH TEST WICKET DURING THE FIFTH TEST AGAINST AUSTRALIA AT THE OVAL, AUGUST 1964

1965-66

It was now 10 years and five series since England had held the Ashes and though they led the series 1-0 after a big victory in the third Test at Sydney, their hopes were snuffed out by Bobby Simpson and Bill Lawry in the following match.

After a rain-affected opening two days at Brisbane in the first Test, Australia set about making a big score. Doug Walters, 19 and playing in his first Test, scored a century (155), the third youngest Australian to score a Test century after Harvey and Jackson, while Bill Lawry top-scored with 166. The two of them came together with Australia 125 for 4 and added 187 in a total of 443 for 6 declared. England began hesitantly but were lifted by a bright innings from Parks and resolute batting from Barrington. Though the tourists failed to avoid the follow-on, they saw out time without serious difficulty with Boycott unbeaten on 63 at the close.

AUSTRALIA FIGHT BACK

Australia seemed doomed on the last day of the second Test at Melbourne when their fourth second-innings wicket fell at 176, when they were still 24 runs behind England's first innings total. Burge and Walters, how-ever, made a stand of 198 after a missed stumping of Burge, and the match was saved. Both Australian openers scored half-centuries in each innings, whilst Bob Cowper in Australia's first knock joined Hill, Macartney, Chipperfield and Miller in being dismissed for 99. For England, both Edrich and Cowdrey hit hundreds in their total of 558, Cowdrey's third at the MCG. Barry Knight, flown out as a reinforcement to the England side, took his four wickets in a spell in which he conceded only 18 runs.

A memorable five-hour innings by left-hander Bob Barber set up an England victory which was made certain by Brown and Jones in a first innings breakthrough, and Titmus and Allen, the off-spinners, as the pitch became more helpful to the turning ball in the second innings. Opening batsmen Barber and Boycott put on 234 for the first wicket in even time before John Edrich made his second successive century in a total of 488. Australian paceman Neil Hawke bowled well to take 7 for 105. In England's innings, Fred Titmus made 14 to take him past the 1,000 run mark to compliment his 100 Test wickets. With the exception of Cowper and Thomas who added 81 for the fifth wicket, Australia had no answer to the pace of Brown and Jones and after being bowled out for 221, had to follow-on. England's off-spinners, supported especially well by Mike Smith, their captain at short-leg, had Australia floundering, with Walters, who batted for over two hours, 35 not out when the tourists picked up the tenth wicket.

ADELAIDE: SIMPSON RETURNS

Having missed the first Test through a broken wrist and the third through chickenpox, Bobby Simpson returned as Australia's captain at Adelaide and reminded everyone what his side had been missing. In a humid atmosphere, Australia soon had England 33 for 3 with Cowdrey's dismissal again shrouded in controversy. A shout from wicket-keeper Grout misled the Kent batsman into thinking he had been called for a run and he was run out. England did well to total 241 but then Simpson and Lawry set a new Australian first-wicket record against England of 244 – this in itself gave Australia the lead. They went on to make 516 with Glamorgan bowler Jeff Jones taking 6 for 118. In England's second innings, Ken Barrington batted

AUSTRALIA'S NUMBER THREE BATSMAN BOB COWPER PLAYS A HOOK SHOT DURING THE THIRD DAY OF THE TEST AT MANCHESTER.

five-and-a-half hours in making 102, but Neil Hawke bowled well to take 5 for 54, enabling Australia to win by an innings and 9 runs.

ALL SQUARE

For the second Australian series in succession, the two sides went into the final Test all-square. Although Barrington made 115 and England declared at 485 for 9, their attack was simply not good enough to force a result. Barrington, as he had in Adelaide in 1962-63, reached his hundred with a six; he remains the only man to bring up a century with a six twice in Ashes Tests. For Australia, Bob Cowper batted for more than 12 hours and scored 307 – Australia's only triple-century in Australia. The series ended with the retirement of Australia's Wally Grout, who made 187 dismissals in 51 Tests. Sadly, by the time England next played Down Under, Grout was dead, having suffered a heart attack at the age of just 41.

1968

This series brought together two new captains in Colin Cowdrey and Bill Lawry, as well as several new players who were destined to play a big part in the shape of cricket in the 1970s. England's hopes of regaining the Ashes received a setback with Australia's win in the opening Test at Old Trafford and despite England's big victory at The Oval, the series was drawn.

The youngest-ever Australian side to visit England used the conditions better than the home side, whose bowling resources for this first Test at Old Trafford were thin. The tourists were 319 for 4 at the end of the first day with Sheahan, Lawry, Walters and Ian Chappell all making valuable contributions. However, after the run out of Chappell, the innings disintegrated and they were all out for 357. Hampered by drizzle and poor light, England stuttered to 165, only the last pair saving the follow-on.

Walters, who never made a Test hundred on four tours of England, made 86 in Australia's second innings and ensured that their lead was over 400 when England began the fourth innings with over nine hours remaining. South African-born Basil D'Oliveira playing his strokes late and very powerfully averted a debacle but Australia still won by 159 runs.

LORD'S: 200TH ASHES TEST

The second Test at Lord's was the 200th Ashes contest. To mark the occasion, the former Australian Prime Minister, Sir Robert Menzies, presented the captains with a gold sovereign for the toss. Cowdrey won the toss and elected to bat. The first day's play was ended at lunch-time by a prodigious hailstorm with England 53 for 1. On the second day, Colin Milburn tore into the Australian attack, hitting a six off Cowper to just under the Father Time weather-vane and one into the Mound Stand off McKenzie. He eventually fell for 83, not surprisingly caught on the boundary. Cowdrey declared England's innings closed at 351 for 7 before Snow, Brown and Knight ripped through the Australian line-up. They were dismissed for 78 – their lowest total in England for more than 50 years, with Warwickshire paceman David Brown taking 5 for 42. Also, Colin Cowdrey created a world record when he took the third of his first innings catches, giving him a Test total of 111. Australia began the final day needing 273 to avoid an innings defeat but with the tourists on 127 for 4, the rain returned to save them.

EDGBASTON: RAIN AGAIN!

Further rain spoilt the third Test at Edgbaston, a contest in which England held the upper hand almost throughout. The records continued for Cowdrey as he became the first cricketer to play in 100 Tests. He celebrated by scoring another century (104) in England's first innings total of 409, with assistance from his runner (Boycott), and during that innings he passed 7,000 Test runs. Australia experienced a grim start with Brown bowling Redpath without a run on the board and Snow breaking Lawry's finger, yet by the third evening they were 109 for 1. However, after Cowper and Chappell were out, only Walters offered any resistance and Australia went from 213 for 4 to 222 all out. With Lawry unable to bat, England extended their lead and Australia were set 330 in 370 minutes. With the tourists on 68 for 1, heavy rain before lunch drove the players from the field and there was no resumption.

The injuries from the Edgbaston match prevented both captains from playing in the fourth Test at Headingley. Their replacements, leading their countries in Tests for the only time, were Tom Graveney and Australian wicket-keeper Barry Jarman. Australia's first innings total of 315 owed much to the ▶

Derek Underwood
(England) 1966-82

Test Average *25.84*
Test Best *8-51 v. Pakistan, Lord's 1974*
Ashes Average *26.38*
Ashes Best *7-50, The Oval 1968*

It soon became the norm to regard Derek Underwood as a very good bowler in English conditions but ineffective on hard pitches overseas. Underwood's greatest triumph occurred in 1968 in the last Test against Australia at The Oval. In the first innings he bowled 59.3 overs with customary steadiness and took 2 for 89 but on the last day there was a thunderstorm and when play became possible again only 75 minutes remained. If the wicket were to become difficult as it dried, then Underwood would clearly be the match-winner. Forty minutes passed before it did and then after one man fell to D'Oliveira, Underwood took the last wickets in 27 balls to win the match with six minutes to spare, level the series and finish with figures of 7 for 50. Though there were those who doubted his effectiveness in Australia, he played an important part in the recovery of the Ashes in 1970-71, containing the Australian batsmen while the pace bowlers recovered and taking 16 wickets.

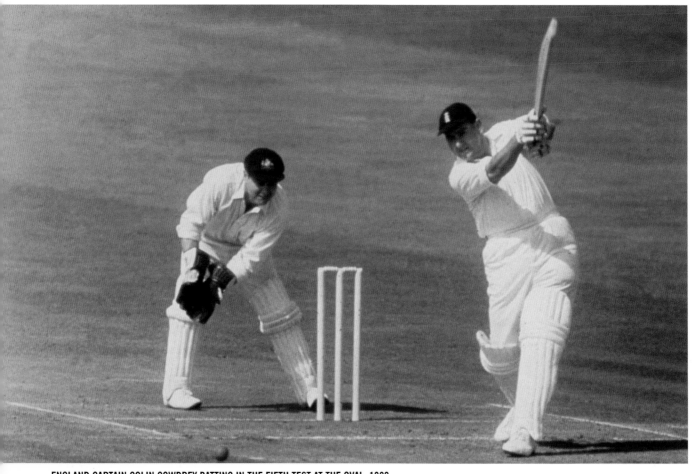

ENGLAND CAPTAIN COLIN COWDREY BATTING IN THE FIFTH TEST AT THE OVAL, 1968

virtue of Redpath, Walters and Chappell, though they were also helped by a number of dropped catches. Roger Prideaux, playing in his first Test for England, top-scored with 64, though the fact that they reached 302 was due to Underwood's unbeaten 45 after he and Brown had added 61 for the last wicket. Australian batsmen Walters and Chappell batted so resolutely in their side's second innings that England's target for victory was 326 in five hours. The risk involved in chasing the bait was too high and the game finished with England on 230 for 4.

Few more dramatic events have occurred on a cricket field than the final scenes at The Oval in the last Test. After England had made 494 – John Edrich 164 and Basil D'Oliveira 158 (this after he had been dropped after the first Test

and recalled for the injured Prideaux) – Australia were dismissed for 324 with Bill Lawry making 135. England then went for quick runs and left Australia 352 to win at 54 an hour. With the tourists 65 for 5 at lunch on the final day, the match was England's. But when a storm turned the field into a lake, an abandonment seemed certain. Then came a miraculous transformation with the groundstaff, helped by volunteers from the crowd, spiking the outfield areas and mopping up countless gallons of water. A resumption was possible at 4.45 pm but England bowled to no avail for 40 minutes until D'Oliveira bowled Jarman. Underwood then came on at the pavilion end and used the drying surface to such effect that he finished with 7 for 50 as Australia lost their last five wickets for 15 runs and England won with just

UNDERWOOD FINISHED WITH FIGURES OF 7 FOR 50 AS AUSTRALIA LOST THEIR LAST FIVE WICKETS FOR JUST 15 RUNS

1970-71

This was the longest Test series in cricket history and went to a seventh Test (although the third Test was abandoned without a ball being bowled). Although Australia had three young players in Greg Chappell, Dennis Lillee and Rod Marsh who were to establish themselves as great players over the coming years, the series belonged to England who won the fourth Test and the seventh to recapture the Ashes.

In the first Test at Brisbane, Keith Stackpole opened the Australian batting for the first time against England and scored a career-best 207. Along with Doug Walters, who made 112, he helped the home side to 418 for 3 before John Snow and Derek Underwood came back to dismiss the last seven batsmen for just 15 runs. Though England's best batsmen were Edrich, Luckhurst and Knott, Colin Cowdrey was still in the side and he became the world run-scoring record holder during the course of the England innings, which totalled 464. With an England first-innings lead of 31 runs, Ken Shuttleworth bowled Australia into trouble until Bill Lawry with 84 led a dour recovery and the game was drawn.

PERTH: GREG CHAPPELL DEBUTS

The second Test was the first to be staged at Perth with Greg Chappell making a memorable debut. England batted first and Boycott and Luckhurst put on 171 for the first wicket, with the Kent batsman going on to make 131, but the middle and lower order collapsed and England were all out for 397. John Snow made early inroads into the Australian batting and they were 107 for 5 when Chappell went in to bat. The No.7 became the sixth Australian to score a century (108) in

his first Test innings but his side's top scorer was Ian Redpath with 171. When England went in to bat for a second time, they were 43 runs in arrears and though they were in trouble against Gleeson, both Knott and Illingworth stayed with Edrich, who made 115 not out. A token declaration was made when safety had been reached and Lawry saw out the 32 overs, making 38 not out which included his 5,000th Test run and his 2,000th against England. After this match, DG Clark, the MCC tour manager, criticised both sides for undue caution in the opening Tests.

MELBOURNE: WASH-OUT

The New Year's Test at Melbourne was washed out without a ball being bowled, though the captains did toss. It was decided to stage an extra Test and so this match at Sydney was to have three to follow it. England seized the chance to go 1-0 up with some high-class batting and Snow's fiery bowling on a pitch that seemed more in favour of spin. Despite the uncertain bounce, Boycott and Luckhurst began the match with a 116-run partnership and the consistent Edrich made another half-century in England's total of 332. Only Redpath and

Walters withstood the varied England attack for long and when the touring side went in again, they had a lead of 96. Quick runs were needed and Boycott obliged with an innings of 142 not out, adding 133 with D'Oliveira after they had lost three wickets for 48. Needing a mammoth 416 for victory, Australia were blasted out for 116 with John Snow taking 7 for 40 in a devastating display of fast bowling. During the course of this spell, McKenzie, who had taken 246 wickets, two short of Benaud's record, had his nose smashed by a rising ball and never played Test cricket again. Bill Lawry carried his bat for 60 not out – the first Australian to do so in Sydney.

FIFTH TEST: MELBOURNE

The fifth Test in Melbourne was a late addition to the fixture, replacing a match against Victoria to make up for the rained-off third Test. In a match notable for unpleasant crowd behaviour, Ian Chappell and Redpath scored quickly in the final session on day one to leave Australia 260 for 1 – Lawry having retired with a damaged finger. Rod Marsh dominated the second day, hitting his way to the verge of becoming the first Australian wicket-keeper to score a Test hundred when Lawry ▶

JOHN SNOW (LEFT) WARNED OVER BOWLING TOO MANY SHORT-PITCHED DELIVERIES DURING THE 1971 TEST AT PERTH. SNOW AND AUSTRALIAN BATSMAN BILL LAWRY AWAIT THE UMPIRE'S VERDICT

John Edrich
(England) 1963-76

Test Average *43.54*
Test Best *310 v. New Zealand, Headingley 1965*
Ashes Average *48.96*
Ashes Best *175, Lord's 1975*

A member of a great cricketing family, John Edrich was a solid and dependable left-handed opening batsman who served England loyally from 1963 to 1976. He had a particular liking for Australian bowling, making seven centuries and scoring 2,644 runs in 32 Tests. The valuable innings he played in Australia in 1965-66 – 109 in the second Test, 103 in the third and 85 in the fifth – were compiled in the more patient, controlled method which he deployed remarkably consistently thereafter. After a fine tour of Australia in 1970-71 he lost some consistency and his Test place but England could not manage without his resolution and he returned in 1974-75 when the Australian pace attack broke hearts as well as fingers. At Sydney, Edrich had two ribs cracked by a short ball from Lillee. Giving not an inch of ground, the 38-year-old then had an outstanding home series against the same tormentors, piling up 175 at Lord's and then being bowled four runs short of yet another century at The Oval.

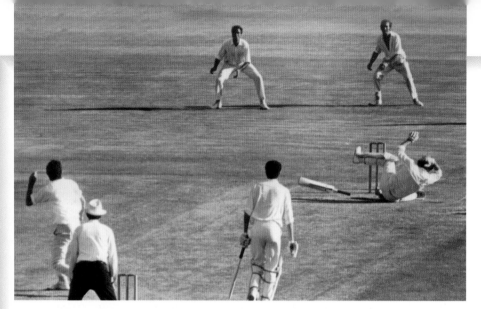

TERRY JENNER IS STRUCK ON THE HEAD BY A BALL FROM JOHN SNOW DURING THE FINAL TEST MATCH AGAINST ENGLAND AT SYDNEY, 20 FEBRUARY 1971

declared. England were in trouble at 88 for 3 but Luckhurst and D'Oliveira both hit centuries and the first innings disparity was less than expected. But Australia were slow to capitalise and England were eventually left four hours in which to score 271 to win. Illingworth's attitude was to decline the invitation and Boycott and Edrich played out time – England 161 for 0 at the close.

ADELAIDE: BLACK MARK FOR BOYCOTT

The sixth Test at Adelaide began well for England with Boycott and Edrich again starting with a century opening stand with the Surrey left-hander going on to record another century. Keith Fletcher made 80, his first notable Test innings, but the most memorable event was the running out of Boycott. His display of petulance was forgivable; his reported refusal to apologise to the umpires, however, was inflammatory. Stackpole continued his good form with 87 but no-one stayed with him and Australia were all out for 235. Unmoved by criticism, Boycott made 119 not out in England's second innings, after Ray Illingworth had decided not to enforce the follow-on. Australia were finally left with 500 minutes and a target of 469. They began the last day on 104 for 1 – the batsman out being Lawry, whose last Test match this was as he was dropped and replaced as skipper by Ian Chappell. Stackpole and Chappell then put 202 on for the second wicket and the home side had at the

close batted for a day and a half without being dismissed.

A great final conflict at Sydney was overshadowed by a long threatened confrontation between Illingworth and the umpires. Jenner was hit by a Snow bouncer; Snow, as had happened several times previously in the series, was warned for intimidation; the crowd demonstrated, a spectator manhandled Snow and Illingworth led his team off the field. Ian Chappell had won the toss and put England in to bat. With spinners Jenner and O'Keeffe taking three wickets apiece, the tourists were bowled out for 184 towards the end of day one. Redpath and Walters halted a collapse and Greg Chappell made 65 as Australia reached 264. The lead of 80 was cleared by the first wicket stand of Edrich and Luckhurst and with the first nine batsmen all reaching double figures, Australia needed 223 to win and were 100 runs adrift of that target with five wickets in hand when the final day began. With Snow unable to bowl after breaking his right forefinger in attempting a catch on the boundary, it was Illingworth and Underwood who carried England's hopes. The skipper drifted one past Greg Chappell's bat to have him stumped and the rest were accounted for with surprising ease. The 38-year-old Illingworth, who became the first to captain England in recapturing the Ashes in Australia since Jardine 38 years earlier, was carried by his players from the field.

1972

Australian captain Ian Chappell was fast developing a reputation as a winner – aggressive, adventurous and inspirational. He was up against the hardened pro in 40-year-old England skipper Ray Illingworth, who had led his side to regaining the Ashes in Australia some 18 months earlier. England, as expected, retained the Ashes but only after a tremendous fight against Chappell's unheralded side.

The cold and damp weather in the first Test at Old Trafford offered encouragement to bowlers throughout the five days. In a low scoring match, England were bowled out for 249 with South African-born Tony Greig top-scoring with 57 on his debut. Despite Keith Stackpole chancing his luck in Australia's first innings – he made 53 – the tourists had no answer to Snow and Arnold who used the conditions to the full, each taking four wickets in bowling Australia out for 142. Greig then repeated his feat of the first innings and led the way with 62, ably supported by Boycott – Dennis Lillee's magnificent 6 for 66 never quite redressing the balance. Rod Marsh had another near-miss in his bid to score a Test century when he made 91 in the second innings, putting Gifford four times into the crowd, but Greig, who had a fine match, and Snow, who took another four wickets, made sure that England were always in command.

LORD'S: ALL SQUARE

The series was squared at Lord's in a remarkable match dominated by the swing bowling of debutant Bob Massie who took 8 for 84 in the first innings and 8 for 53 in the second. No-one has taken as many wickets on debut. Bowling mainly round the wicket, he curved the ball suddenly and late, either way and off a length, and no England player could work out a reliable method of combating him. The other four wickets went to Lillee, who bowled fast and accurately. Greig made his third half-century in as many Test innings and with the help of Knott they took England's first innings score to 272. Australia began their reply disastrously but the Chappells steadied the innings with Greg going on to make 131. Marsh hit a quickfire 50 to gain a lead for the tourists. By Saturday evening, Massie had shattered England again. At 86 for 9, they were only 50 ahead. Massie took his 16th wicket on Monday morning and the runs came with a minimum of fuss.

TRENT BRIDGE: CATCHES GO DOWN

In the third Test at Trent Bridge, Illingworth put Australia in, assured that the wicket would become easier the longer the match went on. The ploy might have worked if the England fielders had held their catches. Peter Parfitt did take four fine slip catches but he dropped Stackpole on 46 and the burly opener went on to make 114. If Snow, who took 5 for 92, had better support, Australia could have been in trouble, but as it was they made 315. England struggled against the bowling of Lillee and Massie and with Marsh taking five catches behind the stumps they were dismissed for 189. With Francis injured, Ross Edwards was asked to open the Australian second innings with Stackpole and grasped his opportunity well, making 170 not out. England needed 451 – a somewhat academic calculation – and with Luckhurst making England's highest score of the entire series, the home side were able to save the game.

HEADINGLEY: A CONTROVERSIAL END

The fate of the Ashes was decided in controversial circumstances in the fourth Test at Headingley. The sub-standard nature of the pitch – put down to devastation of the turf by fusarium disease when heavy rain compelled lengthy protection under covers – allowed the ▶

Dennis Lillee
(Australia) 1971-84

Test Average *23.92*
Test Best *7-83 v. West Indies, Melbourne Cricket Ground 1981*
Ashes Average *21.00*
Ashes Best *7-89 v. England, The Oval 1981*

One of the finest of all fast bowlers, Dennis Lillee was for much of the 1970s, at the forefront of a devastating Australian pace attack alongside Jeff Thomson. On his first tour of England in 1972 he bowled a lengthy 59 overs in the first Test at Old Trafford for match figures of 8 for 106 including an impressive 6 for 66 in the second innings. He ended the series with 31 wickets at 17.87 skittling out a bemused home side and helping to square the series. In 1974-75 he and Thommo destroyed Mike Denness' side whilst in 1977 his 11 for 165 effectively saved the Centenary Test for Australia. After missing the 1977 tour of England he became one of the main drawcards in Packer cricket. On returning to Test cricket he took 39 wickets in 1981 in England but this was Botham's series. In all, Lillee took 355 Test wickets, 167 of which were English, which is the most any bowler has taken against another country.

spinners to achieve turn even before lunch on the opening day. Australia were 79 for 1 at lunch but tumbled to 146 all out as Underwood took 4 for 37 off 31 overs. Edrich and Luckhurst made 43 that evening, but by lunch on the second day, England were struggling at 112 for 6 with Mallett having taken five quality wickets. Illingworth and Snow then added 104 for the eight wicket to give them a lead of 117 on first innings. Australia were given little chance against Underwood and Illingworth and so it transpired. After Edwards had followed his big score at Nottingham with a 'pair' and Arnold had Ian Chappell caught behind without scoring, Underwood tore through the middle-order in a spell of 5 for 18. He returned match figures of 10 for 82 and England were home and dry by nine wickets on the third day.

In the final Test at The Oval, England were humbled by Lillee. Varying his pace and using the bouncer to effect, he took 5 for 58 in their total of 284. Only Knott, batting inventively and bravely for his 92, displayed any resistance. Australia's first innings total of 399 was built upon a third-wicket stand of 201 by the Chappells – the first instance of brothers scoring centuries in the same innings of a Test match. They took their side to within sight of England's total before Edwards steered them to a useful lead on the third day. In England's second knock, Barry Wood batted fearlessly and correctly for 90 on his debut but it was another fine innings from Knott that enabled England to set up a sizeable target for Australia. Set 242, Australia were 116 for 1 on the fifth evening and with three of England's bowlers – Illingworth, Snow and D'Oliveira – all for various reasons unable to bowl, Australia won a great victory by five wickets.

1974-75

With a revitalised Dennis Lillee and new fast bowling sensation Jeff Thomson both at the peak of their powers, Australia crushed England, who could not cope with a barrage of ferocious pace bowling. England's shell-shocked batsmen failed to reach an innings total of 300 until the final Test when the Lillee-Thomson partnership was broken.

The opening Test at Brisbane on a dubious pitch, hastily prepared after storms, was won as much by the bowling of Lillee and Thomson, backed by Walker's medium-pace, as anything else. Ian Chappell saw to it that Australia's first innings rose to some height and his brother Greg made the first of two half-centuries in the match. England's misfortunes were compounded by Amiss's broken thumb and Edrich's broken hand – both caused by very fast balls. The only batsman to conquer the Australian quicks was Tony Greig, who dodged the bouncers to make 110 – England's first century at the Gabba since Maurice Leyland's 38 years earlier. Australia's batsmen then put bat to ball and Ian Chappell declared at 288 for 5, leaving England needing 333 for victory. The England batsmen had no answer to Thomson ferocious pace and well-practiced yorkers: Thomson took 6 for 46 and Australia were 1-0 up and seemed well on the way to regaining the Ashes.

PERTH: COWDREY RETURNS

England called for reinforcements a few days before the start of the second Test in Perth. Colin Cowdrey, just a fortnight short of his 42nd birthday, arrived to boost the England party but the tourists' injury woes against the Australian pacemen continued, with David Lloyd retiring for a time after being hit in the groin by Thomson and Edrich sustaining two fractured ribs in England's second innings. Put in to bat by Ian Chappell, England were bowled out for 208. Australia then batted solidly down the order with Ross Edwards making 115 and Doug Walters 103. Walters' hundred was scored between tea and stumps on the second day – his century being reached when he hit the last ball of the day from Willis for six over square leg. Despite gallant resistance from another 42-year-old, Fred Titmus, in England's second innings, Jeff Thomson reigned supreme and Australia won by nine wickets.

MELBOURNE: NO RESULT

Ian Chappell put England in again – the first time a captain had done that in successive Ashes Tests – before 77,165 spectators on Boxing Day at Melbourne. Edrich and Cowdrey made 76 for the third wicket but there was no other prolonged resistance until Knott went in. England reached 242. Bob Willis, bowling shortish spells,

JEFF THOMSON, LEGENDARY QUICK BOWLER, IN ACTION AGAINST ENGLAND, 1975

was fast and lively and took 5 for 61 as England gained a one-run lead on first innings. Amiss batted well in England's second innings and was out two runs short of Bobby Simpson's record aggregate of 1,381 runs in Tests in a calendar year. He gave England a start of 115 with David Lloyd but the rest of the innings fell away in familiar fashion. Australia, set to make marginally the highest total of the match to win, needed 55 runs in the final hour with four wickets in hand, but dithered, and at the end of an exciting game were still eight runs short with two wickets in hand.

SYDNEY: ASHES REGAINED

Australia regained the Ashes by winning the fourth Test at Sydney, four years after losing them on the same ground, with a decisive victory. Denness dropped himself from this match, Edrich taking over the captaincy. Rick McCosker had a distinguished first Test innings. Opening for the first time in big cricket, he made 80 whilst once more the Chappells contributed valuably in a first innings total of 405. Only Edrich, who batted just under four hours for his 50, and Knott, driving spiritedly, offered any real fight for England. David Lloyd brilliantly caught Ian Chappell as Australia's second innings got under way but then Greg Chappell and Ian Redpath put on 220, enabling the home side to declare at 289 for 4. England were set 400 to win in just over eight hours. A thunderstorm then prevented play for an hour-and-a-half but having progressed to 68 for 0 on the last day, England began to lose wickets at regular intervals, and with Mallett taking 4 for 21, the tourists were all out for 228. The attendance of 178, 027 was a Sydney record.

After the first day of the fifth Test was lost to rain, Australia found themselves put in to bat by Denness, who had returned to the England side. He soon had Underwood bowling on a drying pitch and shortly after lunch, the home side were 84 for 5 – all to Underwood. As the pitch eased, Walters and Jenner played adventurously and Australia's first innings total reached 304. Denness and Fletcher apart, England batted dismally as they were dismissed for 172. Jeff Thomson had taken three wickets at the top of the order but on the rest day, he injured his shoulder while playing tennis. He didn't take any further part in the series, so effectively his 33 wickets had come in four-and-a-half Tests. Australia then increased their lead with Walters and Marsh accelerating to a 112-run stand before the closure. Despite a flamboyant hundred from Alan Knott – only the second century in an Ashes Test by a wicket-keeper – Australia won by 163 runs.

FINAL TEST: CONSOLATION WIN

With Thomson out of the side and Lillee retiring after six overs with a foot injury, England seized the opportunity to come to terms with comparatively ordinary bowling after Peter Lever had routed Australia on a humid morning. The Lancashire paceman took 6 for 38, including four wickets for five runs in one spell as Australia were bowled out for 152. In the face of mounting criticism, Mike Denness was more at home on the slower pitch and made 188 – the highest score by an England captain in Australia – while Keith Fletcher hit 146. Max Walker picked up five quick wickets as the tail subsided and finished with 8 for 143 as England totalled 529. Greg Chappell made another hundred but England won by an innings and four runs. It was a hollow victory at the end of a series in which a lack of quality and character in batting had been cruelly exposed by aggressive, fast and accurate bowling. ▶

1975

Australia retained the Ashes by winning a four-match series arranged to fill a gap in the Test Match calendar. When the series began in July after the first World Cup, it was quite clear that England were still under the clouds of their defeat in Australia the previous winter. Still facing a side led by Denness, Australia batted well and then, with the help of the weather, destroyed the England batting.

FIRST TEST: EDGBASTON

Denness, after consulting his senior players, gambled against an ominous weather forecast by putting Australia in – and lost comprehensively. Turner and McCosker took Australia to 77 without loss at lunch and by the close of play on day one, the tourists were 243 for 5. Hard-hitting by Edwards, Marsh and Thomson took them to a total of 359. England had just begun their innings when a thunderstorm drenched Edgbaston and despite a characteristic fight by Edrich they

NEW ENGLAND CAPTAIN TONY GREIG BOWLING AT LORD'S, SECOND TEST 1975

capitulated to Lillee and Walker for 101. Australia enforced the follow-on and Thomson, erratic in England's first innings, found his rhythm, length and direction. Essex batsman Graham Gooch, on Test debut, made a pair as England were in ruins at 93 for 5 at

the end of the third day. By mid-afternoon on the fourth day, England had suffered their first-ever defeat at Edgbaston by an innings and 85 runs.

LORD'S: GREIG IS CAPTAIN

Denness resigned the England captaincy and Tony Greig, leading the side for the first time at Lord's, made a flamboyant, if not winning debut. Playing in his first game for England was David Steele – grey-haired, bespectacled and looking much older than his 33 years. After getting lost in the Lord's pavilion, Steele found his way quickly in Test cricket, scoring 50 in England's first innings, though it was Greig (96) and Knott (69) who helped England reach 315. Australia were struggling at 81 for 7 when Edwards and Thomson put bat to ball, the former falling one run short of a deserved hundred. Dennis Lillee, not renowned for his batting prowess, made 73 not out, dominating a last wicket stand of 69 as Australia totalled 268. In a much improved batting performance in England's second innings,

THE PITCH AT HEADINGLEY, DUG UP BY 'SUPPORTERS' OF ARMED ROBBER GEORGE DAVIS

John Edrich made 175 – the biggest of his seven Ashes hundreds – as England declared at 436 for 7. After being set 484 to win, Australia started the final day on 97 for 1. England's hoped-for thunderstorm arrived – but before play began. The covered pitch was consequently unharmed and Australia were able to play out time.

At Headingley, the two sides fashioned a Test match of perfect balance which had to be abandoned in unique and controversial circumstances. England had batted first with Steele top-scoring with 73 and adding 112 for the third wicket with the equally consistent Edrich, but Greig apart, there was little resistance to Australia's pace quartet. Playing in his first Test, Gary Gilmour was the pick of Australia's bowlers, taking 6 for 85. Another debutant was Phil Edmonds, the Zambian-born left-arm spinner who took 5 for 17 in his first 12 overs. He got rid of the Chappells, Edwards, Walters and Walker as the tourists slid from 78 for 2 to 107 for 8. England built slowly on their lead on the fourth morning until a concerted effort to score quickly paid off. Chasing 445 for victory, Australia required a further 225 runs to win on the final day with seven wickets in hand. Yet no play was possible due to vandals who overnight dug holes in, and spread oil on, the wicket. They wished to draw attention to the alleged wrongful imprisonment for armed robbery of one George Davis. Not even the rain which finally fell steadily on that last day, and would probably have ruined play in any case, could reduce the disappointment at such an unsatisfactory conclusion to a promising match.

100 YEARS OF TEST CRICKET

After winning the toss at the Oval, Australia made almost certain of holding their series lead by finishing the

first day on 280 for 1. Ian Chappell and Rick McCosker's stand eventually realised 277, the ninth-highest for any wicket in Ashes Tests. Chappell's 192 was his highest score against England as his side went on to make 532 for 9 declared. Thomson, Lillee and Walker then bowled England out for 191 and Chappell enforced the follow-on. But yet again, Edrich and Steele dug in aided by Roope, Knott and finally Woolmer, who occupied the crease for 499 minutes in scoring 149, and in doing so recorded the slowest century made by an Englishman against Australia. The 538 total was England's highest in the second innings of an Ashes Test. This was the longest cricket match ever played in England and a further indictment of over-prepared pitches.

1977

With the 100th anniversary of the first-ever Test match approaching, the authorities in Melbourne set about planning an appropriate celebration, and in March 1977 an ambitious operation supported by big business was carried through with the greatest aplomb. Every surviving cricketer who had played in England-Australia Tests in Australia was invited, expenses paid, and the eyes of the entire cricket world were on Melbourne for the greatest of birthday parties.

100 YEARS OF TEST CRICKET

The match itself, which wasn't for the Ashes, was as fluctuating and thrilling as any in the long saga of England-Australia matches. England excelled themselves by dismissing Australia first for 138 but this was put into perspective when England crashed to Lillee and Walker for just 95, the former taking 6 for 26 and the latter 4 for 54. It then seemed that the ▶

Geoff Boycott
(England) 1964-82

Test Average *47.73*
Test Best *246 v. India, Headingley 1967*
Ashes Average *47.50*
Ashes Best *191, Headingley 1977*

Geoffrey Boycott was one of the most controversial cricketers of modern times. No batsman ever compiled runs in a more single-minded and dedicated manner. The 1970-71 series in Australia was a personal triumph. His 657 Test runs at 93.85 were instrumental in helping England to regain the Ashes. In 1974 he voluntarily withdrew from Test cricket, declining to tour Australia in 1974-75 and did not return to Tests until the summer of 1977. His comeback was dour and nerve-wracking but triumphant, for he made 107 and 80 not out. With his confidence high he made an even more emotional century in the next Test in front of his home crowd at Headingley and his 191 happened to be his 100th first-class century. He was controversial to the end but always insisted his figures spoke for him. His critics claimed that the context was as important as the figures but nobody can take away from him his career average of 56.83, or his 8,114 Test runs, once the highest in the world.

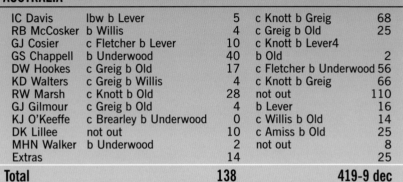

THE CENTENARY TEST

AUSTRALIA v ENGLAND
Played at Melbourne, March 12-17 1977

AUSTRALIA

IC Davis	lbw b Lever	5	c Knott b Greig	68
RB McCosker	b Willis	4	c Greig b Old	25
GJ Cosier	c Fletcher b Lever	10	c Knott b Lever	4
GS Chappell	b Underwood	40	b Old	2
DW Hookes	c Greig b Old	17	c Fletcher b Underwood	56
KD Walters	c Greig b Willis	4	c Knott b Greig	66
RW Marsh	c Knott b Old	28	not out	110
GJ Gilmour	c Greig b Old	4	b Lever	16
KJ O'Keeffe	c Brearley b Underwood	0	c Willis b Old	14
DK Lillee	not out	10	c Amiss b Old	25
MHN Walker	b Underwood	2	not out	8
Extras		14		25
Total		**138**		**419-9 dec**

Fall of wickets 1-11 2-13 3-23 4-45 5-51 6-102 7-114 8-117 9-136 10-138
Second Innings 1-33 2-40 3-53 4-132 5-187 6-244 7-277 8-353 9-407

England Bowling (4-ball overs)

	O	M	R	W	O	M	R	W
JK Lever	12	1	36	2	21	1	95	2
RGD Willis	8	0	32	2	22	0	91	0
CM Old	12	4	39	3	27.6	2	104	4
DL Underwood	11.6	2	16	3	12	2	38	1
AW Greig	-	-	-	-	14	3	66	2

ENGLAND

RA Woolmer	c Chappell b Lillee	9	lbw b Walker	12
JM Brearley	c Hookes b Lillee	12	lbw b Lillee	43
DL Underwood	c Chappell b Walker	7	b Lillee	7
DW Randall	c Marsh b Lillee	4	c Cosier b O'Keeffe	174
DL Amiss	c O'Keefe b Walker	4	b Chappell	64
KWR Fletcher	c Marsh b Walker	4	c Marsh b Lillee	1
AW Greig	b Walker	18	c Cosier b O'Keeffe	41
APE Knott	lbw b Lillee	15	lbw b Lillee	42
CM Old	c Marsh b Lillee	3	c Chappell b Lillee	2
JK Lever	c Marsh b Lillee	11	lbw b O'Keeffe	4
RGD Willis	not out	1	not out	5
Extras		7		22
Total		**95**		**417**

Fall of wickets 1-19 2-30 3-34 4-40 5-40 6-61 7-65 8-78 9-86 10-95
Second Innings 1-28 2-113 3-279 4-290 5-346 6-369 7-380 8-385 9-410 10-417

Australia Bowling

	O	M	R	W	O	M	R	W
DK Lillee	13.3	2	26	6	34.4	7	139	5
MHN Walker	15	3	54	4	22	4	83	1
KJ O'Keeffe	1	0	4	0	33	6	108	3
GJ Gilmour	5	3	4	0	4	0	29	0
GS Chappell	-	-	-	-	16	7	29	1
KD Walters	-	-	-	-	3	2	7	0

AUSTRALIA WON BY 45 RUNS

match might be over in three days and the Queen was due to visit the ground on the fifth. Then the match settled down, Davis and Walters made sixties and David Hookes stroked a delightful 56 with five consecutive fours off Greig's bowling. Finally, to ram home Australia's advantage, Marsh recorded the first Test century by a regular wicket-keeper for Australia against England, having already passed Wally Grout's record of 187 Test catches and stumpings. Marsh was assisted towards the end by McCosker, who batted with a fractured jaw wired up and bandaged, the legacy of an attempted hook which cost him his wicket in the first innings. England were thus set the unlikely target of 463 with plenty of time. By the end of the fourth day, they were a promising 191 for 2 with Nottinghamshire's Derek Randall 87 not out. On a memorable last day, England forged nearer and nearer to their 'impossible' requirement. Amiss made 64 and Greig and Knott made forties; but the star turn was Randall, who scored 174 in his first Test against the old enemy with flashing cuts and drives and spasms of hilarious animation. While he was in, there was always the chance of an England win but when he left, there was but a slender hope. Lillee took the final wicket, that of Underwood, and the jubilant scenes at the end was for the glory of the game as much as for Australia's success. And the margin of victory, as if arranged by the cricketing gods, was 45 runs – as it was in the first Test match, on that same ground 100 years before. ●

1946-1977 RESULTS

1946-47

AUSTRALIA WON SERIES 3-0

1st Test at Brisbane
November 29, 30 December 2, 3, 4
AUSTRALIA 645 (DG Bradman 187 AL Hassett 128 CL McCool 95 KR Miller 79 IW Johnson 47 DVP Wright 5-167)
ENGLAND 141 (KR Miller 7-60) and 172 (ERH Toshack 6-82)
AUSTRALIA WON BY AN INNINGS AND 332 RUNS

2nd Test at Sydney
December 13, 14, 16, 17, 18, 19
ENGLAND 255 (WJ Edrich 71 JT Ikin 60 IW Johnson 6-42) and 371 (WJ Edrich 119 DCS Compton 54 C Washbrook 41 CL McCool 5-109)
AUSTRALIA 659-8 dec (DG Bradman 234 SG Barnes 234 KR Miller 40)
AUSTRALIA WON BY AN INNINGS AND 33 RUNS

3rd Test at Melbourne
January 1, 2, 3, 4, 6, 7
AUSTRALIA 365 (CL McCool 104* DG Bradman 79 SG Barnes 45) and 536 (AR Morris 155 RR Lindwall 100 D Tallon 92 DG Bradman 49 CL McCool 43)
ENGLAND 351 (WJ Edrich 89 C Washbrook 62 NWD Yardley 61 JT Ikin 48 B Dooland 4-69) and 310-7 (C Washbrook 112 NWD Yardley 53* L Hutton 40)
MATCH DRAWN

4th Test at Adelaide
January 31 February 1, 3, 4, 5, 6
ENGLAND 460 (DCS Compton 147 L Hutton 94 J Hardstaff jnr 67 C Washbrook 65 RR Lindwall 4-52) and 340-8 dec (DCS Compton 103* L Hutton 76 WJ Edrich 46 ERH Toshack 4-76)
AUSTRALIA 487 (KR Miller 141* AR Morris 122 AL Hassett 78 IW Johnson 52) and 215-1 (AR Morris 124* DG Bradman 56*)
MATCH DRAWN

5th Test at Sydney
February 28 March 1 (no play), 3, 4, 5
ENGLAND 280 (L Hutton 122 retired ill WJ Edrich 60 RR Lindwall 7-63) and 186 (DCS Compton 76 CL McCool 5-44)
AUSTRALIA 253 (SG Barnes 71 AR Morris 57 DVP Wright 7-105) and 214-5 (DG Bradman 63 AL Hassett 47)
AUSTRALIA WON BY 5 WICKETS

1948

AUSTRALIA WON SERIES 4-0

1st Test at Trent Bridge
June 10, 11, 12, 14, 15
ENGLAND 165 (JC Laker 63 WA Johnston 5-36) and 441 (DCS Compton 184 L Hutton 74 TG Evans 50 J Hardstaff jnr 43 KR Miller 4-125 WA Johnston 4-147)
AUSTRALIA 509 (DG Bradman 139 AL Hassett 137 SG Barnes 62 RR Lindwall 42 JC Laker 4-138) and 98-2 (SG Barnes 64*)
AUSTRALIA WON BY 8 WICKETS

2nd Test at Lord's
June 24, 25, 26, 28, 29
AUSTRALIA 350 (AR Morris 105 D Tallon 53 AL Hassett 47 AV Bedser 4-100) and 460-7 dec (SG Barnes 141 DG Bradman 89 KR Miller 74 AR Morris 62)
ENGLAND 215 (DCS Compton 53 NWD Yardley 44 RR Lindwall 5-70) and 186 (ERH Toshack 5-40)
AUSTRALIA WON BY 409 RUNS

3rd Test at Old Trafford
July 8, 9, 10, 12 (no play), 13
ENGLAND 363 (DCS Compton 145* RR Lindwall 4-99) and 174-3 dec (C Washbrook 85* WJ Edrich 53)
AUSTRALIA 221 (AR Morris 51 AV Bedser 4-81) and 92-1 (AR Morris 54*)
MATCH DRAWN

4th Test at Headingley
July 22, 23, 24, 26, 27
ENGLAND 496 (C Washbrook 143 WJ Edrich 111 L Hutton 81 AV Bedser 79) and 365-8 dec (DCS Compton 66 C Washbrook 65 L Hutton 57 WJ Edrich 54 TG Evans 47* WA Johnston 4-95)
AUSTRALIA 458 (RN Harvey 112 SJE Loxton 93 RR Lindwall 77 KR Miller 58) and 404-3 (AR Morris 182 DG Bradman 173*)
AUSTRALIA WON BY 7 WICKETS

5th Test at The Oval
August 14, 16, 17, 18
ENGLAND 52 (RR Lindwall 6-20) and 188 (L Hutton 64 WA Johnston 4-40)
AUSTRALIA 389 (AR Morris 196 SG Barnes 61 WE Hollies 5-131)
AUSTRALIA WON BY AN INNINGS AND 149 RUNS

1950-51

AUSTRALIA WON SERIES 4-1

1st Test at Brisbane
December 1, 2 (no play), 4, 5
AUSTRALIA 228 (RN Harvey 74 RR Lindwall 41 AV Bedser 4-45) and 32-7 dec (TE Bailey 4-22)
ENGLAND 68-7 dec (WA Johnston 5-35) and 122 (L Hutton 62* JB Iverson 4-43)
AUSTRALIA WON BY 70 RUNS

2nd Test at Melbourne
December 22, 23, 26, 27
AUSTRALIA 194 (AL Hassett 52 RN Harvey 42 TE Bailey 4-40 AV Bedser 4-37) and 181 (KA Archer 46 FR Brown 4-26)
ENGLAND 197 (FR Brown 62 TG Evans 49 JB Iverson 4-37) and 150 (L Hutton 40 WA Johnston 4-26)
AUSTRALIA WON BY 28 RUNS

3rd Test at Sydney
January 5, 6, 8, 9
ENGLAND 290 (FR Brown 79 L Hutton 62 RT Simpson 49 KR Miller 4-37) and 123 (JB Iverson 6-27)
AUSTRALIA 426 (KR Miller 145* IW Johnson 77 AL Hassett 70 KA Archer 48 AV Bedser 4-107 FR Brown 4-153)
AUSTRALIA WON BY AN INNINGS AND 13 RUNS

4th Test at Adelaide
February 2, 3, 5, 6, 7, 8
AUSTRALIA 371 (AR Morris 206 KR Miller 44 AL Hassett 43 RN Harvey 43 DVP Wright 4-99) and 403-8 dec (JW Burke 101* KR Miller 99 RN Harvey 68)
ENGLAND 272 (L Hutton 156*) and 228 (RT Simpson 61 L Hutton 45 DS Sheppard 41 WA Johnston 4-73)
AUSTRALIA WON BY 274 RUNS

5th Test at Melbourne
February 23, 24 (no play), 26, 27, 28
AUSTRALIA 217 (AL Hassett 92 AR Morris 50 AV Bedser 5-46 FR Brown 5-49) and 197 (GB Hole 63 RN Harvey 52 AL Hassett 48 AV Bedser 5-59)
ENGLAND 320 (RT Simpson 156* L Hutton 79 KR Miller 4-76) and 95-2 (L Hutton 60*)
ENGLAND WON BY 8 WICKETS

1953

ENGLAND WON SERIES 1-0

1st Test at Trent Bridge
June 11, 12, 13, 15(no play), 16
AUSTRALIA 249 (AL Hassett 115 AR Morris 67 KR Miller 55 AV Bedser 7-55) and 123 (AR Morris 60 AV Bedser 7-44)
ENGLAND 144 (L Hutton 43 RR Lindwall 5-57) and 120-1 (L Hutton 60*)
MATCH DRAWN

2nd Test at Lord's
June 25, 26, 27, 29, 30
AUSTRALIA 346 (AL Hassett 104 AK Davidson 76 RN Harvey 59 AV Bedser 5-105 JH Wardle 4-77) and 368 (KR Miller 109 AR Morris 89 RR Lindwall 50 GB Hole 47 FR Brown 4-82)
ENGLAND 372 (L Hutton 145 TW Graveney 78 DCS Compton 57 RR Lindwall 5-66) and 282-7 (W Watson 109 TE Bailey 71)
MATCH DRAWN

3rd Test at Old Trafford
July 9, 10, 11, 13 (no play) 14
AUSTRALIA 318 (RN Harvey 122 GB Hole 66 JH de Courcy 41 AV Bedser 5-115) and 35-8 (JH Wardle 4-7)
ENGLAND 276 (L Hutton 66 DCS Compton 45 TG Evans 44*)
MATCH DRAWN

4th Test at Headingley
July 23, 24, 25, 27, 28
ENGLAND 167 (TW Graveney 55 RR Lindwall 5-54) and 275 (WJ Edrich 64 DCS Compton 61 JC Laker 48 KR Miller 4-63)
AUSTRALIA 266 (RN Harvey 71 GB Hole 53 AV Bedser 6-95) and 147-4
MATCH DRAWN

5th Test at The Oval
August 15, 17, 18, 19
AUSTRALIA 275 (RR Lindwall 62 AL Hassett 53 FS Trueman 4-86) and 162 (RG Archer 49 GAR Lock 5-45 JC Laker 4-75)
ENGLAND 306 (L Hutton 82 TE Bailey 64 RR Lindwall 4-70) and 132-2 (WJ Edrich 55*)

1954-55

ENGLAND WON SERIES 3-1

1st Test at Brisbane
November 26, 27, 29, 30 December 1
AUSTRALIA 601-8 dec (RN Harvey 162 AR Morris 153 RR Lindwall 64* GB Hole 57 KR Miller 49)
ENGLAND 190 (TE Bailey 88 MC Cowdrey 40) and 257 (WJ Edrich 88 PBH May 44)
AUSTRALIA WON BY AN INNINGS AND 154 RUNS

2nd Test at Sydney
December 17, 18, 20, 21, 22
ENGLAND 154 and 296 (PBH May 104 MC Cowdrey 54)
AUSTRALIA 228 (RG Archer 49 JW Burke 44 TE Bailey 4-59 FH Tyson 4-45) and 184 (RN Harvey 92* FH Tyson 6-85)
ENGLAND WON BY 38 RUNS

3rd Test at Melbourne
December 31 January 1, 3, 4, 5
ENGLAND 191 (MC Cowdrey 102 RG Archer 4-33) and 279 (PBH May 91 L Hutton 42 WA Johnson 5-85)
AUSTRALIA 231 (LV Maddocks 47 JB Statham 5-60) and 111 (FH Tyson 7-27)
ENGLAND WON BY 128 RUNS

4th Test at Adelaide
January 28, 29, 31 February 1, 2
AUSTRALIA 323 (LV Maddocks 69 CC McDonald 48 KR Miller 44 IW Johnson 41) and 111
ENGLAND 341 (L Hutton 80 MC Cowdrey 79 DCS Compton 44 R Benaud 4-120) and 97-5
ENGLAND WON BY 5 WICKETS

5th Test at Sydney
February 25(no play) 26(no play) 28(no play) March 1,,2, 3
ENGLAND 371-7 dec (TW Graveney 111 DCS Compton 84 PBH May 79 TE Bailey 72)
AUSTRALIA 221 (CC McDonald 72 JH Wardle 5-79) and 118-6
Captains L Hutton (E) IW Johnson (A)
MATCH DRAWN

1956

ENGLAND WON SERIES 2-1

1st Test at Trent Bridge
June 7, 8(no play) 9, 11l, 12
ENGLAND 217-8 dec (PE Richardson 81 PBH May 73 KR Miller 4-69) and 188-3 dec (MC Cowdrey 81 PE Richardson 73)
AUSTRALIA 148 (RN Harvey 64 JC Laker 4-58) and 120-3 (JW Burke 58*)
Captains PBH May (E) IW Johnson (A)
MATCH DRAWN

2nd Test at Lord's
June 21, 22, 23, 25, 26
AUSTRALIA 285 (CC McDonald 78 JW Burke 65) and 257 (R Benaud 97 FS Trueman 5-90 TE Bailey 4-64)
ENGLAND 171 (PBH May 63 KR Miller 5-72) and 186 (PBH May 53 KR

Miller 5-80 RG Archer 4-71)

AUSTRALIA WON BY 185 RUNS

3rd Test at Headingley

July 12, 13, 14(no play), 16, 17
ENGLAND 325 (PBH May 101 C Washbrook 98 TG Evans 40)
AUSTRALIA 143 (JW Burke 41 KR Miller 41 JC Laker 5-58 GAR Lock 4-41) and 140 (RN Harvey 69 JC Laker 6-55)

ENGLAND WON BY AN INNINGS AND 42 RUNS

4th Test at Old Trafford

July 26, 27, 28, 30, 31
ENGLAND 459 (Rev DS Sheppard 113 PE Richardson 104 MC Cowdrey 80 TG Evans 47 PBH May 43 IW Johnson 4-151)
AUSTRALIA 84 (JC Laker 9-37) and 205 (CC McDonald 89 JC Laker 10-53)

ENGLAND WON BY AN INNINGS AND 170 RUNS

5th Test at The Oval

August 23, 24, 25, 27(no play), 28
ENGLAND 247 (DCS Compton 94 PBH May 83* RG Archer 5-53 KR Miller 4-91) and 182-3 dec (Rev DS Sheppard 62)
AUSTRALIA 202 (KR Miller 61 JC Laker 4-80) and 27-5

MATCH DRAWN

1958-59

AUSTRALIA WON SERIES 4-0

1st Test at Brisbane

December 5, 6, 8, 9, 10
ENGLAND 134 and 198 (TE Bailey 68, R Benaud 4-66)
AUSTRALIA 186 (CC McDonald 42 PJ Loader 4-56) and 147-2 (NC O'Neill 71*)

AUSTRALIA WON BY 8 WICKETS

2nd Test at Melbourne

December 31 January 1, 2, 3, 5
ENGLAND 259 (PBH May 113 TE Bailey 48 MC Cowdrey 44 AK Davidson 6-64) and 87 (I Meckiff 6-38)
AUSTRALIA 308 (RN Harvey 167 CC McDonald 47 JB Statham 7-57) and 42-2

AUSTRALIA WON BY 8 WICKETS

3rd Test at Sydney

January 9, 10, 12, 13, 14, 15
ENGLAND 219 (PBH May 42 R Swetman 41 R Benaud 5-83) and 287-7 dec (MC Cowdrey 100* PBH May 92 R Benaud 4-94)
AUSTRALIA 357 (NC O'Neill 77 AK Davidson 71 KD Mackay 57 LE Favell 54 CC McDonald 40 JC Laker 5-107 GAR Lock 4-130) and 54-2

MATCH DRAWN

4th Test at Adelaide

January 30, 31 February 2, 3, 4, 5
AUSTRALIA 476 (CC McDonald 170 JW Burke 66 NC O'Neill 56 R Benaud 46 AK Davidson 43 RN Harvey 41 FS Trueman 4-90) and 36-0
ENGLAND 240 (MC Cowdrey 84 TW Graveney 41 R Benaud 5-91) and 270 (PBH May 59 TW Graveney 53* PE Richardson 43 W Watson 40 R Benaud 4-82)

AUSTRALIA WON BY 10 WICKETS

5th Test at Melbourne

February 13, 14, 16, 17, 18
ENGLAND 205 (PE Richardson 68 JB Mortimore 44* R Benaud 4-43) and 214 (TW Graveney 54 MC Cowdrey 46)
AUSTRALIA 351 (CC McDonald 133 ATW Grout 74 R Benaud 64 FS Trueman 4-92 JC Laker 4-93) and 69-1 (CC McDonald 51*)

AUSTRALIA WON BY 9 WICKETS

1961

AUSTRALIA WON SERIES 2-1

1st Test at Edgbaston

June 8, 9, 10, 12, 13
ENGLAND 195 (R Subba Row 59 KD Mackay 4-57) and 401-4 (ER Dexter 180 R Subba Row 112 KF Barrington 48*)
AUSTRALIA 516-9 dec (RN Harvey 114 NC O'Neill 82 RB Simpson 76 KD Mackay 64 WM Lawry 57)

MATCH DRAWN

2nd Test at Lord's

June 22, 23, 24, 26
ENGLAND 206 (R Subba Row 48 AK Davidson 5-42) and 202 (KF Barrington 66 G Pullar 42 GD McKenzie 5-37)
AUSTRALIA 340 (WM Lawry 130 KD Mackay 54 PJP Burge 46 FS Trueman 4-118) and 71-5

AUSTRALIA WON BY 5 WICKETS

3rd Test at Headingley

July 6, 7, 8
AUSTRALIA 237 (RN Harvey 73 CC McDonald 54 FS Trueman 5-58) and 120 (RN Harvey 53 FS Trueman 6-30)
ENGLAND 299 (MC Cowdrey 93 G Pullar 53 AK Davidson 5-63) and 62-2

ENGLAND WON BY 8 WICKETS

4th Test at Old Trafford

July 27, 28, 29, 31 August 1
AUSTRALIA 190 (WM Lawry 74 BC Booth 46 JB Statham 5-53) and 432 (WM Lawry 102 AK Davidson 77* NC O'Neill 67 RB Simpson 51 DA Allen 4-58)
ENGLAND 367 (PBH May 95 KF Barrington 78 G Pullar 63 DA Allen 42 RB Simpson 4-23) and 201 (ER Dexter 76 R Subba Row 49 R Benaud 6-70)

AUSTRALIA WON BY 54 RUNS

5th Test at The Oval

August 17, 18, 19, 21, 22
ENGLAND 256 (PBH May 71 KF Barrington 53 AK Davidson 4-83) and 370-8 (R Subba Row 137 KF Barrington 83 DA Allen 42* JT Murray 40 KD Mackay 5-121)
AUSTRALIA 494 (PJP Burge 181 NC O'Neill 117 BC Booth 71 RB Simpson 40 DA Allen 4-133)

MATCH DRAWN

1962-63

SERIES DRAWN 1-ALL

1st Test at Brisbane

November 30, December 1, 3, 4, 5
AUSTRALIA 404 (BC Booth 112 KD

Mackay 86* R Benaud 51 RB Simpson 50) and 362-4 dec (WM Lawry 98 RB Simpson 71 RN Harvey 57 NC O'Neill 56 PJP Burge 47*)
ENGLAND 389 (PH Parfitt 80 KF Barrington 78 ER Dexter 70 R Benaud 6-115) and 278-6 (ER Dexter 99 G Pullar 56 Rev DS Sheppard 53)

MATCH DRAWN

2nd Test at Melbourne

December 29, 31, January 1, 2, 3
AUSTRALIA 316 (WM Lawry 52 KD Mackay 49 AK Davidson 40 FJ Titmus 4-43) and 248 (BC Booth 103 WM Lawry 57 FS Trueman 5-62)
ENGLAND 331 (MC Cowdrey 113 ER Dexter 93 TW Graveney 41 AK Davidson 6-75) and 237-3 (Rev DS Sheppard 113 MC Cowdrey 58* ER Dexter 52)

ENGLAND WON BY 7 WICKETS

3rd Test at Sydney

January 11, 12, 14, 15
ENGLAND 279 (MC Cowdrey 85 G Pullar 53 RB Simpson 5-57 AK Davidson 4-54) and 104 (AK Davidson 5-25)
AUSTRALIA 319 (RB Simpson 91 BK Shepherd 71* RN Harvey 64 FJ Titmus 7-79) and 67-2

AUSTRALIA WON BY 8 WICKETS

4th Test at Adelaide

January 25, 26, 28, 29, 30
AUSTRALIA 393 (RN Harvey 154 NC O'Neill 100 AK Davidson 46) and 293 (BC Booth 77 RB Simpson 71 R Benaud 48 FS Trueman 4-60)
ENGLAND 331 (KF Barrington 63 ER Dexter 61 FJ Titmus 59* GD McKenzie 5-89) and 223-4 (KF Barrington 132*) Captains R Benaud (A) ER Dexter (E)

MATCH DRAWN

5th Test at Sydney

February 15, 16, 18, 19, 20
ENGLAND 321 (KF Barrington 101 ER Dexter 47) and 268-8 dec (KF Barrington 94 Rev DS Sheppard 68 MC Cowdrey 53)
AUSTRALIA 349 (PJP Burge 103 NC O'Neill 73 R Benaud 57 FJ Titmus 5-103) and 152-4 (PJP Burge 52* WM Lawry 45*)

MATCH DRAWN

1964

AUSTRALIA WON SERIES 1-0

1st Test at Trent Bridge

June 4, 5, 6(no play), 8, 9
ENGLAND 216-8 dec (G Boycott 48) and 193-9 dec (ER Dexter 68 GD McKenzie 5-53)
AUSTRALIA 168 (RB Simpson 50) and 40-2

MATCH DRAWN

2nd Test at Lord's

June 18(no play),19(no play), 20,22,23
AUSTRALIA 176 (TR Veivers 54 FS Trueman 5-48) and 168-4 (PJP Burge 59)
ENGLAND 246 (JH Edrich 120 GE Corling 4-60)

MATCH DRAWN

3rd Test at Headingley

July 2, 3, 4, 6
ENGLAND 268 (JM Parks 68 ER Dexter 66 NJN Hawke 5-75 GD McKenzie 4-74) and 229 (KF Barrington 85)
AUSTRALIA 389 (PJP Burge 160 WM Lawry 78 FJ Titmus 4-69) and 111-3 (IR Redpath 58*)

AUSTRALIA WON BY 7 WICKETS

4th Test at Old Trafford

July 23, 24, 25, 27, 28
AUSTRALIA 656-8 dec (RB Simpson 311 WM Lawry 106 BC Booth 98 NC O'Neill 47) and 4-0
ENGLAND 611 (KF Barrington 256 ER Dexter 174 JM Parks 60 G Boycott 58 GD McKenzie 7-153)

MATCH DRAWN

5th Test at The Oval

August 13, 14, 15, 17, 18(no play)
ENGLAND 182 (KF Barrington 47 NJN Hawke 6-47) and 381-4 (G Boycott 113 MC Cowdrey 93* FJ Titmus 56 KF Barrington 54*)
AUSTRALIA 379 (WM Lawry 94 BC Booth 74 TR Veivers 67* IR Redpath 45 FS Trueman 4-87)

MATCH DRAWN

1965-66

SERIES DRAWN 1-1

1st Test at Brisbane

December 10, 11(no play) 13, 14, 15
AUSTRALIA 443-6 dec (WM Lawry 166 KD Walters 155 TR Veivers 56*)
ENGLAND 280 (FJ Titmus 60 KF Barrington 53 JM Parks 52 G Boycott 45 PI Philpott 5-90) and 186-3 (G Boycott 63*)

MATCH DRAWN

2nd Test at Melbourne

December 30, 31 January 1, 3, 4
AUSTRALIA 358 (RM Cowper 99 WM Lawry 88 RB Simpson 59 BR Knight 4-84) and 426 (PJP Burge 120 KD Walters 115 WM Lawry 78 RB Simpson 67)
ENGLAND 558 (JH Edrich 109 MC Cowdrey 104 JM Parks 71 KF Barrington 63 FJ Titmus 56* G Boycott 51 RW Barber 48 MJK Smith 41 GD McKenzie 5-134) and 5-0

MATCH DRAWN

3rd Test at Sydney

January 7, 8, 10, 11
ENGLAND 488 (RW Barber 185 JH Edrich 103 G Boycott 84 DA Allen 50* NJN Hawke 7-105)
AUSTRALIA 221 (RM Cowper 60 G Thomas 51 DJ Brown 5-63) and 174 (FJ Titmus 4-40 DA Allen 4-47)

ENGLAND WON BY AN INNINGS AND 93 RUNS

4th Test at Adelaide

January 28, 29, 31 February 1
ENGLAND 241 (KF Barrington 60 JM Parks 49 GD McKenzie 6-48) and 266 (KF Barrington 102 FJ Titmus 53 NJN Hawke 5-54)

AUSTRALIA 516 (RB Simpson 225 WM Lawry 119 G Thomas 52 KR Stackpole 43 IJ Jones 6-118)

AUSTRALIA WON BY AN INNINGS AND 9 RUNS

5th Test at Melbourne

February 11, 12, 14, 15(no play), 16
ENGLAND 485-9 dec (KF Barrington 115 JM Parks 89 JH Edrich 85 MC Cowdrey 79 FJ Titmus 42* KD Walters 4-53) and 69-3
AUSTRALIA 543-8 dec (RM Cowper 307 WM Lawry 108 KD Walters 60)

MATCH DRAWN

1968

SERIES DRAWN 1-1

1st Test at Old Trafford

June 6, 7, 8, 10, 11
AUSTRALIA 357 (AP Sheahan 88 WM Lawry 81 KD Walters 81 IM Chappell 73 JA Snow 4-97) and 220 (KD Walters 86 BN Jarman 41 PI Pocock 6-79)
ENGLAND 165 (JH Edrich 49 RM Cowper 4-48) and 253 (BL D'Oliveira 87* RW Barber 46)

AUSTRALIA WON BY 159 RUNS

2nd Test at Lord's June 20, 21, 22, 24, 25
ENGLAND 351-7 dec (C Milburn 83 KF Barrington 75 G Boycott 49 MC Cowdrey 45)
AUSTRALIA 78 (DJ Brown 5-42) and 127-4 (IR Redpath 53)

MATCH DRAWN

3rd Test at Edgbaston

July 1(no play), 12, 13, 15, 16
ENGLAND 409 (MC Cowdrey 104 TW Graveney 96 JH Edrich 88 EW Freeman 4-78) and 142-3 (JH Edrich 64*)
AUSTRALIA 222 (IM Chappell 71 RM Cowper 57 KD Walters 46) and 68-1

MATCH DRAWN

4th Test at Headingley

July 25, 26, 27, 29, 30
AUSTRALIA 315 (IR Redpath 92 IM Chappell 65 KD Walters 42 DL Underwood 4-41) and 312 (IM Chappell 81 KD Walters 56 IR Redpath 48 R Illingworth 6-87)
ENGLAND 302 (RM Prideaux 64 JH Edrich 62 KF Barrington 49 DL Underwood 45* AN Connolly 5-72) and 230-4 (JH Edrich 65 KF Barrington 46*)

MATCH DRAWN

5th Test at The Oval

August 22, 23, 24, 26, 27
ENGLAND 494 (JH Edrich 164 BL D'Oliveira 158 TW Graveney 63) and 181 (AN Connolly 4-65)
AUSTRALIA 324 (WM Lawry 135 IR Redpath 67 AA Mallett 43*) and 125 (RJ Inverarity 56 DL Underwood 7-50)

RESULT   ENGLAND WON BY 226 RUNS

1970-71

ENGLAND WON SERIES 2-0

1st Test at Brisbane

November 27, 28, 29 December 1, 2
AUSTRALIA 433 (KR Stackpole 207

KD Walters 112 IM Chappell 59 JA Snow 6-14) and 214 (WM Lawry 84 K Shuttleworth 5-47)
ENGLAND 464 (JH Edrich 79 BW Luckhurst 74 APE Knott 73 BL D'Oliveira 57) and 39-1

MATCH DRAWN

2nd Test at Perth

December 11,12, 13, 15, 16
ENGLAND 397 (BW Luckhurst 131 G Boycott 70 JH Edrich 47* MC Cowdrey 40 GD McKenzie 4-66) and 287-6 dec (JH Edrich 115* G Boycott 50)
AUSTRALIA 440 (IR Redpath 171 GS Chappell 108 IM Chappell 50 RW Marsh 44 JA Snow 4-143) and 100-3

MATCH DRAWN

The 3rd Test scheduled for Melbourne, was abandoned without a ball being bowled.

4th Test at Sydney

January 9, 10, 11, 13, 14
ENGLAND 332 (G Boycott 77 JH Edrich 55 JW Gleeson 4-83 AA Mallett 4-40) and 319-5 dec (G Boycott 142* BL D'Oliveira 56* R Illingworth 53)
AUSTRALIA 236 (IR Redpath 64 KD Walters 55 DL Underwood 4-66) and 116 (WM Lawry 60* JA Snow 7-40)

ENGLAND WON BY 299 RUNS

5th Test at Melbourne

January 21, 22, 23, 25, 26
AUSTRALIA 493-9 dec (IM Chappell 111 RW Marsh 92* IR Redpath 72 WM Lawry 56 KD Walters 55) and 169-4 dec (WM Lawry 42)
ENGLAND 392 (BL D'Oliveira 117 BW Luckhurst 109 R Illingworth 41) and 161-0 (G Boycott 76* JH Edrich 74*)

MATCH DRAWN

6th Test at Adelaide

January 29, 30 February 1, 2, 3
ENGLAND 470 (JH Edrich 130 KWR Fletcher 80 G Boycott 58 JH Hampshire 55 BL D'Oliveira 47 DK Lillee 5-84) and 233-4 dec (G Boycott 119 R Illingworth 48* JH Edrich 40)
AUSTRALIA 235 (KR Stackpole 87 P Lever 4-49) and 328-3 (KR Stackpole 136 IM Chappell 104)

MATCH DRAWN

7th Test at Sydney

February 12, 13, 14, 16, 17
ENGLAND 184 (R Illingworth 42) and 302 (BW Luckhurst 59 JH Edrich 57 BL D'Oliveira 47)
AUSTRALIA 264 (GS Chappell 65 IR Redpath 59 KD Walters 42) and 160 (KR Stackpole 67)

ENGLAND WON BY 62 RUNS

1972

SERIES DRAWN 2-2

1st Test at Old Trafford

June 8, 9, 10, 12, 13
ENGLAND 249 (AW Greig 57 JH Edrich 49) and 234 (AW Greig 62 G Boycott 47 DK Lillee 6-66)
AUSTRALIA 142 (KR Stackpole 53 JA Snow 4-41 GG Arnold 4-62) and 252 (RW Marsh 91 KR Stackpole 67 JA Snow 4-87 AW Greig 4-53)

ENGLAND WON BY 89 RUNS

2nd Test at Lord's

June 22, 23, 24, 26
ENGLAND 272 (AW Greig 54 APE Knott 43 RAL Massie 8-84) and 116 (RAL Massie 8-53)
AUSTRALIA 308 (GS Chappell 131 IM Chappell 56 RW Marsh 50 JA Snow 5-57) and 81-2 (KR Stackpole 57*)

AUSTRALIA WON BY 8 WICKETS

3rd Test at Trent Bridge

July 13, 14, 15, 17, 18
AUSTRALIA 315 (KR Stackpole 114 DJ Colley 54 RW Marsh 41 JA Snow 5-92) and 324-4 dec (R Edwards 170* GS Chappell 72 IM Chappell 50)
ENGLAND 189 (DK Lillee 4-35 RAL Massie 4-43) and 290-4 (BW Luckhurst 96 BL D'Oliveira 50* PH Parfitt 46)

MATCH DRAWN

4th Test at Headingley

July 27, 2, 29
AUSTRALIA 146 (KR Stackpole 52 DL Underwood 4-37) and 136 (AP Sheahan 41* DL Underwood 6-45)
ENGLAND 263 (R Illingworth 57 JA Snow 48 JH Edrich 45 AA Mallett 5-114) and 21-1

ENGLAND WON BY 9 WICKETS

5th Test at The Oval

August 10, 11, 12, 14, 15, 16
ENGLAND 284 (APE Knott 92 PH Parfitt 51 JH Hampshire 42 DK Lillee 5-58) and 356 (B Wood 90 APE Knott 63 BL D'Oliveira 43 DK Lillee 5-123)
AUSTRALIA 399 (IM Chappell 118 GS Chappell 113 R Edwards 79 DL Underwood 4-90) and 242-5 (KR Stackpole 79 AP Sheahan 44* RW Marsh 43*)

AUSTRALIA WON BY 5 WICKETS

1974-75

AUSTRALIA WON SERIES 4-1

1st Test at Brisbane

November 29, 30 December 1, 3, 4
AUSTRALIA 309 (IM Chappell 90 GS Chappell 58 MHN Walker 41* RGD Willis 4-56) and 288-5 dec (GS Chappell 71 KD Walters 62* R Edwards 53 RW Marsh 46)
ENGLAND 265 (AW Greig 110 JH Edrich 48 MHN Walker 4-73) and 166 (JR Thomson 6-46)

AUSTRALIA WON BY 166 RUNS

2nd Test at Perth

December 13, 14, 15, 17
ENGLAND 208 (APE Knott 51 D Lloyd 49) and 293 (FJ Titmus 61 CM Old 43 MC Cowdrey 41 JR Thomson 5-93)
AUSTRALIA 481 (R Edwards 115 KD Walters 103 GS Chappell 62 IR Redpath 41 RW Marsh 41) and 23-1

AUSTRALIA WON BY 9 WICKETS

3rd Test at Melbourne

December 26, 27, 28, 30, 31
ENGLAND 242 (APE Knott 52 JH Edrich 49 JR Thomson 4-72) and 244 (DL Amiss 90 AW Greig 60 D Lloyd 44 JR Thomson 4-71 AA Mallett 4-60)
AUSTRALIA 241 (IR Redpath 55 RW Marsh 44 RGD Willis 5-61) and 238-6 (GS Chappell 61 RW Marsh 40 AW Greig 4-56)

MATCH DRAWN

4th Test at Sydney

January 4, 5, 6, 8, 9
AUSTRALIA 405 (GS Chappell 84 RB McCosker 80 IM Chappell 53 GG Arnold 5-86 AW Greig 4-104) and 289-4 dec (GS Chappell 144 IR Redpath 105)
ENGLAND 295 (APE Knott 82 JH Edrich 50 JR Thomson 4-74) and 228 (AW Greig 54 AA Mallett 4-21)

AUSTRALIA WON BY 171 RUNS

5th Test at Adelaide

January 25 (no play), 26, 27, 29, 30
AUSTRALIA 304 (TJ Jenner 74 KD Walters 55 MHN Walker 41 DL Underwood 7-113) and 272-5 dec (KD Walters 71* RW Marsh 55 IR Redpath 52 IM Chappell 41 DL Underwood 4-102)
ENGLAND 172 (MH Denness 51 KWR Fletcher 40 DK Lillee 4-49) and 241 (APE Knott 106* KWR Fletcher 63 DK Lillee 4-69)

AUSTRALIA WON BY 163 RUNS

6th Test at Melbourne

February 8, 9, 10, 12, 13
AUSTRALIA 152 (IM Chappell 65 P Lever 6-38) and 373 (GS Chappell 102 IR Redpath 83 RB McCosker 76 IM Chappell 50 AW Greig 4-88)
ENGLAND 529 (MH Denness 188 KWR Fletcher 146 AW Greig 89 JH Edrich 70 MHN Walker 8-143)

ENGLAND WON BY AN INNINGS AND 4 RUNS

1975

AUSTRALIA WON SERIES 1-0

1st Test at Edgbaston

July 10, 11, 12, 14
AUSTRALIA 359 (RW Marsh 61 RB McCosker 59 R Edwards 56 IM Chappell 52 JR Thomson 49)
ENGLAND 101 (DK Lillee 5-15 MHN Walker 5-48) and 173 (KWR Fletcher 51 JR Thomson 5-38)

AUSTRALIA WON BY AN INNINGS AND 85 RUNS

2nd Test at Lord's

July 31 August 1, 2, 4, 5
ENGLAND 315 (AW Greig 96 APE Knott 69 DS Steele 50 DK Lillee 4-84) and 436-7 dec (JH Edrich 175 B Wood 52 DS Steele 45 AW Greig 41)
AUSTRALIA 268 (R Edwards 99 DK Lillee 73* R Edwards 52*)

MATCH DRAWN

3rd Test at Headingley

August 14, 15, 16, 18, 19(no play)
ENGLAND 288 (DS Steele 73 JH Edrich 62 AW Greig 51 GJ Gilmour 6-85) and 291 (DS Steele 92 AW Greig 49)
AUSTRALIA 135 (PH Edmonds 5-28) and 220-3 (RB McCosker 95* IM Chappell 62)

MATCH DRAWN

4th Test at The Oval

August 28, 29, 30 September 1, 2, 3
AUSTRALIA 532-9 dec (IM Chappell 192 RB McCosker 127 KD Walters 65 R Edwards 44) and 40-2
ENGLAND 191 (JR Thomson 4-50 MHN Walker 4-63) and 538 (RA Woolmer 149 JH Edrich 96 GRJ Roope 77 DS Steele 66 APE Knott 64 DK Lillee 4-91 KD Walters 4-34)

MATCH DRAWN

THE MODERN ERA

1977

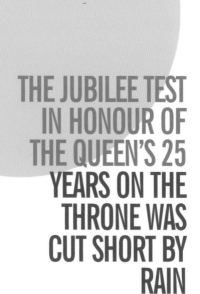

THE JUBILEE TEST IN HONOUR OF THE QUEEN'S 25 YEARS ON THE THRONE WAS CUT SHORT BY RAIN

This series was staged in the shadow of the most dramatic shake-up in cricket history. Kerry Packer's World Series Cricket was set to split the game wide open, involving most of the world's top players. Most of the Australian touring side were about to defect, while Tony Greig's close involvement cost him the England captaincy and he was replaced by Mike Brearley. Played amid such acrimony, the cricket was of secondary interest as England regained the Ashes by 3-0, Australia's biggest drubbing since the turn of the century.

The first Test at Lord's, known as the Jubilee Test in honour of the Queen's 25 years on the throne, was curtailed by rain, with honours even. England's first innings total of 216 owed everything to Bob Woolmer (79) and Derek Randall (53) while Jeff Thomson took four wickets, as he was to do in the second innings. The tourists took a first innings lead of 80 thanks to a fine knock of 66 by Greg Chappell and newcomer Craig Sergeant's 81, though Bob Willis returned figures of 7 for 87. Woolmer, with 120, and Brearley steadied England's second innings with 132 for the second wicket and Greig made a swashbuckling 91. Australia needed 226 to win in 165 minutes, and wickets fell during the charge until a Willis bouncer to Marsh prompted the umpires to 'offer the light' to the batsmen, who accepted.

SECOND TEST: ENGLAND LEAD

A fine all-round performance by England in the second Test at Old Trafford gave them the lead in the series. Australia's first innings of 297 included 88 by Doug Walters, his highest score in England, but it was Bob Woolmer, making a century in his third consecutive home Test against Australia, who led the way in England's total of 437. His stand of 160 with Greig beat the previous best for the fourth wicket at Old Trafford. However, the most delightful demonstration of batting came from Greg Chappell when Australia went in again, 140 behind. He made a brilliant 112, but the cause was lost as England made the 79 needed for victory for the loss of Brearley on 44.

England's first victory over Australia at Trent Bridge was memorable for the comeback after three years of self-imposed exile Geoff Boycott, the batting of Alan Knott and the Test debut of Ian Botham. The sensation of Australia's first innings was Botham, who took 5 for 74. Boycott, who ran out local hero Derek Randall, then dominated the scene with an innings of 107 before Knott's 135 took England to 364. Rick McCosker returned to form, adding 107 to his first-

GEOFF BOYCOTT ON HIS WAY TO HIS 100TH FIRST CLASS CENTURY, FOURTH TEST, HEADINGLEY

innings 51, but Australia's second knock of 309 left England needing just 189: 81 from Brearley and an unbeaten 80 by Boycott ensured victory. The Yorkshireman became the first England player to bat each day of a five-day Test.

England demolished Australia in the fourth Test at Headingley to go 3-0 up and so recover the Ashes. The ground provided a dramatic background to Geoff Boycott's 100th hundred in first-class cricket. Long and loud was the acclamation from his Yorkshire crowd when he straight-drove Chappell to bring up his century. His innings of 191 was the highest of his seven Ashes hundreds as England totalled 436. In less than 32 overs, the tourists were bowled out for 103 with Botham taking 5 for 21 and Mike Hendrick 4 for 41. Following-on, Australia made 248 thanks in the main to 63 by Rodney Marsh who was last man out, caught at cover by Randall, who did a cartwheel to celebrate the recapture of the Ashes.

At last Greg Chappell's Australian side lived up to promise in the final Test at The Oval. With Mick Malone in his first Test taking 5 for 63, England were bowled out for 214. The debutant then made 46 in a ninth wicket stand of 100 with Max Walker, who finished on 78 not out. Earlier in their innings, David Hookes showed some fine-off-side strokes in an innings of 85. Bob Willis's 27 wickets in the series was a record for a pace bowler against Australia in England.

1978-79

Both sides were without the players who had joined Kerry Packer's World Series Cricket. Without Greg Chappell and the established stars, Australia were the more handicapped and they were ill-prepared for an Ashes battle against an England side headed by Mike Brearley. As a batsman, the Middlesex opener was a flop, failing to reach double figures in

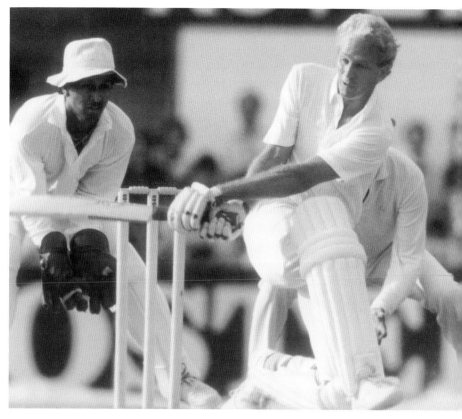

six of his 10 innings, but as a skipper he was a huge success, leading England to a 5-1 win in the six Ashes Tests pitted against the WSC razzmatazz.

In the first Test at Brisbane, Yallop won the toss and unwisely elected to bat. Australia were 26 for 6 before Maclean and Hogg dragged the score into three figures – the England seam bowlers having done an admirable job. England made 286 with Randall top-scoring with 75, while Rodney Hogg, who was making his Test debut, took 6 for 74. Australia's other debutant was John Maclean, who took five catches behind the wicket to equal the record for most in an innings in Ashes matches. In the first innings, Bob Taylor, himself making his debut in an Ashes Test, had also equalled the record. Yallop (102) and Kim Hughes (129) added 170 for the fourth wicket, over half of Australia's total of 339. Yallop's century marked a unique feat in that it was by a player not only playing in his first Ashes Test but also captaining his side. England ▶

DAVID GOWER, MUCH-ADMIRED LEFT-HAND BATSMAN. HIS ENGLAND CAPTAINCY WAS MORE CONTROVERSIAL, HOWEVER

FOR THE 1978-79 SERIES, BOTH SIDES WERE WITHOUT THE PLAYERS WHO HAD JOINED KERRY PACKER'S WORLD SERIES CRICKET

needed 170 to win and made them for the loss of three wickets, Randall being unbeaten on 74.

At Perth, Yallop put England in and seemed justified with the score 41 for 3 but then a rescue operation was mounted by Boycott, who scored 77 from 337 balls without a boundary and Gower, who at 21 became the youngest England century-maker against Australia since Compton in 1938. Rodney Hogg took 5 for 65 but England scored 309. Australia's batting was abysmal and only Toohey, with an unbeaten 81, resisted the fire of Willis, who took 5 for 44 as Australia totalled 190. After an opening stand of 58, England made 208 in their second innings with Hogg producing another five-wicket return for the third time in three completed innings. Australia were left to make 328 for victory on the final day but only Graeme Wood offered any resistance and they were all out for 161.

Australia won the toss and batted first on a wicket that rapidly deteriorated. Graeme Wood reached a painstaking hundred after batting throughout the whole of the first day.

AUSTRALIAN QUICK BOWLER RODNEY HOGG CONTEMPLATES THE WICKET, JUNE 1980

There was an enterprising knock from Yallop (41) and a gritty maiden Test innings of 29 by Allan Border as Australia made 258. England were destroyed by Hogg's opening burst when he removed Boycott and Brearley for a single apiece and they made only 143. During the course of Australia's second innings, wickets fell steadily to the accuracy and movement of Botham and off-spinners Miller and Emburey, and England were left 283 to win. The loss of two early wickets dispelled any reasonable expectation and the bowlers, spearheaded again by Hogg, worked their way through the order to give the home side victory by 103 runs.

ENGLAND RETAIN THE ASHES

A great tactical victory at Sydney in the face of illness, terrific heat and a large first-innings deficit ensured England's retention of the Ashes and earned Mike Brearley the honour of being the first captain to win successive series against Australia at home and away since Hutton in 1953 and 1954-55. England batted first and were quickly out for 152, with Alan Hurst taking 5 for 28. Darling, backed by Hughes, set up a reasonable score for Australia as the wicket became a little more subdued. The England bowlers didn't give runs away but Australia's lead was extended at a vital time by Border. When England went in a second time, 142 behind the home side and Boycott was dismissed first ball, it seemed Australia would level the series. But Randall came in and made the slowest century – 353 balls – in Ashes history. He went on to score 150 in stifling heat, Brearley 53 and England 346, setting Australia 205 to win. Fine bowling by Emburey and Miller saw England dismiss the hosts for just 111 and so retain the Ashes.

As in the previous Test, Australia

threw away a position of distinct advantage. Yallop put England in and his fast bowlers Hogg and Hurst reduced the tourists to 27 for 5 before Botham's swashbuckling 74 effected a recovery. Even so, they were all out for 169 and Hogg, who had 4 for 26, finished the innings with 37 wickets in the series, thus passing Thomson's 33 as a fast-bowling series record and Mailey's 36 for any Australian bowler in an Ashes series. Australia made more even progress to 164. During the course of that innings, Darling was carried from the field on a stretcher. He had been struck under the heart by a ball from Willis and received life-saving treatment by England's John Emburey and umpire Max O'Connell. The match turned when England, 132 for 6 in their second innings, managed to reach 360 with Bob Taylor making 97 and his Derbyshire team-mate Geoff Miller 64. Faced with a victory target of 366, Australia were bowled out for 160 with only Hughes and Yallop putting up any resistance.

FINAL TEST: SYDNEY

In the final Test at Sydney, Graham Yallop decided to bat and was forced to hold Australia together as wickets tumbled around him. Coming in at 19 for 2, Yallop made 100 out of 150 in four hours and was eventually dismissed for 121 as Australia totalled 198. England batted consistently throughout their first innings total of 308 with Gooch making 74 and Gower 65. In their second innings, Australia were skittled out for 143 with Geoff Miller taking 5 for 44, but it could have been much worse if Bruce Yardley, coming in at 48 for 5, hadn't scored 61 not out to save the innings defeat. England needed 34 and won by nine wickets. Hogg's aggregate of wickets for the series was 41, an Australian Ashes record.

1979-80

With peace made between the Packer organisation and established cricket, England and West Indies both went to Australia and each played a three-match Test series against the home country. The Australians, with Greg Chappell regaining the captaincy, picked their Packer stars, but England took only Underwood of the English World Series party. England insisted beforehand that the Ashes would not be at stake in the short series, which Australia dominated, winning 3-0.

THE 'ALUMINIUM BAT' AFFAIR

In the course of Australia's first innings during the first Test at Perth, Dennis Lillee strode out to the crease with an aluminium bat, and was ordered to change it for a more traditional appliance. England put Australia in and dismissed them for 244 with Kim Hughes top-scoring with 99 and Botham taking 6 for 78. England made a disastrous start to their innings with openers Boycott and Randall both dismissed by Lillee for a duck. England failed by 16 runs to reach the home side's total with Brearley making 64. In Australia's second innings, Border made 115 and in doing so, reached 1,000 runs just under 12 months after his debut, the quickest Australian to do so in the 103 years of Test cricket to that date. Again Botham was England's best bowler with 5 for 98, but with the tourists needing 354 to win, they were never seriously in with a chance. In England's total of 215, Geoff Boycott finished unbeaten on 99, becoming the first England batsman to carry his bat through a completed innings without reaching a century. He was also the first player to finish 99 not out in a Test.

ENGLAND'S BOB TAYLOR KEEPS WICKET TO AUSTRALIAN CAPTAIN ALAN BORDER

The Sydney pitch for the second Test was the subject of controversy. Soaked by rain for a good number of days beforehand, it was underprepared and, according to Greg Chappell before the match, utterly unfit for Test cricket. However, he won the toss and asked England to bat and in effect, the toss decided the match. At the close of a shortened first day, England were 90 for 7 and all out for 123 early the next day. Australia didn't fare much better, making 145 with Ian Chappell, on his return to Test cricket after his retirement in 1975-76 and subsequent Packer adventures, being top-scorer with 42. England, 38 for 3 overnight, improved when night-watchman Derek Underwood made 43 and Gower, batting at No.7, then scored 98 not out. But he ran out of partners and England's 237 left Australia only 216 to make. The wicket had by now improved and with Greg Chappell emulating Gower in making 98 not out, the home side won comfortably by six wickets.

In the final Test at Melbourne, England made 306 and this total owed much to Brearley, who batted over four hours for 60 not out and Graham Gooch, who on 99 in the final over before tea, missed his maiden Test century by inches when Hughes hit the bowler's stumps from mid-on as the batsmen tried to scramble a single. In reply, all the Australian batsmen except Hughes scored well, with Greg Chappell reaching 114 in a total of 477. Despite an unbeaten 119 by Botham, Dennis Lillee took 5 for 78 to go with his first innings 6 for 60 and Australia needed a mere 103 to win and did so by eight wickets.

1980 CENTENARY TEST

After the huge success of the 1977 Centenary Test in Melbourne, celebrating 100 years of Test cricket, another was held at Lord's in 1980, this time marking the centenary of the first Test match played in England. The Ashes were not at stake, and with rain interruptions, the match failed to live up to the drama of the match three years earlier. In fact, it will always be remembered not for its cricket but for the behaviour of some MCC members when the start of play was delayed on Saturday. The England captain Ian Botham was struck and the umpires were jostled as they returned to the pavilion from inspecting the wicket.

Greg Chappell won the toss and decided to bat; by close of the first day, Australia were 227 for 2. On Friday, this was increased to 278 for 4 in the hour and fifteen minutes that was played, and Chappell declared at 385 for 5 at tea on Saturday. Graeme Wood scored 112 on the first two days while Kim Hughes batted on all three to reach 117.

England were all out for 205 on the Monday with Boycott making 62 and Gower 45, and Chappell declared at 189 for 4 on Tuesday, setting England to score 370 runs at just over a run a minute. The chase was soon given up but Boycott enjoyed himself, batting out time for 128 not out and passing 7000 Test runs along the way. Proceedings ended with England on 244 for 3.

1980 CENTENARY TEST at Lord's

August 28, 29, 30 September 1, 2
AUSTRALIA 385-5 dec (KJ Hughes 117, GM Wood 112, AR Border 56* GS Chappell 47) and 189-4 dec (KJ Hughes 84 GS Chappell 59)
ENGLAND 205 (G Boycott 62 DI Gower 45 LS Pascoe 5-59 DK Lillee 4-43) and 244-3 dec (G Boycott 128* MW Gatting 51*)
Captains GS Chappell (A) IT Botham (E)

MATCH DRAWN

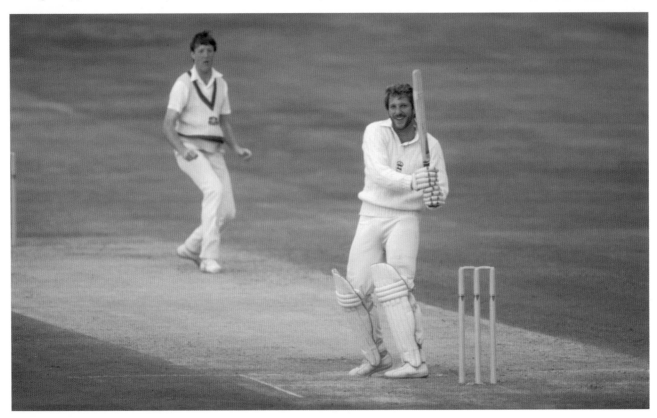

IAN BOTHAM TAKES ANOTHER BOUNDARY OF GEOFF LAWSON, HEADINGLEY, 3RD TEST 1981

1981

One of the most memorable series in cricket history began with Ian Botham struggling for form as England captain. After two Tests, Australia led 1-0 and seemed on course to regain the Ashes. But when Mike Brearley took over for the third Test, Botham cut loose, leading England to remarkable fightback victories at Headingley and Edgbaston. With a third win at Old Trafford, England clinched the series 3-1.

FIRST STRIKE TO AUSTRALIA

After more than a century of cricket in England, the first Test at Trent Bridge was the first time a Test was played without a scheduled rest day – and with play on a Sunday. With Greg Chappell not touring, Kim Hughes led the Australians and on a wicket and in conditions which helped seam and swing bowling, he won the toss and put England in. Only Gatting made more than 50 and it took 34 from Dilley batting at No. 9 to get England up to 185 all out. However, before the first day was over, Australia had sunk to 33 for 4. The next day was interrupted by rain and bad light and was distinguished by the home side dropping several catches.

Nevertheless, Australia were finally all out on Saturday for 179 with Border top-scoring with 63. By the time play ended in mid-afternoon, England had been reduced to 94 for 6. Marsh took his 100th Ashes wicket when he held Woolmer for his second duck of the match. England were eventually dismissed for 125 with Terry Alderman taking 5 for 42 – the West Australian protégé went on to take a record 42 wickets for the series. Australia had a few alarms reaching 132 for 6 but went 1-0 up in the series.

The second Test at Lord's always looked a draw. Hughes put England in again but after a bright start by Gooch, the innings proceeded slowly. With an interruption for bad light, the home side were 191 for 4 at the end of the first day and there was more time lost on the second, when England were dismissed for 311, with Peter Willey leading the way with 82. For Australia, Geoff Lawson took 7 for 81, his best figures against England. There were scenes of crowd dissatisfaction for the second year running at Lord's when, after Australia's innings had been suspended for bad light and the players had been 'dismissed' for the day, the sun shone brightly. Next day, after Wood made 44 out of 62 in an hour, Australia suddenly slumped to 81 for 4 but Hughes, Border, Marsh, Bright and Lillee made good contributions as Australia reached 345. In that total, extras contributed a record 55, including 32 no-balls – 28 from Willis. It was now well into the fourth day and England's hopes of setting a target were not helped by Boycott, in his 100th Test, taking 279 minutes for 60. Botham, the England captain, was out first ball on the last morning attempting a sweep, thereby bagging a pair. He declared at 265 for 8, leaving Australia just under three hours to make 232. But three wickets went down for 17 runs and Australia went on the defensive, ending on 90 for 4. Shortly after the game had finished, it was announced that Botham had resigned the captaincy and Mike Brearley was appointed to resume the duties for the remainder of the series.

THE MOST EXCITING TEST

The third Test at Headingley was the most exciting of modern times and featured the biggest reversal of fortune anyone can remember. As if to make a point, the main hero was Ian Botham. Australia won the toss, batted, and made 401 for 9 declared, using up almost all of the first two rain-interrupted days. John Dyson made his first Test century, 102, skipper Hughes 89, while ex-captain Botham took 6 for 98. On the ▶

GREAT PLAYERS

Ian Botham
(England) 1976-92

BATTING
Test Average 33.55
Test Best 208 v. India – Oval 1982
Ashes Average 29.35
Ashes Best 149, Headingley 1981
BOWLING
Test Average 28.40
Test Best 8-34 v. Pakistan, Lord's 1978
Ashes Average 27.66
Ashes Best 6-78, W.A.C.A, 1979

Ian Botham is one of the greatest cricketers the world has seen. It is a measure of his stature that although he became the most prolific wicket-taker in history, he is likely to be remembered for his batting. Botham was a man who could turn Test matches on his own, the man whose entry to bat was enough to excite crowds to expectancy, the most charismatic cricketer of all. In the 1981 Headingley Test, Botham's all-round performance was one of the greatest ever seen. With the ball he took 6 for 95 and with the bat he scored 50 and the match-winning 149 not out. The series continued with Botham in similar form: a match-winning 5 for 11 at Edgbaston and a superb 118 at Old Trafford. Though a knee injury later ended a run of 65 consecutive Tests, he returned for the 1984 series against the West Indies, becoming the first player to complete the double of 3,000 Test runs and 300 Test wickets. In 1986 he achieved his greatest statistical feat in becoming the leading wicket-taker in Test cricket when he passed Dennis Lillee's total of 355.

Saturday, England were shot out by Lillee, Alderman and Lawson for 174. Botham was top-scorer with 50 – extras came next with 34. The home side were forced to follow-on and Gooch was out for the second time on the same day for a total of two runs. England's situation was so bleak that, on the morning of the fourth day, with them 6 for 1 in their second innings – still 221 runs in arrears – the bookmakers offered odds of 500-1 against an England win. Lillee and Marsh both placed bets in the unlikely event of their opponents turning things around. England slid to 41 for 4 before Boycott and Willey took the score to 105 for 5. Botham came in to join Boycott but the Yorkshire opener soon fell, and was quickly followed by Taylor to leave England 135 for 7, still 92 runs short of avoiding an innings defeat. Dilley joined Botham and the pair added 117 in 18 overs. When Dilley was out for 56, Old continued in the same vein of sensible aggression and with Botham blasting 149 not out, England made 356. The last session of the fourth day had seen 175 runs scored – it was one of the most thrilling sessions in Test cricket, as unexpected as it was exciting. Australia needed 130 to win. Wood hit Botham's first two deliveries to the boundary but at 13 he was caught behind off the Somerset all-rounder. Bob Willis was then switched to the Kirkstall Lane end and with hair streaming and knees pumping he dismissed Chappell, Hughes and Yallop within the space of a few minutes just before lunch. After lunch, the rout continued as Old bowled Border and Dilley held a Marsh hook on the boundary – 74 for 7. Willis then beat Lawson for speed – 75 for 8 and then Lillee and Bright took 35 off four overs before Lillee popped a ball from Willis towards mid-on and Gatting dived for-

BOB WILLIS LAUNCHES ANOTHER BOUNCER AT ALLAN BORDER, ON HIS WAY TO 8 FOR 43, THIRD TEST

ward to take the catch – 110 for 9. Old twice missed Alderman at third slip off Botham before a Willis yorker accounted for Bright. He had taken a career best 8 for 43 and England had won the most remarkable game of cricket by 18 runs.

FOURTH TEST: EDGBASTON

The fourth Test at Edgbaston began in Australia's favour after England batted first and were dismissed in five hours for 189. Alderman took 5 for 42, including the wicket of the hero of the previous Test, Botham, for 26. Chris Old had two Australians out for 14 but night-watchman Bright, along with Hughes, Yallop and Kent managed to get the tourists' score to 258, a lead of 69. Brearley was out overnight and on the Saturday, England batted grimly to try and repair the damage. At 167 for 8, they were only 98 ahead, but a stand of 50 between Emburey and Old meant England totalled 219. Set 151 to win, Australia soon lost Wood and on Sunday (Edgbaston's first Test

Sunday), 142 were needed with nine wickets left. After slipping to 29 for 3, Border and Yallop put bat to ball but both were out to Emburey. At 105 for 5, Australia needed 46 but then Brearley called on Botham. The last five wickets fell for just seven runs, all to Botham, and Australia were all out for 121. England won by 29 runs and Botham, who had taken 5 for 11, was, for the second time running, Man of the Match.

The Old Trafford Test was a match of contrasts – high and low innings, fast and slow scoring. England batted first and were bowled out for 231, with 94 of the runs coming from the last two wickets, including an unbeaten 52 from debutant Paul Allott. Kent's Chris Tavare on his Ashes debut batted 287 minutes for 69 before he was out to Mike Whitney, the young New South Wales bowler called-up from league cricket with Fleetwood to bolster Australia's attack for the last two Tests. Australia were then dismissed for 130 with Willis picking up his 100th wicket in

Ashes cricket and Knott becoming the first England wicket-keeper to make 100 dismissals. In the pre-lunch session on the Saturday, England scored just 29 runs in 28 overs but as they also lost three wickets, this period of consolidation appeared mistaken, especially as they then slid to 104 for 5. However, Botham joined Tavare and he passed 100 in 86 balls with a six. When he was out he had scored 118 from the 149 runs added by the pair in 123 minutes, and had hit an Ashes record 6 sixes as well as 13 fours. Tavare scored the slowest 50 in an English first-class match (75 overs, 306 minutes). With Knott and Emburey playing well down the order, England reached 404. Australia needed 506 to win – Yallop played a beautiful and gallant innings of 114 and Border, with a broken finger, a brave and dogged one of 123 not out. Australia were all out for 402 with Botham, for the third successive time since giving up the captaincy, the Man of the Match.

FINAL TEST: THE OVAL

The final Test at The Oval could not live up to the previous three. Australia were put in by Brearley and responded by making 352 with Border top-scoring with an unbeaten 106. England replied with 314, Geoff Boycott making 137. Dennis Lillee's 7 for 89 was his best Test bowling to date. On the Monday, England had a great chance of victory, with Australia reduced to 110 for 4 and Dirk Wellham offering an easy chance to Willis. It was dropped however, and Wellham, who became the only player to captain three Sheffield Shield sides, went on to score 104 – the first Australian since Harry Graham in 1893 to make a hundred on Test debut in England. Hughes declared at 344 for 9, leaving England to make 383 on the last day. Boycott was out to Lillee without a run on the board but with Knott making 70 not out, they survived comfortably in the end to finish on 261 for 7. ▶

THE RESULTS

ENGLAND v AUSTRALIA
Played at Headingley July, 16-21 1981

AUSTRALIA

J Dyson	b Dilley	102	c Taylor b Willis	34
GM Wood	lbw b Botham	34	c Taylor b Botham	10
TM Chappell	c Taylor b Willey	27	c Taylor b Willis	8
KJ Hughes	c and b Botham	89	c Botham b Willis	0
RJ Bright	b Dilley	7	b Willis	19
GN Yallop	c Taylor b Botham	58	c Gatting b Willis	0
AR Border	lbw b Botham	8	b Old	0
RW Marsh	b Botham	28	c Dilley b Willis	4
GF Lawson	c Taylor b Botham	13	c Taylor b Willis	1
DK Lillee	not out	3	c Gatting b Willis	17
TM Alderman	did not bat		not out	0
Extras		32		18
Total		**401-9 dec**		**111**

Fall of wickets 1-55 2-149 3-196 4-220 5-332 6-354 7-357 8-396 9-401
Second Innings 1-13 2-56 3-58 4-58 5-65 6-68 7-74 8-75 9-110 10-111

England Bowling

	O	M	R	W	O	M	R	W
RGD Willis	30	8	72	0	15.1	3	43	8
CM Old	43 1	4	91	0	9	1	21	1
GR Dilley	27	4	78	2	2	0	11	0
IT Botham	38.2	11	95	6	7	3	14	1
P Willey	13	2	31	1	3	1	4	0
G Boycott	3	2	2	0	-	-	-	-

ENGLAND

GA Gooch	lbw b Alderman	2	c Alderman b Lillee	0
G Boycott	b Lawson	12	lbw b Alderman	46
JM Brearley	c Marsh b Alderman	10	c Alderman b Lillee	14
DI Gower	c Marsh b Lawson	24	c Border b Alderman	9
MW Gatting	lbw b Lillee	15	lbw b Alderman	1
P Willey	b Lawson	8	c Dyson b Lillee	33
IT Botham	c Marsh b Lillee	50	not out	149
RW Taylor	c Marsh b Lillee	5	c Bright b Alderman	1
GR Dilley	c and b Lillee	13	b Alderman	56
CM Old	c Border b Alderman	0	b Lawson	29
RGD Willis	not out	1	c Border b Alderman	2
Extras		34		16
Total		**174**		**356**

Fall of wickets 1-12 2-40 3-42 4-84 5-87 6-112 7-148 8-166 9-167 10-174
Second Innings 1-0 2-18 3-37 4-41 5-105 6-133 7-135 8-252 9-319 10-356

Australia Bowling

	O	M	R	W	O	M	R	W
DK Lillee	18.5	7	49	4	25	6	94	3
TM Alderman	19	4	59	3	35.3	6	135	6
GF Lawson	13	3	32	3	23	4	96	1
RJ Bright	-	-	-	-	4	0	15	0

ENGLAND WON BY 18 RUNS

1982-83

With Mike Brearley's reign as captain over, England, without South African 'rebels' Gooch, Boycott, Emburey, Knott and Underwood, headed to Australia for a five-match Test series under Bob Willis. The Australians still had their ageing stars Dennis Lillee and Rodney Marsh, while Greg Chappell was back as captain in place of Kim Hughes. Wins in Brisbane and Adelaide followed by a narrow defeat in Melbourne, enabled Australia to regain the Ashes.

The series began at Perth on a batsman's wicket, on which England, put in, made 411. There were attractive knocks from Gower and Randall and while Chris Tavare top-scored with 89, it took him 466 minutes including a period of an hour-and-a-half when he froze on 66.

When England reached 400 there was a pitch invasion by drunken England supporters, which developed into a skirmish and Alderman, who tried to do some personal policing, dislocated a shoulder and stretched a nerve. He took no further part in the series. Australia moved faster than England in overhauling their total and with Greg Chappell making 117, and Hughes, Hookes, Dyson and Lawson all making half-centuries, they were able to declare at 424 for 9. With England in their second innings at one stage 80 for 4, there was a possibility of a result but Randall (115) and Lamb (56) helped the tourists recover to 358 and the match ended in a tame draw with Australia on 73 for 2.

With Lillee having bone flakes removed from his knee, Jeff Thomson and Carl Rackemann joined the Australian attack for the second Test at

WHEN ENGLAND REACHED 400 AT PERTH, THERE WAS A PITCH INVASION BY DRUNKEN ENGLAND SUPPORTERS

ENGLAND OPENER CHRIS TAVARE PLAYS THE STRAIGHT BAT , FIFTH TEST 1981

Brisbane. England were again put in and though Lamb hit a brave 72, Geoff Lawson with 6 for 47 wrecked the tourists' innings as they were bowled out for 219. South African-born Kepler Wessels, making his debut for Australia, then scored 162, this after he had been dropped on 15. On a pitch that seemed to be getting easier, Chappell and Yardley each made 53 and Australia had a lead of 122 on first innings. Though England debutant Graeme Fowler often played and missed, he fought gamely for over six hours to score 83 and with Miller making 60, England totalled 309 in their second knock. Rodney Marsh took an Ashes record six catches, giving him nine for the match; his total of 28 for the series was a world record. Geoff Lawson took 5 for 87 and Jeff Thomson 5 for 73, the former becoming the first to take 11 wickets in a Brisbane Ashes Test. With Wessels dropped before he had scored, Dyson retired hurt and with three men out for 93, there was just a hint of a collapse but Hughes and Hookes saw Australia home by seven wickets.

THIRD TEST: ADELAIDE

Bob Willis failed to respect history when he won the toss in the third Test at the Adelaide Oval. Peter May in 1958-59 and Mike Denness in 1974-75 had won the toss on this ground and sent Australia in to bat. Willis did the same and again it backfired as Australia totalled 438. Greg Chappell made 115, his first century at Adelaide and the last of his nine against England, while Kim Hughes scored 88. Only Lamb, Gower and Botham batted well for England and the tourists last seven wickets fell for 35 runs; England all out for 216 followed on. This time, Gower made 114 and Botham 58 but the lower order was again disappointing, the last seven wickets doing little better by adding 68. Australia made the 83 needed for the loss of two wickets. ▶

THE RESULTS

AUSTRALIA v ENGLAND
Played at Melbourne December 26-30 1982

ENGLAND

G Cook	c Chappell b Thomson	10	c Yardley b Thomson	26	
G Fowler	c Chappell b Hogg	4	b Hogg	65	
CJ Tavare	c Yardley b Thomson	89	b Hogg	0	
DI Gower	c Marsh b Hogg	18	c Marsh b Lawson	3	
AJ Lamb	c Dyson b Yardley	83	c Marsh b Hogg	26	
IT Botham	c Wessels b Yardley	27	c Chappell b Thomson	46	
G Miller	c Border b Yardley	10	lbw b Lawson	14	
DR Pringle	c Wessels b Hogg	9	c Marsh b Lawson	42	
RW Taylor	c Marsh b Yardley	1	lbw b Thomson	37	
RGD Willis	not out	6	not out	8	
NG Cowans	c Lawson b Hogg	3	b Lawson	10	
Extras		24		17	
Total		**284**		**294**	

Fall of wickets 1-11 2-25 3-56 4-217 5-227 6-259 7-262 8-268 9-278 10-284
Second Innings 1-40 2-41 3-45 4-128 5-129 6-160 7-201 8-262 9-282 10-294

Australia Bowling

	O	M	R	W	O	M	R	W
GF Lawson	17	6	48	0	21.4	6	66	4
RM Hogg	23.3	6	69	4	22	5	64	3
B Yardley	27	9	89	4	15	2	67	0
JR Thomson	13	2	49	2	21	3	74	3
GS Chappell	1	0	5	0	1	0	6	0

AUSTRALIA

KC Wessels	b Willis	47	b Cowans	14	
J Dyson	lbw b Cowans	21	c Tavare b Botham	31	
GS Chappell	c Lamb b Cowans	0	c sub b Cowans	2	
KJ Hughes	b Willis	66	c Taylor b Miller	48	
AR Border	b Botham	2	not out	62	
DW Hookes	c Taylor b Pringle	53	c Willis b Cowans	68	
RW Marsh	b Willis	53	lbw b Cowans	13	
B Yardley	b Miller	9	b Cowans	0	
GF Lawson	c Fowler b Miller	0	c Cowans b Pringle	7	
RM Hogg	not out	8	lbw b Cowans	4	
JR Thomson	b Miller	1	c Miller b Botham	21	
Extras		27		18	
Total		**287**		**288**	

Fall of wickets 1-55 2-55 3-83 4-89 5-180 6-261 7-276 8-276 9-278 10-287
Second Innings 1-37 2-39 3-71 4-171 5-173 6-190 7-190 8-202 9-218 10-288

England Bowling

	O	M	R	W	O	M	R	W
RGD Willis	15	2	38	3	17	0	57	0
IT Botham	18	3	69	1	25.1	4	80	2
NG Cowans	16	0	69	2	26	6	77	6
DR Pringle	15	2	40	1	12	4	26	1
G Miller	15	5	44	3	16	6	30	1

ENGLAND WON BY 3 RUNS

Rod Marsh
(Australia) 1982-83

Test Average *26.52*
Test Best *132 v. New Zealand, Adelaide Oval 1974*
Ashes Average *27.22*
Ashes Best *110, Melbourne 1977*

Rodney Marsh did not become the most successful wicket-keeper in Test cricket by supreme natural talent. Marsh first earned preference because of his batting but he fumbled so often in his early Tests that he earned the nickname 'Old Irongloves'. By the end of his career his wicket-keeping was so outstanding that his batting was a bonus. Against Pakistan in 1972-73 Marsh became the first Australian wicket-keeper to score a century. The 1976-77 Centenary Test saw Marsh pass Wally Grout's Australian record of 187 Test victims and he made 110 not out in the second innings – the first Australian wicket-keeper to score a century in the Ashes series. Marsh began passing some of last milestones during the tour of 1981. At Trent Bridge he became the first keeper to take 100 wickets in the Ashes series, whilst in the last match he passed 3000 Test runs. In 1982-83, Marsh who was awarded the MBE for his services to cricket, took 28 catches, another world record.

The Boxing Day Test in Melbourne provided one of cricket's great finishes. Put in again, England made 284, with Tavare batting at No.3, scoring 89 in very untypical manner (5 fours in 8 balls off Yardley) and Botham 83. At one time, England were 217 for 3 but again the last seven wickets disappointed, adding just 67 runs, giving them a total which was fewer than hoped. Australia passed it only by three, however, with Hughes making 66 and Hookes and Marsh 53 each. Fowler top-scored in England's second innings, when from 129 for 5 they recovered to reach 294, leaving Australia 292 to win. The home side were struggling at 71 for 3 when Hughes (48) and Hookes (68) added exactly 100, putting Australia on top. Six wickets then fell for 47 runs, leaving Border and Thomson to make 74 for the last wicket. Half of these were made by the close of play on the fourth day and 18,000 entered the ground free on the last day to see if they could make the other 37. They almost did. When three runs short of the target, Thomson nicked Botham to Tavare at second slip. Tavare could only knock the ball up over his head but Miller at first slip came round the back of him to hold the ball just above the ground. The decisive ball brought Botham his 100 wickets against Australia and gave him the fastest 1,000 turns/100 wickets double (22 Tests).

Australia won the toss for the final Test at Sydney and for the first time, the winning captain elected to bat. Throughout the series, television replays had highlighted some bad umpiring decisions. Now on the sixth ball of the match, came the worst. Dyson, palpably run out by almost a yard, was allowed to stay and he went on to make 79. Border made 89 and Australia totalled 314.

England replied with 237 with Gower and Randall both scoring 70. In Australia's second innings, Hughes made 137, Border 83 and Wessels 53 as the home side made 382. England lost Cook overnight and began the last day needing a virtually impossible 452 to win. Nottinghamshire off-spinner Eddie Hemmings, who had been sent in as night-watchman, made 95 and the day ended with England on 315 for 7. An anonymous donor presented the Australians with a silver urn containing a burnt bail – the 'new Ashes' or as the newspapers put it, 'Urnie'.

1985

With the ghosts of their 1981 tour still lingering, Australia, under the captaincy of Allan Border, returned to England for this six-Test series. Ultimately, Border was to become the first Australian captain since Woodfull in 1934 to regain the Ashes in England, but not on this occasion. With the scores standing at 1-1 with two Tests to play, England won them both by an innings and so, under David Gower, regained the Ashes lost two years earlier.

ROBINSON'S CENTURY

In the first Test at Headingley, Australia batted first, and overcoming the early life in the wicket reached 201 for 2, but they collapsed later and were all out for 331 with Andrew Hilditch making 119. Graham Gooch, along with Willey and Emburey, had returned to the England side after the lifting of the three-year ban for touring South Africa, but he was soon out. Tim Robinson, playing his first Test, became the 15th England batsman to score a century (175) in his first Ashes appearance and was well supported by Botham (60) Downton (54)

David Gower
(England) 1978-92

Test Average *44.25*
Test Best *215 v. Australia – Edgbaston 1985*
Ashes Average *44.78*
Ashes Best *(as above)*

David Gower has been described as the most accomplished English batsman of his generation and his languid, graceful style has been likened to that of Frank Woolley, another great left-hander born in Kent. In the World Series Cup in Australia in 1982-83, a bonanza of one-day matches which followed the Test series, he made three centuries against New Zealand. Having made over 1000 runs in five Tests and 10 WSC matches, he was named Benson and Hedges International Cricketer of the Year. In 1985, Gower regained the Ashes from an Australian side weakened by the defection to a rebel tour of South Africa. In the third Test at Trent Bridge he made his first century as England skipper, whilst at Edgbaston he hit his highest-ever Test score of 215 and in the final Test, 157. He scored 732 runs in the series at 81.33. Having been deprived of the captaincy he joined Gooch's team to tour Australia in 1990-91 and though he made two centuries, he was guilty of a breach of discipline with an ill-judged flying escapade !

ENGLAND'S TIM ROBINSON ON HIS WAY TO A TEST CENTURY IN HIS DEBUT MATCH, HEADINGLEY

and Gatting (53) in a total of 533, England's highest at the Yorkshire ground. With intermittent rain and bad light, the match became a race against time. Australia's second innings eventually closed at 324 with Wayne Phillips making 91, Hilditch 80 and Wessels 64, leaving England 200 minutes to score 123, a target they achieved but not without losing five wickets. There was a minor controversy on the last ball as the crowd invaded the pitch and came extremely close to Lawson, who was attempting a difficult catch.

Australia put England in at Lord's and early on the second day had them all out for 290 with David Gower top-scoring with 86. Australia's best bowler was Craig McDermott who took 6 for 70. After losing a couple of early wickets, Australia batted well and Border and Ritchie added 216 for the fifth wicket, the Australian captain going on to make

196 in a total of 425. This meant a lead of 135 runs for the tourists who had England 98 for 6 in their second innings before a stand of 131 between Gatting (75 not out) and Botham (85) promised recovery. Botham's dismissal by Bob Holland, who took 5 for 68, virtually meant the end. All out for 261, England set Australia 127 to win. At 65 for 5, memories of the 1981 Headingley Test were in the minds of the English supporters, but Australia won by four wickets.

THE DAVID GOWER SHOW

England batted first on a flat wicket in the third Test at Trent Bridge, scoring 456, an insurance against defeat. It was nevertheless slightly disappointing, as at one stage they were 358 for 2. Gatting was then run out by a Gower drive which Holland touched and the momentum was lost. Gower, leading from the front, scored an elegant 166, Gatting 74 and ▶

Gooch 70 while Geoff Lawson rediscovered his earlier form to take 5 for 103. When Australia batted, Graeme Wood asserted himself, making an uncharacteristically steady 172. Later Ritchie, batting at No.7, made a more aggressive 146, adding 161 with Wood for the sixth wicket. Australia reached 569 but the pitch was too good and the weather breaks too frequent for a result. There was just time for the local hero, Tim Robinson, to make an unbeaten 77 in England's total of 196 for 2.

RAIN AT OLD TRAFFORD

Despite the frequent interruptions for rain in the fourth Test at Old Trafford, England were pressing for a result until the last day. Australia were put in and with only David Boon, who top-scored with 61, showing any form, they were bowled out for 257. England passed this total for the loss of just three wickets and finally declared at 482 for 9 with Gatting making 160 – his first Test century in England – Gooch 74 and Lamb 67. Craig McDermott bowled brilliantly to take 8 for 141 and was the only Australian to take a wicket in the match. Beginning their second innings 225 runs in arrears, Australia initially struggled against the spin of Edmonds and Emburey, and when the last day began, England needed six Australian wickets. Play started late and Border was missed in the first over. He went on to make 146 not out and Australia, who finished on 340 for 5, drew the match.

RICHARD ELLISON RETURNS

England won the toss at Edgbaston and put Australia in, but when after the first two interrupted days, Australia were apparently safe at 335 for 8, the decision seemed a mistake. However, Saturday's play turned the series and established the pattern for the remaining matches. The last two wickets fell without addition in the first over with Richard Ellison, recalled to the England team,

GRAHAM GOOCH OF ESSEX AND ENGLAND, ENGLAND CAPTAIN FOR 11 ASHES MATCHES 1990-93

taking 6 for 77. Robinson and Gower then batted so well that at the close of the day, England were 355 for 1.

Robinson went on to 148 and Gower to 215 as they added 331 for the second wicket. Gatting scored another hundred before Gower declared at 595 for 5. Ellison then took 4 for 1 in the evening to reduce Australia to 35 for 5 at the close. On the final day, rain delayed the start until mid-afternoon. The breakthrough came in controversial

IAN BOTHAM TRAPS CRAIG McDERMOTT TO SEAL VICTORY IN THE FIFTH TEST AT EDGBASTON 1985

1986-87

After their succession of defeats, England went to Australia regarded by the press as underdogs, but the journalists seemed to have forgotten that many of the Australian team would be absent, being in South Africa. For the first time, England were without a single tourist from Lancashire or Yorkshire. After England won the first Test, victory in the fourth ensured the retention of the Ashes, despite Australia's belated win in the final match.

BOTHAM AT BRISBANE

In the opening Test at Brisbane, England's senior all-rounder Ian Botham stole the show with a fine innings of 138 including 22 off one over from Merv Hughes – their first innings total of 456 remains England's highest score at the Gabba. There were other useful contributions down the order with debutant Phil de Freitas, batting at No.9, making a rapid 40. Graham Dilley with 5 for 68 then helped bowl Australia out for 248 and Gatting became the first England captain to enforce the follow-on while playing in his first Test match in Australia. It was also the first time Australia had suffered this indignity in a home Ashes Test since 1965-66. Geoff Marsh, in his first Ashes Test, made 110 in Australia's second innings but only Greg Ritchie with 45 stayed with him and England went on to win by seven wickets.

At Perth, England's 592 for 8 declared was their highest score in Australia for almost 60 years, with opener Chris Broad's 162 the highest by an England player at the WACA. His partner Bill Athey scored 96 in an England opening stand of 223. England also had other centurions in David Gower (136) and Jack Richards (133) – the Surrey wicket-keeper joining Les Ames and Alan Knott as England keepers to score an Ashes ▶

fashion. Phillips, batting aggressively, was on 69 when he slashed square, Lamb at silly point jumped, the ball hit his instep and was caught by Gower. The umpire at the bowler's end was unsighted but after consulting his colleague at square-leg, gave him out. The remaining wickets soon went down and England had won by an innings and 118 runs. It was the first time in Ashes history that a side had won a match without losing more than five wickets.

Australia had to win at The Oval to square the series and retain the Ashes. This looked impossible after the first day, on which England batted. After Robinson had departed early, Gooch (196) and Gower (157) added 351, England making 376 for 3 by the close of the opening day. After they collapsed to 464 all out it seemed that a fightback was on the cards, but Australia were bowled out for 241. Gower applied the follow-on and although rain on Saturday delayed the end, only Allan Border, with 58, put up much resistance. Early Monday morning – a day when for the first time in England, all seats were sold in advance for a fourth day – the Australians were dismissed for 129. England captain David Gower took his series aggregate to 732 at 81.3 – passing Compton's record aggregate for an Ashes series in England.

AT EDGBASTON ENGLAND WON, LOSING THAN FEWER THAN FIVE WICKETS IN THE PROCESS, AN ASHES RECORD

hundred. Allan Border then held Australia together with a gritty innings of 125 in their total of 401 – it was Australia's 200th century in an Ashes Test, but any hope of a definite result disappeared when England scored far too slowly in their second innings.

The third Test in Adelaide resulted in more high scoring, and another draw. Australia reached 514 for 5 before declaring, with David Boon making 103, whilst all the top order made useful contributions. England then did almost as well with Broad and Gatting making hundreds. The pick of the Australian bowlers was Bruce Reid, the tallest man to play in an Ashes series, with 4 for 64. Border made an unbeaten 100 as the last part of the match turned into a formality.

MELBOURNE: SMALL IN CHARGE

Gladstone Small, who had played Sheffield Shield cricket for South Australia, came into the England side in place of Dilley for the fourth Test at Melbourne and, taking 5 for 48, helped Ian Botham (5 for 41) bowl out the home side for just 141. Chris Broad hit his third hundred in successive Tests to give England a commanding lead and Australia, needing 208 to make England bat again, fell apart in their second innings. Their last eight wickets went down for 81, mainly to the spin of Emburey and Edmonds. England won by an innings and 14 runs inside three days and Mike Gatting joined Chapman, Hutton and Brearley as the only England captains to retain the Ashes in Australia that century.

Little known spinner Peter Taylor was chosen for his Test debut for Australia in the final Test at Sydney and he confounded the critics by taking 6 for 78 and removing England for 275, this after Dean Jones had scored the first and biggest

ALLAN LAMB LEADS AN ENGLAND FIGHT BACK AT HEADINGLEY, BUT AUSTRALIA WIN BY 200 RUNS

of his three Ashes hundreds – 184 not out. It was a magnificent effort as Australia totalled 343. Middlesex's John Emburey, in the home side's second knock, then produced his best performance against Australia, taking 7 for 78 in a total of 251. Needing 320 to win, England started well and with Gatting making 96, the game was evenly poised at lunch on the fifth day. But then Peter Sleep's leg-breaks confused the tourists and Australia ended a sequence of 14 matches without winning with a 55-run victory.

BICENTENARY TEST

This Test match was staged in Sydney in January and February 1988 to celebrate the 200th anniversary of white settlement in Australia, but unfortunately it failed to live up to all the pre-match hype. For the first three days England were in control but then a rearguard fightback by the hosts ensured that the match would be drawn.

Mike Gatting won the toss for England and batted, reaching a slowish 221 for 2 by the close of play on day one. England eventually totalled 425 with only the not out batsman, Eddie Hemmings, failing to reach double figures. Chris Broad top-scored with 139 but annoyed with his dismissal, he knocked his off stump from the ground and was heavily fined by the England tour management. Australia were then dismissed for 214 and the follow-on was enforced but then David Boon (184 not out) and Geoff Marsh (56) put on 162 for the first wicket to thwart England's hopes of victory. This remains Australia's highest-opening partnership against England in Sydney.

1989

An evenly fought series was expected, but the array of young Australian batting talent found the dry pitches to their liking, as did Terry Alderman, back for the first time since his record-breaking tour of 1981. Australia steam-rolled through the series, winning 4-0 and regaining the Ashes lost four years earlier. It was the first time Australia had regained the Ashes in England since 1934.

The Headingley pitch was a new one and played without the early life, which in past Tests had made batting there very difficult on the first morning. No Australian wickets went down before lunch and by the end of the first day, Australia were 207 for 3. Mark Taylor, making his Ashes debut, went on to 136, Steve Waugh bettered this with his first century (177 not out) and skipper Allan Border (66) Dean Jones (79) and Merv Hughes (71) helped their side to 601 for 7 declared, a record for all Tests at the Yorkshire ground. Allan Lamb played a magnificent innings for England of 125, which included 24 fours; the proportion of his score coming from boundaries was thus 75.51%, a record for an Ashes century. Kim Barnett (80) and Robin Smith (66) gave him support, and in making 430, England avoided the follow-on. Australia rattled up 230 for 3 declared and England went in again with a minimum 83 overs to survive for a draw. Though Gooch stayed three hours for his 68, the innings crashed to 191 all out with Terry Alderman taking 5 for 44 – the first time he had taken ten wickets in a Test match.

In the second Test at Lord's, England won the toss and decided to bat, but this time wickets did fall before lunch, and the home side were all out for 286 well before the close of play. England's main scorers were Gooch (60), Gower (57) and Russell (64 not out). At the end of day two, with Taylor having made 62 and Boon 94, Australia were 276 for 6 and the match well poised. Steve Waugh went on to make an unbeaten 152 and, helped mainly by Geoff Lawson (74), he took Australia to 528. Gower (106) and Smith (96) fought back well for the home side after early wickets but a total of 359, in which Terry Alderman took 6 for 128, left the tourists only 118 to win – a total they achieved without unduly struggling for the loss of four wickets. ▶

At Edgbaston, Dean Jones was Australia's batting hero as he scored 157 of a total of 424. But with numerous interruptions for rain, Border had already batted into the fourth morning. Steve Waugh was out for the first time in the series after scoring 393 runs, a record unbeaten run in Ashes cricket, second only to Sobers in all Test cricket. England then made 242, avoiding the follow-on with the last pair together and Australia were 158 for 2 when the match ended in a draw.

The fourth Test at Old Trafford saw England batting first after winning the toss and Robin Smith holding the innings together with his first Test century. But with Geoff Lawson taking 7 for 62, England were all out for 260, a poor total soon put into perspective when Australia reached 135 for the first wicket. Taylor (84), Border (80), Jones (69), and Waugh (92),

took the total to 447 before England went in a second time. They collapsed to 59 for 6 before Jack Russell (128 not out) and John Emburey (64) gave the score some respectability. Russell also became the first England player to score his maiden first-class century in an Ashes Test. England made 264 but Australia needed only 78 to win and won with nine wickets in hand. Drama on the final morning came with the news that Emburey, Foster and Robinson were among players signed to join a rebel tour of South Africa and they were overlooked for the final two Tests.

TAYLOR AT TRENT BRIDGE

The fifth Test was dominated by Australia's openers, Geoff Marsh (138) and Mark Taylor (219), who became the first pair to bat throughout a full day in England. They ended up with 329 – an Ashes record and a record for all Tests in England. Taylor's double-century was Australia's first against England since Stackpole's 207 in 1970-71. With Boon adding 73, Border 65 and extras a record 61 in Ashes Tests, Australia declared at 602 for 6. During his innings, Border passed Boycott's Test aggregate of runs to move into second place on the all-time list behind Gavaskar. England, with a much changed side, made a disastrous start with Alderman dismissing Moxon and Atherton in his first over and Curtis in his next to leave England 14 for 3. He went on to take 5 for 69 but another century by Robin Smith (101) took the home team to 255. Following on, they were bundled out for 167 and were beaten by an innings and 180 runs.

For the final Test at the Oval, England brought the number of players selected to 29, one fewer than the record 30 of 1921. Australia by contrast made only one change in the

MARK TAYLOR OF AUSTRALIA IN ACTION DURING HIS INNINGS OF 219 IN THE FIFTH TEST AT TRENT BRIDGE. AUSTRALIA WON THE MATCH BY AN INNINGS AND 180 RUNS

whole series. Australia batted first and made 468 with Jones (122) Border (76) and Taylor (71) leading the way. After 79 from Gower, England made 285 but only avoided the follow-on after Gladstone Small (59) and Nick Cook (31) had added 73 for the ninth wicket. Border declared Australia's second innings at 219 for 4 and England had one or two anxious moments before gaining the draw at 143 for 5, with Smith again top-scoring with 77 not out. Mark Taylor's aggregate of 839 runs was the third highest-ever recorded in Tests and Alderman, with 41 wickets, became the first bowler to take 40 wickets in a series twice.

1990-91

When it comes to an Ashes series, the Baron de Coubertin principle scarcely enters into it – it is not the taking part, but the winning. Unlike 1989, England, as they say, were fortunate to get nil! They did at least take part this time, but the overall results mirrored the original qualification for a trip to Australia – a criminal record! Australia deservedly won the series 3-0.

FIRST TEST: BRISBANE

There was moisture beneath the surface when the captains tossed prior to the first Test at Brisbane. Acting captain Allan Lamb called incorrectly and in text-book conditions ideal for swing bowling, it was a triumph for the tourists to lose only two wickets before lunch. Yet from 117 for 2, eight wickets fell for 77 and England were all out for 194 with Bruce Reid full value for his figures of 4 for 53 – the ball that bowled Smith being the best of many good ones. Next day, the cloud cover had given way to blue sky, theoretically making batting simpler. But with Fraser and Small making good use of the movement off the seam and the team giving a fine exhibition of catching, Australia were bowled out for 152. Though they had a lead of 42, England never recovered after losing Larkins to Reid's first ball and with Alderman bowling a number of unplayable outswingers to take 6 for 47, they were dismissed for 114. Needing 157 for victory, Australian openers Marsh and Taylor knocked off the runs with disdainful ease.

Until teatime on the fourth day of a tense, toughly contested and memorable second Test in Melbourne, England were not only on level terms with Australia but were actually making more of the pace. Then superb fast bowling by Bruce Reid, along with Marsh and Boon batting heroically all through what was supposed to be an intensely difficult last day,

DAVID BOON OF AUSTRALIA IN ACTION DURING THE FOURTH TEST AT SYDNEY, 1991

Australia all but assured themselves of the Ashes for three more years. Reid took 6 for 97 in England's first innings after Gooch had had the good fortune to win the toss on what for the first two days was a beautiful batting pitch. Gower made 100 with Stewart (79) ▶

89

ANGUS FRASER OF ENGLAND WAS AN ASHES REGULAR THROUGHOUT THE 1990S

IN THE FIFTH TEST AT THE WACA, CRAIG McDERMOTT PRODUCED THE SPECTACULAR MATCH FIGURES OF 11 FOR 157

and Larkins (64) giving good support. Australia were bowled out for 306 with Angus Fraser taking 6 for 82 and Jack Russell taking six catches in the innings – an England record in Australia. Though Gooch and Larkins hit half-centuries, nobody else in England's second innings reached double figures and with Reid taking 7 for 51, Australia needed 197 to win. Despite the early loss of Taylor and unnecessary night-watchman Healy, Marsh (79 not out) and Boon (94 not out) put together their sixth hundred-plus partnership for the home side.

Though the third Test at Sydney was drawn and the Ashes retained by Australia, England at least restored some honour. The toss was important, as it had been in the first two Tests and it was Australia's turn. England could not prevent the home side from taking advantage of an excellent pitch and with Greg Matthews making 128, Boon 97, Border 78 and Jones 60, Australia totalled 518. Atherton then batted all through the third day and was eventually out for 105, whilst Gower (123) reached his third hundred in four Tests. Stewart fell nine runs short before Gooch declared at 469 for 8. Enterprise is usually rewarded in cricket and with the ball now turning sharply for Tufnell and Hemmings, Australia were bowled out for 205. Night-watchman Healy (who had had five stitches in a wound over his left eye), made 69. Needing 254 to win, England ended on 113 for 4 in a game watched by a crowd of 106,304, who provided the record receipts for a Test in Australia.

MARK WAUGH MAKES HIS DEBUT

No-one felt robbed of their money in a fourth Test match at Adelaide attracting 78,676 spectators and restored to its traditional Australia Day weekend. The game is especially remembered for a wonderful first innings in Test cricket by Mark Waugh. His 138 in Australia's total of 386 was an innings of the purest

pedigree. When he came in, the home side were 104 for 4 but when he reached his hundred less than three hours later, they were 252 for 5 and the match transformed. After losing Atherton and Lamb – both of whom failed to trouble the scorers – England through Gooch and Robin Smith reached 137 for 2 before Reid (4-53) and McDermott (5-97) dismissed them for 229. In reply, David Boon (121) and Allan Border (83 not out) put their immense limited-overs experience to good use, enabling the Australian captain to declare the second innings closed at 314 for 6. Gooch (117) and Atherton (87) played so well that there were visions of England getting somewhere near the improbable target of 472. But after the second new ball had been taken, the scoring rate dropped and England ended on 335 for 5.

McDERMOTT AT THE WACA

Australia's tougher, more resilient, thoughtful and, in the field, aggressive cricket had its reward with a nine-wicket win in the fifth Test at the WACA. Craig McDermott produced the spectacular match figures of 11 for 157 to underline the wisdom of his recall. After a good start, England, from 191 for 2, were all out for 244 as McDermott, who had been hit for 23 runs off two overs after lunch, took 5 for 17 in 40 balls to finish with 8 for 97. For Australia, Boon again made a solid contribution, but for once he had little support. Only Greg Matthews' dogged approach helped his side to a total of 307. Persistent and accurate fast bowling proved too much for England in their second innings with only Smith (43) and Newport (40 not out) offering any resistance. Newport and Malcolm actually added 38 for the last wicket and brief visions of Headingley 1981 arose. Australia needed 120 to win. DeFreitas dismissed Taylor with a beauty but Marsh and Boon saw Australia through to a nine-wicket victory just before lunch on the fourth day.

1993

After their success in 1989, the Australian tourists of 1993 had a tough act to follow. Though their attack didn't seem as menacing, this was to be Border's Ashes. Australia retained the Ashes with a 3-0 lead after four Tests, then made it 4-0 at Edgbaston before England broke through for a long-awaited win at The Oval.

'BALL OF THE CENTURY'

In the first Test at Old Trafford, England and Australia produced a match of rare quality. The measure of Australia's eventual superiority was better reflected by the 179-run margin of their win than

HOWZAT: MIKE GATTING SUCCUMBS TO THE 'BALL OF THE CENTURY' BY SHANE WARNE AT OLD TRAFFORD

England's bold effort to save the game which lasted until the fifth over of the mandatory final 15. It was Mark Taylor (124) who held together Australia's first innings as both spinners were in action before lunch on the opening day. Peter Such (6 for 67) did the damage as the tourists were eventually all out for 289. With Gooch showing a return to form, England started well, he and Atherton putting on 71 for the first wicket. After Atherton had succumbed to Hughes, Gatting was bowled by Warne's first ball in Ashes cricket – a ball that pitched wide of leg stump by a foot, and turned viciously out of the rough to clip the outside of the off stump. The remainder of the innings was wrecked by Warne (4 for 51) and Australia had a lead of 79. As the weather improved, so did the pitch and Australia declared their second innings on 432 for 5 with Ian Healy hitting an unbeaten 102 and useful contributions coming from Boon (93), Steve Waugh (78 not out) and Mark Waugh (64). Needing 512 to win, Gooch's legside play was faultless in an innings of 133 and though most players produced useful knocks, the classical leg-spin of Warne and the bustling hostility of Hughes was too much.

In the second Test at Lord's, Australia, batting first, obtained an advantage they never looked like relinquishing once Taylor (111) and Slater (152) had posted a century opening partnership. The second day belonged to David Boon (164), firstly in the company of Mark Waugh (99) and then Allan Border (77) as Australia declared their first innings closed at 632 for 4. England's bid to save the game devolved upon Atherton (80) but he received little support and they were bowled out for 205. Invited to follow on, England lost Gooch to a perfectly pitched leg-break before Atherton and Gatting put together a century partnership. Nearing his hundred, Atherton set off for a third run to deep mid-wicket but slipped on turning after Gatting ▶

declined it and was run out for 99. After half-centuries from Gatting, Hick and Stewart, the tail was no match for the quality of Australia's spinner and they won by an innings and 62 runs.

At Trent Bridge Gooch won the toss and, to the surprise of many, decided to bat. With Robin Smith (86) and Nasser Hussain (71) batting well, a substantial total seemed possible until the latter batsmen contrived to get themselves out and England were all out for 321. Australia's first innings was almost a mirror image of England's. Debutants McCague (4 for 121) and Ilott (3 for 108) bowled well as David Boon (101) top-scored in Australia's total of 373. Warne and Hughes grabbed early wickets in the second innings but further inroads were denied by Gooch and Thorpe. Gooch fell to Warne for 120 whilst Thorpe, with an unbeaten 114,

became the 14th England player to score a hundred on Test debut and only the third against Australia in England. Gooch declared England's second innings closed at 422 for 6, setting Australia 371 to win. Wickets fell at a steady rate until Steve Waugh and Brendan Julien came together at 115 for 6 and thereafter the penetration of the attack was unsustainable and unable to match England's excitement at the prospect of winning a Test match.

GRAHAM GOOCH RESIGNS

The fourth Test was momentous in several respects – not the least of which was that the outcome, a win for Australia by an innings and 148 runs, heralded the resignation of England captain Graham Gooch. Australia's innings of 653 for 4 declared set a new record for an innings of a Test match at Headingley. The undefeated fifth wicket partnership of 432 between Allan Border and Steve Waugh was the highest stand for any Australian wicket in a Test match at the Yorkshire ground. Border's 200 not out was the highest score by an Australian at Headingley other than Bradman's two scores of over 300 in the 1930s. Though Atherton and Gooch hit half-centuries, Paul Reiffel took 5 for 65 as England, 453 runs adrift of Australia's total, were made to follow on. Despite some gritty performances in their second innings, Tim May took 4 for 45 as England's tail failed to wag.

Though Edgbaston has often been kind to England, it could not prevent Mike Atherton from becoming the eighth captain in succession to lose his first Test in command. England won the toss in this fifth Test and elected to bat on a wicket described by Allan Border as the driest he had ever seen in England. Atherton was heading for a lovely hundred until Reiffel bowled him

a grubber, but all the other batsmen who got a footing threw away their wickets through ill-judged forcing strokes. Dismissed for 276, England made early inroads into the Australian batting to leave them at 80 for 4, but Mark Waugh (137) and Ian Healy (80) helped them to a total of 408. A deficit of 132 might not have been irretrievable had England built on an opening stand of 60, and though Thorpe scored 60, May and Warne shared the 10 wickets, leaving Australia just 120 to win, a target which they achieved for the loss of two wickets.

Four up in the series and looking forward to holidays and going home after a long season, Australia did not easily summon motivation, especially on the first morning after losing the toss of the final Test at The Oval. Gooch (56) and Atherton (50) put on 88 for the first wicket before Hick (80) and Stewart (76) added their contributions to a useful total of 380.

ENGLAND'S GRAHAM THORPE HAS SHOWN HIM-SELF TO BE A CONSISTENTLY STYLISH BATSMAN

1994-95

A crucial difference throughout this series was the fielding of the two sides – Australia's was routinely excellent while England's ground fielding was predictably laborious. Though England had a chance to level the series in the final Test at Perth, they dropped 10 catches of varying degrees of difficulty.

WARNE GOES TO WAR

This series was launched at Brisbane with two Australian centuries and the rehabilitation of the home side's key fast bowler, McDermott But it will forever be remembered for the devastating performance of Shane Warne, whose record-breaking spin bowling snuffed out England's lingering hope of a miraculous fightback. Both Michael Slater (176) and Mark Waugh (140) made their highest Test centuries in adding 182 for the third wicket as Australia totalled 426. With Craig McDermott determined to prove the doubters wrong, he bowled an unwavering line to finish with 6 for 53 in England's poor total of 167 – only Michael Atherton with 54 showing any real resistance. Australia set about stretching their giant lead and with useful contributions from Taylor (58), Slater (45) and Healy (45 not out), they declared their second innings closed at 248 for 8. Needing an unlikely 508 for victory, England's top order put up a brave fight with Hick (80), Thorpe (67) and Gooch (56) the pick of the batsmen. Survival was the name of the game but Shane Warne was in devastating form and his 8 for 71 was his best in Tests and the best by an Australian in any Test at Brisbane. His analysis included three wickets in four balls as he led his side to a 184-run victory.

The weather conditions for the second Test at Melbourne conspired to make England feel more at home, as grey skies and scudding showers surrounded the ▶

Atherton's astute handling of his bowlers contained the Australian batsmen, with only Ian Healy, with an unbeaten 83 in a total of 303, showing any form. Angus Fraser, recalled to the side after a two-year absence, took 5 for 87. Growing in confidence, England's rate of scoring at the start of their second innings exceeded that of the first until it was curtailed by Warne. During the course of his 79, Gooch became England's all-time leading run-scorer, whilst Ramprakash with 64 made a useful contribution lower down the order. Needing 391 to win, Australia lost three early wickets to Glamorgan's Steve Watkin before Mark Waugh and Border made a recovery. Malcolm then removed them and Steve Waugh in a productive burst after lunch and though Reiffel and Warne added 74 for the ninth wicket, Fraser dismissed them both to give England their first win in 18 Tests against the old enemy.

SHANE WARNE IS CONGRATULATED AFTER HIS FIRST EVER BALL IN ASHES CRICKET IS REALLY 'QUITE GOOD'!

THE UNDEFEATED PARTNERSHIP OF 432 BETWEEN BORDER AND WAUGH AT HEADINGLEY WAS THE HIGHEST EVER AT THE YORKSHIRE GROUND

MCG. Atherton duly won the toss and decided to field, but the pitch on the first morning did not afford the pace or movement that had been envisaged. Wickets fell steadily and at 100 for 4, many sides would buckle, but not Australia and with the Waugh twins at the crease, they edged themselves towards safety. Mark Waugh (71) and Steve Waugh (94 not out) along with Boon (41) helped Australia reach 279 with Darren Gough (4 for 60) the pick of the England bowlers. England batted well on the second day as Atherton and Hick and then Atherton and Thorpe took them to 119 for 1, this after Alec Stewart had his finger broken with the first ball after lunch. After this though, the English batsmen submitted to Warne and McDermott and were all out for 212. Australia built on their lead of 67 with ease, that is except when Darren Gough had the ball in his hand. David Boon hardly played a false stroke as he scored his first century for his country at the MCG. Declaring at 320 for 7, Australia set England a total of 389 to win. In their second innings, the English batsmen capitulated again to McDermott and Warne, the latter performing the hat-trick as England were dismissed for just 92.

DARREN GOUGH DIGS IN

Michael Atherton's team turned the form book upside down as the third Test at Sydney climaxed in a gut-wrenching and nerve-jangling mammoth final session lasting four minutes short of four hours. England batted first but with McDermott and Fleming seaming and swinging the new ball away from the upper order, they were reduced to 20 for 3. Atherton was then joined by Crawley and the two Lancashire batsmen added 174 for the fourth wicket. However, with the exception of a swashbuckling innings of 51 from Gough, the remaining English batsmen played indifferently and they were all out for 309. Thick grey cloud on the third day helped the English bowlers and

DARREN GOUGH HITS A BOUNDARY OFF CRAIG MCDERMOTT, SYDNEY 1994

at lunch, Australia were 57 for 6 and in danger of having to follow-on. Gough followed his 50 with 6 for 49 but with Taylor (49) and McDermott (21 not out) hitting some lusty blows, they edged themselves clear of 110 necessary to avert the follow on. England led by 193 runs and after another good stand by Atherton and Gooch, the England captain was joined by Hick. Atherton had a target for Australia of 450 in mind and a declaration time of 3.00pm and Hick found himself the first batsman to have the innings declared whilst on 98 in a Test match. Set 449 to win, Australia, courtesy of Taylor and Slater, cruised to 139 for 0 to set up an intriguing final day. Over 25,000 turned up to record the highest fifth day crowd at a Sydney Test and they witnessed a showdown of epic proportions. Lunching on 206 for 0, Australia were on the brink of history, but though rain after lunch meant one-and-a-half hours were lost, there was still the provision of an extra hour's play. On the resumption, Fraser tempted Slater

GRAEME HICK: THE BEST BATSMAN NEVER TO SCORE AN ASHES CENTURY?

GREG BLEWETT PULLS
ANGUS FRASER TO
THE BOUNDARY AT
ADELAIDE, 1995

by hitting 164 runs. Dismissed for 419, they led England by 66 runs but with Thorpe (83) and Crawley (71) batting aggressively, the game was kept alive. Then came an astonishing innings by Phil DeFreitas, who responded to being hit in the box by McDermott by cracking the pace bowler for 22 runs in one over. His 88 was his highest and most valuable innings for England as they made 328 in their second knock. Needing 262 to win, Australia collapsed to 83 for 8 thanks to some fine bowling by Malcolm and Lewis. An English victory looked a formality but then Healy and Fleming resisted for 26 overs until the latter was defeated by a ball from Lewis and Malcolm was recalled to dispose of the hapless McIntyre, who bagged a pair.

FINAL TEST: PERTH

The final Test at Perth offered England the chance to level the series but they were well beaten by 329 runs. Slater (124) went on to score his third hundred of the series – a frenetic, exhilarating affair. Mark Waugh's innings of 88 was more polished but brother Steve, who remained unperturbed as he progressed towards his century, was left on 99 not out after last man Craig McDermott was deemed run out. In fact, having ricked his back in the nets, he needed a runner – Mark Waugh – who in trying to help his brother reach three figures, failed to reach the crease after being sent back by his brother. Australia's total of 402 was a formidable one, especially after England slumped to 77 for 4. Thorpe (123) and Ramprakash (72) added 158 for the fifth wicket and a quickfire 40 by Chris Lewis helped England to 295. With a lead of 107, Australia then stumbled to 123 for 5 before Blewett (115) and Steve Waugh (80) assaulted a weary England attack. Declaring at 345 for 8, the Australian bowlers exploited the new ball and a now fit again Craig McDermott took 6 for 38 as England were bowled out for just 123. ▶

(103) into pulling and Taylor (13) and Boon immediately shut up shop, abandoning all hopes of victory. Fraser bowled magnificently to remove the middle order but with the light now deteriorating, Atherton could only employ Hick and Tufnell. England were valiant to the last; the tourist's pride was salvaged, but the Ashes were retained by Australia.

The fourth Test at Adelaide was one that confounded the critics and stunned Australia. England openers Atherton (80) and Gooch (47) put on 93 on a benign wicket before the skipper was joined by Mike Gatting, who had resigned himself to a couple of weeks sunbathing before being drafted into the side. His innings of 117 was his 10th Test hundred and his first for seven-and-a-half years. However, wickets fell steadily at the other end and England were all out for 353. In reply, Slater (67) and Taylor (90) put on 128 for the first wicket and though Australia were then stuttering a little at 232 for 5, Greg Blewett, who hit his maiden Test century, and Ian Healy, caused mayhem

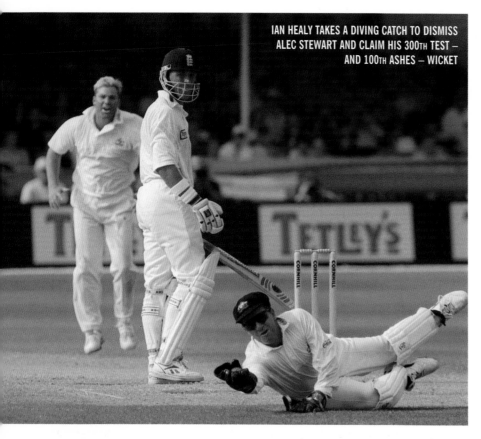

IAN HEALY TAKES A DIVING CATCH TO DISMISS ALEC STEWART AND CLAIM HIS 300TH TEST – AND 100TH ASHES – WICKET

1997

Coming into the series, Australia were riding high on the back of six straight series wins, including defeats of West Indies and South Africa, in which they reconfirmed their status as the world's best Test-playing team. Meanwhile, a revitalised England team, fresh from a successful tour of New Zealand, won the one-day internationals and the opening Test but the Australians showed their pedigree by coming back to win the series 3-2.

Mark Taylor won the toss and elected to bat in very humid conditions on the opening day of the first Test at Edgbaston – it was a difficult decision and within a couple of hours Australia were 54 for 8. The England bowlers, Gough, Malcolm and Caddick, bowled in exactly the right place and got prodigious swing and though Shane Warne hit a belligerent

47, the tourists were all out for 118 with Andy Caddick finishing with 5 for 50. England lost two early wickets, debutant Mark Butcher and Mike Atherton, who was playing in his 41st Test as captain, to equal Peter May's record. But then Hussain and Thorpe put on 288 runs for the third wicket before the Surrey left-hander mistimed a pull shot. Hussain went on to make 207, his first double century, and with Mark Ealham hitting an unbeaten 53, England declared at 478 for 9. Australia batted well at the start of their second innings and at one stage were 327 for 1 with both Taylor (129) and Blewett (125) making centuries. In doing so, Blewett became the first man to score a century in each of his first three Ashes Tests. There were useful contributions all down the order before an inspired spell of bowling by Gough got England back on track. Needing 118 for victory, Atherton and Stewart saw

England home with a day to spare.

The opening day of the second Test at Lord's was abandoned without a ball being bowled and though most of day two was also lost to the rain, Australia, who had put the home side into bat, had England at 38 for 3. Glenn McGrath and Paul Reiffel then bowled unchanged throughout the morning of the third day with McGrath destroying England with 8 for 38 in their total of just 77. These were the best figures by an Australian at Lord's and the third best by an Australian in Ashes contests. Though Gough removed Mark Taylor early on, Matthew Elliott made 112 with Australia looking for quick runs, and Steve Waugh declared at 213 for 7. In England's second innings, Butcher and Atherton opened with a first wicket partnership of 162 and though both men were denied centuries, England ended on 266 for 4 at the close of play.

HEADLEY KEEPS IT IN THE FAMILY

On an Old Trafford wicket that was in a poor state, Mark Taylor opted to bat first in the third Test, but he was soon back in the pavilion, the first of Dean Headley's four victims. In making his debut, the Kent paceman became the first third-generation Test cricketer, following father Ron and grandfather George, both of whom appeared for the West Indies. Though gradually the ball dominated the bat, Steve Waugh, who made a gutsy 108, and Paul Reiffel contributed a valuable eighth wicket stand of 70 to take Australia to 235. England, through Butcher and Stewart took the score to 74 for 1 before Warne struck, taking 6 for 48 to dismiss the home side for 162. Perhaps the highlight of the day for the tourists was the freakish leg-side stumping of top-scorer Butcher for 51. Headley again claimed early wickets and Australia in their second knock

GLENN McGRATH CELEBRATES TAKING MICHAEL ATHERTON'S WICKET AT LORD'S, SECOND TEST, 1997

ADAM (L) AND BEN HOLLIOAKE RECEIVE THEIR NEW TEST CAPS FROM CAPTAIN MICHAEL ATHERTON, THE FIFTH PAIR OF BROTHERS TO PLAY FOR ENGLAND. BEN'S TRAGIC DEATH IN A CAR ACCIDENT IN MARCH 2002 WOULD SHOCK THE CRICKET – AND THE WIDER – WORLD

were reeling at 39 for 3, but the Waugh twins turned the game round and Steve went on to record his second century of the match – a superb performance. With useful knocks from Healy, Warne, Reiffel and Gillespie, Australia declared at 395 for 8, setting England 469 to win. Though John Crawley made 83, Shane Warne took early wickets and Glenn McGrath took four of the five wickets to fall on the final day in a 268 run win for Australia.

RAIN AT HEADINGLEY

On a rain-affected first day at Headingley, England reached 103 for 2 but then collapsed following a fine spell of bowling by Jason Gillespie, who ran through the remaining batsmen to finish with figures of 7 for 37 from 13.4 overs. England had given a debut to Gloucestershire's Mike Smith in place of Andy Caddick but the ball didn't swing and with Matthew Elliott making a magnificent 199 and Ricky ▶

Ponting 127, Australian captain Mark Taylor (who went without troubling the scorers) was able to declare at 501 for 9. It was Ponting's maiden century and this meant that all the first seven Australian batsmen had made their maiden Test century against England. Needing 329 to make Australia bat a second time, England started badly and were 89 for 4 when Crawley joined Nasser Hussain. They both batted bravely, taking the score to 222 when Warne dismissed Hussain for 105. Crawley made 72 but Paul Reiffel was brought back into the attack and ran through the tail to finish with 5 for 49 as Australia won by an innings and 51 runs.

THE HOLLIOAKES TAKE A BOW

The fifth Test at Trent Bridge saw Adam and Ben Hollioake become the fifth set of brothers to play together for England – but the first time this century that two brothers had made their debuts in the same Test, other than in the inaugural Test of a country. Mark Taylor again guessed correctly and Australia batted first on a fairly docile track and though Dean Headley was again the pick of the England bowlers, all the first five batsmen in the Australian side scored half-centuries in a total of 427. Atherton and Stewart posted 106 runs for the first wicket before the England skipper became the first of Shane Warne's four victims. Stewart went on to top-score with 87 and there were useful contributions from Thorpe and the Hollioake brothers. The tourists then set about extending their 114-run lead from the first innings and whilst there were many cameo innings, only Greg Blewett recorded his second half-century of the match. England were left needing 451 runs for victory but with only Thorpe (82 not out) batting to potential, McGrath, Gillespie and Warne took three wickets apiece in a 264 run win.

For the first time in this series, Mike

JUSTIN LANGER REACHES 175 IN THE THIRD TEST, ADELAIDE, 1998

Atherton won the toss at the Oval, but Glenn McGrath and Shane Warne bowled well in tandem to restrict the home side to 180. McGrath returned figures of 7 for 76 from 21 overs of distinguished quality while Warne went a little under-rewarded with two wickets. After Australia had ended the first day on 77 for 2, Phil Tufnell got the ball to turn prodigiously to take 7 for 66 off 34.3 overs, though Warne came in and putting bat to ball, gave the Australians a useful lead. When England batted a second time, the only batsmen to get to grips with the bowling were Thorpe and Ramprakash, who put on 79 for the fifth wicket. For the third time in the match, a bowler took seven wickets – this time it was Mike Kasprowicz, who finished with 7 for 36. Australia required 124 runs to win but Andy Caddick ran in and bowled everything in the right area to take 5 for 42 and Phil Tufnell took 4 for 27 – finishing with 11 for 93 – the best return in an Ashes Test at The Oval since Fred Martin with 12 for 102 in 1890, and England won by 19 runs.

MIKE KASPROWICZ BECAME THE THIRD BOWLER TO TAKE SEVEN WICKETS IN THE TRENT BRIDGE TEST

1998-99

With Australia dominating the Ashes scene in recent years, there were calls from some people suggesting that the series be cut from five to three matches, especially after the home side took the lead. But England came back to win the fourth Test at the MCG and had they won the final Test, would have squared the series.

In the first Test at Brisbane, England escaped with a draw, thanks mainly to a thunderstorm which flooded the ground. Making his 100th Test appearance, Mark Taylor won the toss and elected to bat. England were instantly disciplined with Gough, Cork and Mullally bowling a tight line. Slater lost patience and started a slide which left Australia 106 for 4. However, Steve Waugh (112) and Ian Healy (134) both scored centuries and with Damien Fleming hitting an unbeaten 71, Australia totalled 485.

Though Atherton failed to trouble the scorers, Hussain, Thorpe and Ramprakash were resolute while Butcher (116) was exceptional. Then Glenn McGrath took 5 for 9 in 35 balls to present Taylor with an unexpected lead of 110. After Slater had become the fourth centurion in Australia's second knock, a declaration which seemed to surprise the Waughs, who were batting together, set England a target of 348 in a probable 98 overs. Wickets fell at regular intervals before all eyes swivelled to the skies where clouds were building. The umpires consulted. England had vetoed the use of floodlights, so off they came shortly before tea – just in time!

England paid the full price of being dismissed in the first two sessions of the second Test match at Perth. Their total of 112 was their lowest total at the WACA, and the third-lowest total ever in Perth Tests. Damien Fleming kept putting the ball in the right place and was rewarded with figures of 5 for 46. ▶

NASSER HUSSAIN DEMONSTRATES THE PULL SHOT THAT HE MADE HIS OWN

MARK RAMPRAKASH, A CONSISTENTLY STYLISH PERFORMER OF THE NINETIES

HUSSAIN PLAYS OFF HIS LEGS, FOURTH TEST, HEADINGLEY 2001. MARK BUTCHER WATCHES

By the end of the first day, Australia were 38 ahead with seven wickets in hand. On the second day, debutant Alex Tudor ran through the Waughs and the tail with the second new ball to leave Australia 240 all out. In England's second innings, Fleming bowled a spell of 4 for 16 and though Ramprakash (47*) and Hick, with a Bothamesque innings of 68, carried the fight to Australia, the home side were left with just 64 runs for victory, which they achieved for the loss of three wickets.

THIRD TEST: ADELAIDE

At Adelaide, Australia won the toss and opted to bat. Justin Langer's innings of 179 not out was an effort of outstanding calibre, and though Mark Taylor and Steve Waugh both scored 59, the English bowlers worked their way through the others very niftily. Australia's total of 391 was barely a par total against an England team bowling in great heat and when England were 187 for 3 the next day, nothing was decided. Then came the Sunday morning massacre – Hussain remained unbeaten on 89 as the last seven England wickets fell for just 40 runs. Australia kicked on, with Slater

making 103 and Langer and Mark Waugh half-centuries, enabling Taylor to declare at 278 for 5. Though there were moments when England could fantasise about a draw, they were bowled out for 237. Australia had retained the Ashes. It was 15 December, 13 days earlier than the Ashes had ever been settled before in Australia, partly a reflection of the earlier scheduling, and partly not.

The fourth Test match at Melbourne was so nearly the Test match of the 90s – the game had it all. The city's mercurial climate had gone from monsoon to midwinter and though McGrath claimed two early wickets, most of the greenness that had encouraged Taylor to put England in, had gone. Alec Stewart batted with bravado and no little luck to score 107, his first hundred in 23 Tests against Australia, but England were all out for 270. Darren Gough (5 for 96) bowled well when Australia battled, but though the tourists could have taken a first innings lead, they faced a deficit of 70 after Steve Waugh (122 not out) reached 7,000 Test runs to move past Don Bradman into fifth place in Australia's all-time list. His ninth wicket stand of 88 with MacGill was the tenth 50 partnership he had masterminded for the seventh, eighth,

or ninth wicket against England. In their second innings, three English batsmen – Stewart, Hussain and Hick – all scored fifties but Australia were left with just 175 to win. Early wickets fell but at 103 for 2, Australia looked favourites, but then Dean Headley had a spell of 4 for 4 in 16 balls. With Steve Waugh still there, Australia claimed the extra half-hour but Headley (6 for 60) and Darren Gough polished off the tail to leave England the winners by 12 runs.

DARREN GOUGH'S ASHES HAT-TRICK

The final Test at Sydney was a boy's own adventure. For three wonderful days, in front of record crowds, the momentum swung from one side to the other. Mark Taylor won the toss and in doing so, became the first captain to win the toss in every game of an Ashes series in Australia. England, bowling tightly, made early inroads until they entered the 'Waugh Zone'. Steve Waugh was bowled by Such for 96 and Mark Waugh fell to Headley for 121 before Gough produced three beauties to dismiss Healy, MacGill and Miller in successive balls.

Australia 322 all out. It was the first hat-trick for England in an Ashes Test this century. England's batsmen struggled against Stuart MacGill (5 for 57) and were dismissed for 220. The third day belonged to Mark Slater – his 123 was twice as many as all his team-mates made together and his proportion of 66.8 per cent of the total of 184 was the highest since the very first Test in 1876-77 when Australia's Charlie Bannerman made 165 out of 245 (67.3 per cent). Needing 287 to win, England ended the third day on 104 for 2 and though Hussain went on to make 53, he couldn't find anyone to stay with him and with Stuart MacGill taking 7 for 50 (match figures of 12 for 107), Australia won by 98 runs.

MARK BUTCHER CELEBRATES HIS UNBEATEN 173, AND ENGLAND CELEBRATE THE WIN AT HEADINGLEY, THEIR ONLY SUCCESS OF THE SUMMER

2001

Australia totally dominated the 2001 English season, winning the series 4-1. Damien Martyn and the Waugh twins contributed a brace of hundreds apiece, Glenn McGrath and Shane Warne shared 63 wickets and Adam Gilchrist played two match-winning innings. Yet it was at Headingley when acting captain Gilchrist set England the task of scoring 315 runs from 110 overs that Mark Butcher played one of the finest knocks ever seen in Ashes cricket.

Australian captain Steve Waugh won the toss in the first Test at Edgbaston and asked England to bat. Trescothick departed without troubling the scorers before Atherton (57) and Butcher (38) put on 104 for the second wicket. Shane Warne took 5 for 71 as England lurched to 191 for 9. Then came a remarkable 10th wicket stand of 103 between Alec Stewart (65) and Andy Caddick, who ended one run short of what would

have been a well-deserved half-century. Though the English bowlers made a couple of early inroads, three Australian batsmen scored centuries – with Steve Waugh and Damien Martyn each scoring 105 and Adam Gilchrist 152. England's best bowler was the much under-used Mark Butcher, who took 4 for 42. Australia's total of 576 gave them a lead of 282 and though Trescothick (76) and Butcher (41) batted well, Warne and Gillespie saw to it that no other England batsman reached double figures – Australia winning by an innings and 118 runs.

McGRATH ON SONG

Steve Waugh again asked England to bat first in the Lord's Test and with Glenn McGrath's steep bounce and unerring accuracy making things difficult, the home side were all out for 187. Caddick and Gough grabbed a couple of early wickets before Mark Waugh with 108 and Adam Gilchrist with 90 put Australia in the driving seat. Andy Caddick took 5 for 101 as

the tourists lost their last wicket at 401. In England's second innings, only Mark Butcher (83), who was one of Jason Gillespie's five victims, showed any form as the home side were dismissed for 227. Needing just 14 for victory, Australia lost Slater and Ponting in reaching their target off 3.1 overs.

In the third Test at Trent Bridge, Mike Atherton, again replacing Nasser Hussain, who was injured, as captain, won the toss and elected to bat. He failed to get off the mark and only Trescothick (69) and Stewart (46) showed any form in England's 185. For Australia, Glenn McGrath bagged another five wickets. On a bowler-friendly wicket, Alex Tudor took 5 for 44 but Australia, who were at one time struggling at 102 for 7, still managed to pass England's total by five runs. Atherton held the England second innings together with a fighting half-century but he was one of Shane Warne's six victims, caught behind by Adam Gilchrist. Australia still needed 158 to win on a wicket that was beginning to break up but though they lost a couple of wickets early on, Hayden and Mark Waugh, both of whom made 42, helped the tourists to a seven-wicket win.

The Headingley Test saw centuries by Ricky Ponting (144) and Damien Martyn (118) help Australia to a first innings total of 447. Darren Gough on what was then his home ground bowled manfully to finish with 5 for 103. All England's top order batsmen made useful scores with Alec Stewart making 76 not out. With a lead of 138, the Australian batsmen set about the England attack, with Ponting again leading the way with an innings of 72. Australia's acting captain Adam Gilchrist, who had replaced the injured Steve Waugh, declared their second innings closed at 176 for 4. England needed 315 to win – and ▶

only on one occasion, at Melbourne in 1928-29, had England achieved a fourth innings target in excess of 300. In scoring his undefeated 173 off 227 balls, Mark Butcher – against one of Australia's strongest-ever attacks – played magnificently to lead his side home by six wickets.

For the final test at The Oval, Steve Waugh was back to lead Australia and showed just how much he had been missed at Headingley by making an unbeaten 157. Brother Mark made 120 and Justin Langer 102 whilst there were other useful contributions from Hayden (68), Martyn (64 not out) and Ponting (62). Waugh eventually declared at 641 for 4. Warne

then removed England's first three batsmen and went on to finish with 7 for 165 off 44.2 overs, but not before Mark Ramprakash had made a splendid 133 in a total of 432 – just nine runs off avoiding the follow-on. In a disappointing showing second time round, England were bowled out for 184 with McGrath (5 for 43) and Warne (4 for 64, match figures of 11 for 229) causing the damage. Glenn McGrath, whose tally of victims was one more than Warne, was named Man of the Series. One of his victims was Mike Atherton, whose shy twirl of the bat as he left the international stage provided the summer's most poignant memory.

PERHAPS THE SUMMER'S MOST POIGNANT MEMORY WAS PROVIDED BY MIKE ATHERTON'S RETIREMENT FROM TEST CRICKET

MICHAEL VAUGHAN SALUTES THE SYDNEY CROWD AFTER THE FINAL TEST OF 2003

2002-03

The last time the two countries met, England, for whom current captain Michael Vaughan was in fine form, just avoided a whitewash by winning the last game of the series at Sydney. While there was a danger of reading too much into this result, England have since become serious challengers for the 2005 Ashes.

FIRST TEST: BRISBANE

The first Test at Brisbane saw England captain Nasser Hussain win the toss but then throw away any advantage by defying all conventional wisdom and choosing to field despite the sight of a dry, flat pitch and a cloudless sky in drought-ridden Queensland. When Australia were 364 for 2 at the close of the first day, England were already in a hopeless position just six hours into the series. With Hayden (197) and Ponting (123) dominating the England attack, Australia reached 492 before Giles claimed his fourth wicket to end the innings. Simon Jones, who had snapped up the wicket of Justin Langer, suffered a cruel knee injury which not only ruled him out of the match but out of any form of cricket for nigh on a year.

England required a monumental innings from one of their batsmen but though all the specialists played diligently, none was forthcoming. Trescothick, Butcher, Hussain and Crawley all hit half-centuries in a total of 325. Matthew Hayden smashed another hundred and after extending their lead to 463 midway through the fourth afternoon, Australia declared their second innings at 296 for 5. With the cracks now widening, Vaughan and Trescothick departed within two overs after tea and McGrath (4 for 36) and Warne (3 for 29) ran through the remaining bats-

men as England collapsed to 79 all out – Alec Stewart bagging his first pair in Test cricket.

SECOND TEST: ADELAIDE

At Adelaide, Michael Vaughan, who had hit a magnificent 177, was dismissed off the final delivery of the first day and from that moment, the Australians took charge. From 295 for 3, England slumped to 342 all out with Gillespie (4 for 78) and Warne (4 for 93) the leading wicket-takers. Then Langer and Matthew Hayden soon posted a century stand against an impotent English attack before Ricky Ponting and Damien Martyn added 242, with the former hitting

SINCE THE 2002-3 SERIES IN AUSTRALIA, ENGLAND HAVE BECOME SERIOUS CHALLENGERS FOR THE 2005 ASHES

his fifth century in seven Tests. With useful lower order contributions from Gilchrist and Bichel, Australia eventually declared at 552 for 9. Australia effectively wrapped up the match on the third evening when England lost three early wickets and though on the fourth morning there was a good stand between Vaughan and Stewart, the former's dismissal showed the difference between the sides. After Vaughan swept at a ball from Warne, Glenn McGrath on the square-leg boundary held an astonishing catch, diving to his left. It told the story – exuberant Australian brilliance as they

won by an innings and 51 runs – English disbelief and despair.

ENGLAND IN TROUBLE

At Perth, Hussain won the toss for the third time in succession and had little option but to bat. At 69 for 1, all was reasonably well, but after Steve Waugh ran out Butcher by hitting the stumps directly from cover, only Robert Key with 47 showed any bottle in an innings total of 185. Australia remorselessly built an invincible lead though nobody exceeded Damien Martyn's measured 71. For England, Craig White took 5 for 127 though Steve Harmison was his side's best bowler. After half-an-hour on the Sunday morning, England, 271 behind, had slumped to 34 for 4 and though Stewart (66 not out) and Hussain (61) batted well in a total of 223, there was never much likelihood of Australia suffering the indignity of having to bat a second time. Alex Tudor ducked into a bouncer from Brett Lee and had to be stretchered off. For a moment, he thought he had lost an eye; fortunately, it was no worse than a nasty gash that required stitches and a terrible headache.

FOURTH TEST: MELBOURNE

The fourth Test at Melbourne saw Australia scramble home for their least convincing victory of the series. Victory it was, however, in a match they were winning throughout, although Michael Vaughan scored his sixth century of 2002 and went past Dennis Amiss's record for the number of runs in a calendar year by an England batsman. At the end of the first day, Australia were 356 for 3 from 90 overs as the first wicket stand of 195 between Langer, who went on to make 250, and Hayden (102) got them off to a flying start. Steve Waugh (77) and Martin Love (62 not out) on his debut allowed them to declare their first innings at 551 for 6. England's top order failed miserably but Craig White, badly short of form, salvaged the innings with a fighting 85 not out, though avoidance of the follow-on was never probable. The centrepiece of England's second innings was Vaughan, with an innings of 145 and though Key made 52, England did not assemble a single three-figure partnership. Needing just 107 for victory, Harmison and Caddick bowled with plenty of fire to remove five frontline Australian batsmen but it wasn't long before Steve Waugh was celebrating his 33rd win as captain, beating Allan Border's record and seemingly firmly en route to only the second Ashes whitewash and the first for 82 years. But it was not to be as England saved their best until with a consolation victory at Sydney.

ENGLAND TURN THE TIDE?

Suddenly, at last, a well beaten side found themselves possessing the highest run-scorer in the series and the bowler with the best innings and match analysis. In their first innings, England eked out a total of 362 with Mark Butcher, at last enjoying the rub of the green, leading the way with 124. Alec Stewart rolled back the years to score 71, after Hussain had scored 75. For Australia, Steve Waugh reached his 29th Test hundred to draw level with Sir Donald Bradman. Yet that, and a characteristically buccaneering hundred from Adam Gilchrist, batting under pressure for the first time in the series, gave Australia a lead of only one run. Batting for a second time, England made 452 for 9 declared with Michael Vaughan making 183. His aggregate for the rubber was 663 and he was voted the Man of the Series. A target of 451 was just the sort of run chase that Australia fancied but they had spent a long time in the field and with Caddick taking 7 for 94, England won by 225 runs. For the sixth consecutive series, England had secured a win when the Ashes were gone.●

RETIRING AUSTRALIAN CAPTAIN STEVE WAUGH HOLDS ALOFT THE NEW ASHES TROPHY, SYDNEY, 2003

1977-2003 RESULTS

1977

ENGLAND WON SERIES 3-0

1st Test at Lord's
June 16, 17, 18, 20, 21
ENGLAND 216 (RA Woolmer 79 DW Randall 53 JR Thomson 4-41) and 305 (RA Woolmer 120 AW Greig 91 JM Brearley 49 JR Thomson 4-86)
AUSTRALIA 296 (CS Serjeant 81 GS Chappell 66 KD Walters 53 RGD Willis 7-78) and 114-6 (DW Hookes 50)

MATCH DRAWN

2nd Test at Old Trafford
July 7, 8, 9, 11, 12
AUSTRALIA 297 (KD Walters 88 GS Chappell 44) and 218 (GS Chappell 112 DL Underwood 6-66)
ENGLAND 437 (RA Woolmer 137 DW Randall 79 AW Greig 76) and 82-1 (JM Brearley 44) Captains GS Chappell (A) JM Brearley (E)

ENGLAND WON BY 9 WICKETS

3rd Test at Trent Bridge
July 28, 29, 30 August 1, 2
AUSTRALIA 243 (RB McCosker 51 KJ O'Keeffe 48* IT Botham 5-74) and 309 (RB McCosker 107 DW Hookes 42 RGD Willis 5-88)
ENGLAND 364 (APE Knott 135 G Boycott 107 LS Pascoe 4-80) and 189-3 (JM Brearley 81 G Boycott 80*)

ENGLAND WON BY 7 WICKETS

4th Test at Headingley
August 11, 12, 13, 15
ENGLAND 436 (G Boycott 191 APE Knott 57 AW Greig 43 JR Thomson 4-113 LS Pascoe 4-91)
AUSTRALIA 103 (IT Botham 5-21 M Hendrick 4-41) and 248 (RW Marsh 63 M Hendrick 4-54)

ENGLAND WON BY AN INNINGS AND 85 RUNS

5th Test at The Oval
August 25 (no play), 26, 27, 29, 30
ENGLAND 214 (MF Malone 5-63 JR Thomson 4-87) and 57-2
AUSTRALIA 385 (DW Hookes 85 MHN Walker 78* RW Marsh 57 MF Malone 46 RGD Willis 5-102)

MATCH DRAWN

1978-79

ENGLAND WON SERIES 5-1

1st Test at Brisbane
December 1,2,3,5,6
AUSTRALIA 116 (RGD Willis 4-44) and 339 (KJ Hughes 129 GN Yallop 102)
ENGLAND 286 (DW Randall 75 IT Botham 49 DI Gower 44 RM Hogg 6-74 AG Hurst 4-93) and 170-3 (DW Randall 74 DI Gower 48*)

ENGLAND WON BY 7 WICKETS

2nd Test at Perth
December 15, 16, 17, 19, 20
ENGLAND 309 (DI Gower 102 G Boycott 77 G Miller 40 RM Hogg 5-65) and 208 (DW Randall 45 GA Gooch 43 RM Hogg 5-57)
AUSTRALIA 190 (PM Toohey 81* RGD Willis 5-44) and 161 (GM Wood 64 GJ Cosier 47 JK Lever 4-28)

ENGLAND WON BY 166 RUNS

3rd Test at Melbourne
December 29, 30 January 1, 2, 3
AUSTRALIA 258 (GM Wood 100 GN Yallop 41) and 167 (KJ Hughes 48)
ENGLAND 143 (RM Hogg 5-30) and 179 (DI Gower 49 GA Gooch 40 RM Hogg 5-36)

AUSTRALIA WON BY 103 RUNS

4th Test at Sydney
January 6, 7, 8, 10, 11
ENGLAND 152 (IT Botham 59 AG Hurst 5-28) and 346 (DW Randall 150 JM Brearley 53 JD Higgs 5-148 RM Hogg 4-67)
AUSTRALIA 294 (WM Darling 91 AR Border 60* KJ Hughes 48 GN Yallop 44) and 111 (AR Border 45* JE Emburey 4-46)

ENGLAND WON BY 93 RUNS

5th Test at Adelaide
January 27, 28, 29, 31 February 1
ENGLAND 169 (IT Botham 74 RM Hogg 4-26) and 360 (RW Taylor 97 G Miller 64 G Boycott 49 JE Emburey 42 AG Hurst 4-97)
AUSTRALIA 164 (IT Botham 4-42) and 160 (KJ Hughes 46)

ENGLAND WON BY 205 RUNS

6th Test at Sydney
February 10, 11, 12, 14
AUSTRALIA 198 (GN Yallop 121 IT Botham 4-57) and 143 (B Yardley 61* G Miller 5-44 JE Emburey 4-52)
ENGLAND 308 (GA Gooch 74 DI Gower 65 JM Brearley 46 JD Higgs 4-69) and 35-1

ENGLAND WON BY 9 WICKETS

1979-80

AUSTRALIA WON SERIES 3-0

1st Test at Perth
December 14, 15, 16, 18, 19
AUSTRALIA 244 (KJ Hughes 99 RW Marsh 42 IT Botham 6-78) and 337 (AR Border 115 JM Wiener 58 GS Chappell 43 IT Botham 5-98)
ENGLAND 228 (JM Brearley 64 DK Lillee 4-73) and 215 (G Boycott 99* G Dymock 6-34)

AUSTRALIA WON BY 138 RUNS

2nd Test at Sydney
January 4, 5, 6, 8
ENGLAND 123 (DK Lillee 4-40 G Dymock 4-42) and 237 (DI Gower 98* DL Underwood 43)
AUSTRALIA 145 (IM Chappell 42 IT Botham 4-29) and 219-4 (GS Chappell 98* KJ Hughes 47 RB McCosker 41)

AUSTRALIA WON BY 6 WICKETS

3rd Test at Melbourne
February 1, 2, 3, 5, 6
ENGLAND 306 (GA Gooch 99 JM Brearley 60* G Boycott 44 DK Lillee 6-60) and 273 (IT Botham 119* GA Gooch 51 DK Lillee 5-78 LS Pascoe 4-80)
AUSTRALIA 477 (GS Chappell 114 IM Chappell 75 BM Laird 74 AR Border 63 JK Lever 4-111) and 103-2 (GS Chappell 40*)

AUSTRALIA WON BY 8 WICKETS

1981

ENGLAND WON SERIES 3-1

1st Test at Trent Bridge
June 18, 19, 20, 21
ENGLAND 185 (MW Gatting 85 TM Alderman 4-68) and 125 (DK Lillee 5-46 TM Alderman 5-62)
AUSTRALIA 179 (AR Border 63) and 132-6 (GR Dilley 4-24)

AUSTRALIA WON BY 4 WICKETS

2nd Test at Lord's
July 2, 3, 4, 6, 7
ENGLAND 311 (P Willey 82 MW Gatting 59 GA Gooch 44 GF Lawson 7-81) and 265-8 dec (DI Gower 89 G Boycott 60)
AUSTRALIA 345 (AR Border 64 RW Marsh 47 GM Wood 44 KJ Hughes 42 DK Lillee 40*) and 90-4 (GM Wood 62*)

MATCH DRAWN

3rd Test at Headingley
July 16, 17, 18, 20, 21
AUSTRALIA 401-9 dec (J Dyson 102 KJ Hughes 89 GN Yallop 58 IT Botham 6-95) and 111 (RGD Willis 8-43)
ENGLAND 174 (IT Botham 50 DK Lillee 4-49) and 356 (IT Botham 149* GR Dilley 56 G Boycott 46 TM Alderman 6-135)

ENGLAND WON BY 18 RUNS

4th Test at Edgbaston
July 30, 31 August 1, 2
ENGLAND 189 (JM Brearley 48 TM Alderman 5-42) and 219 (RJ Bright 5-68)
AUSTRALIA 258 (KJ Hughes 47 MF Kent 46 JE Emburey 4-43) and 121 (AR Border 40 IT Botham 5-11)

ENGLAND WON BY 29 RUNS

5th Test at Old Trafford
August 13, 14, 15, 16, 17
ENGLAND 231 (CJ Tavare 69 PJW Allott 52* DK Lillee 4-55 TM Alderman 4-88) and 404 (IT Botham 18 CJ Tavare 78 APE Knott 59 JE Emburey 57 TM Alderman 5-109)
AUSTRALIA 130 (MF Kent 52 RGD Willis 4-63) and 402 (AR Border 123* GN Yallop 114 RW Marsh 47 KJ Hughes 43)

ENGLAND WON BY 103 RUNS

6th Test at The Oval
August 27, 28, 29, 31 September 1
AUSTRALIA 352 (AR Border 106* GM Wood 66 MF Kent 54 IT Botham 6-125 RGD Willis 4-91) and 344-9 dec (DM Wellham 103 AR Border 84 RW Marsh 52 M Hendrick 4-82 IT Botham 4-128)

ENGLAND 314 (G Boycott 137 MW Gatting 53 DK Lillee 7-89) and 261-7 (APE Knott 70* MW Gatting 56 JM Brearley 51 DK Lillee 4-70)

MATCH DRAWN

1982-83

AUSTRALIA WON SERIES 2-1

1st Test at Perth
November 12, 13, 14, 16, 17
ENGLAND 411 (CJ Tavare 89 DW Randall 78 DI Gower 72 AJ Lamb 46 B Yardley 5-107) and 358 (DW Randall 115 AJ Lamb 56 DR Pringle 47* GF Lawson 5-108)
AUSTRALIA 424-9 dec (GS Chappell 117 KJ Hughes 62 DW Hookes 56 J Dyson 52 GF Lawson 50 G Miller 4-70) and 73-2

MATCH DRAWN

2nd Test at Brisbane
November 26, 27, 28, 30 December 1
ENGLAND 219 (AJ Lamb 72 IT Botham 40 GF Lawson 6-47) and 309 (G Fowler 83 G Miller 60 GF Lawson 5-87 JR Thomson 5-73)
AUSTRALIA 341 (KC Wessels 162 GS Chappell 53 B Yardley 53 RGD Willis 5-66) and 190-3 (DW Hookes 66* KC Wessels 46)

AUSTRALIA WON BY 7 WICKETS

3rd Test at Adelaide
December 10, 11, 12, 14, 15
AUSTRALIA 438 (GS Chappell 15 KJ Hughes 88 KC Wessels 44 J Dyson 44 IT Botham 4-112) an 83-2
ENGLAND 216 (AJ Lamb 82 DI Gower 60 GF Lawson 4-56) and 304 (DI Gower 114 IT Botham 58 GF Lawson 5-66)

AUSTRALIA WON BY 8 WICKETS

4th Test at Melbourne
December 26, 27, 28, 29, 30
ENGLAND 284 (CJ Tavare 89 AJ Lamb 83 RM Hogg 4-69 B Yardley 4-89) and 294 (G Fowler 65 IT Botham 46 DR Pringle 42 GF Lawson 4-66)
AUSTRALIA 287 (KJ Hughes 66 DW Hookes 53 RW Marsh 53 KC Wessels 47) and 288 (DW Hookes 68 AR Border 62* KJ Hughes 48 NG Cowans 6-77)

ENGLAND WON BY 3 RUNS

5th Test at Sydney
January 2, 3, 4, 6, 7
AUSTRALIA 314 (AR Border 89 J Dyson 79 IT Botham 4-75) and 382 (KJ Hughes 137 AR Border 83 KC Wessels 53 RW Marsh 41)
ENGLAND 237 (DI Gower 70 DW Randall 70 JR Thomson 5-50) and 314-7 (EE Hemmings 95 DW Randall 44 B Yardley 4-139)

MATCH DRAWN

1985

ENGLAND WON SERIES 3-1

1st Test at Headingley
June 13, 14, 15, 17, 18
AUSTRALIA 331 (AMJ Hilditch 119 GM Ritchie 46) and 324 (WB Phillips 91 AMJ Hilditch 80 KC Wessels 64 JE Emburey 5-82 IT Botham 4-107)
ENGLAND 533 (RT Robinson 175 IT Botham 60 PR Downton 54 MW Gatting 53 CJ McDermott 4-134) and 123-5

ENGLAND WON BY 5 WICKETS

2nd Test at Lord's

June 27, 28, 29, July 1, 2
ENGLAND 290 (DI Gower 86 AJ lamb 47 CJ McDermott 6-70) and 261 (IT Botham 85 MW Gatting 75* RG Holland 5-68)
AUSTRALIA 425 (AR Border 196 GM Ritchie 94 SP O'Donnell 48 IT Botham 5-109) and 127-6 (AR Border 41*)

AUSTRALIA WON BY 4 WICKETS

3rd Test at Trent Bridge

July 11, 12, 13. 15, 16
ENGLAND 456 (DI Gower 166 MW Gatting 74 GA Gooch 70 GF Lawson 5-103) and 196-2 (RT Robinson 77* GA Gooch 48)
AUSTRALIA 539 (GM Wood 172 GM Ritchie 146 AMJ Hilditch 47 SP O'Donnell 46)

MATCH DRAWN

4th Test at Old Trafford

August 1, 2, 3, 5, 6
AUSTRALIA 257 (DC Boon 61 AMJ Hilditch 49 SP O'Donnell 45 IT Botham 4-79 PH Edmonds 4-40) and 340-5 (AR Border 146* KC Wessels 50 AMJ Hilditch 40 JE Emburey 4-99)
ENGLAND 482-9 dec (MW Gatting 160 GA Gooch 74 AJ Lamb 67 DI Gower 47 CJ McDermott 8-141)

MATCH DRAWN

5th Test at Edgbaston

August 15, 16, 17, 19, 20
AUSTRALIA 335 (KC Wessels 83 GF Lawson 53 AR Border 45 RM Ellison 7-66) and 142 (WB Phillips 59 RM Ellison 4-27)
ENGLAND 595-5 dec (DI Gower 215 RT Robinson 148 MW Gatting 100* AJ Lamb 46)

ENGLAND WON BY AN INNINGS AND 118 RUNS

6th Test at The Oval

August 29,30, 31 September 2
ENGLAND 464 (GA Gooch 196 DI Gower 157 GF Lawson 4-101 CJ McDermott 4-108)
AUSTRALIA 241 (GM Ritchie 64*) and 129 (AR Border 58 RM Ellison 5-46)

ENGLAND WON BY AN INNINGS AND 94 RUNS

1986-87
ENGLAND WON SERIES 2-1

1st Test at Brisbane

November 14, 15, 16, 18, 19
ENGLAND 456 (IT Botham 138 CWJ Athey 76 MW Gatting 61 DI Gower 51 AJ Lamb 40 PAJ DeFreitas 40) and 77-3
AUSTRALIA 248 (GR Marsh 56 GRJ Matthews 56* GM Ritchie 41 GR Dilley 5-68) and 282 (GR Marsh 110 GM Ritchie 45 JE Emburey 5-80)

ENGLAND WON BY 7 WICKETS

2nd Test at Perth

November 28, 29, 30 December 2, 3
ENGLAND 592-8 dec (BC Broad 162 DI Gower 136 CJ Richards 133 CWJ Athey 96 BA Reid 4-115) and 199-8 dec (MW Gatting 70 DI Gower 48 SR Waugh 5-69)

AUSTRALIA 401 (AR Border 125 SR Waugh 71 GRJ Matthews 45 GR Dilley 4-79) and 197-4 (DM Jones 69 GR Marsh 49)

MATCH DRAWN

3rd Test at Adelaide

December 12, 13, 14, 15, 16
AUSTRALIA 514-5 dec (DC Boon 103 DM Jones 93 SR Waugh 79* GRJ Matthews 73* AR Border 70 GR Marsh 43) and 201-3 dec (AR Border 100* GM Ritchie 46* GR Marsh 41)
ENGLAND 455 (BC Broad 16 MW Gatting 100 CWJ Athey 55 JE Emburey 49 BA Reid 4-64 PR Sleep 4-132) and 39-2

MATCH DRAWN

4th Test at Melbourne

December 26, 27, 28
AUSTRALIA 141 (DM Jones 59 GC Small 5-48 IT Botham 5-41) and 194 (GR Marsh 60 SR Waugh 49)
ENGLAND 349 (BC Broad 112 AJ Lamb 43 MW Gatting 40 CJ McDermott 4-83 BA Reid 4-78)

ENGLAND WON BY AN INNINGS AND 14 RUNS

5th Test at Sydney

January 10, 11, 12, 14, 15
AUSTRALIA 343 (DM Jones 184* GC Small 5-75) and 251 (SR Waugh 73 AR Border 49 PL Taylor 42 JE Emburey 7-78)
ENGLAND 275 (DI Gower 72 JE Emburey 69 CJ Richards 46 PL Taylor 6-78) and 264 (MW Gatting 96 PR Sleep 5-72)

AUSTRALIA WON BY 55 RUNS

1989
AUSTRALIA WON SERIES 4-0

1st Test at Headngley

June 8, 9, 10, 12, 13
AUSTRALIA 601-7 dec (SR Waugh 177* MA Taylor 136 DM Jones 79 MG Hughes 71 AR Border 66) and 230-3 dec (MA Taylor 60 AR Border 60* DC Boon 43 DM Jones 40*)
ENGLAND 430 (AJ Lamb 125 KJ Barnett 80 RA Smith 66 TM Alderman 5-107) and 191 (GA Gooch 68 TM Alderman 5-44)

AUSTRALIA WON BY 210 RUNS

2nd Test at Lord's

June 22, 23, 24, 26, 27
ENGLAND 286 (RC Russell 64* GA Gooch 60 DI Gower 57 MG Hughes 4-71) and 359 (DI Gower 106 RA Smith 96 TM Alderman 6-128)
AUSTRALIA 528 (SR Waugh 152* DC Boon 94 GF Lawson 74 MA Taylor 62 JE Emburey 4-88) and 119-4 (DC Boon 58*)

AUSTRALIA WON BY 6 WICKETS

3rd Test at Edgbaston

July 6, 7, 8, 10, 11
AUSTRALIA 424 (DM Jones 157 MA Taylor 43 SR Waugh 43 GR Marsh 42 TV Hohns 40 ARC Fraser 4-63) and 158-2 (MA Taylor 51 GR Marsh 42)
ENGLAND 242 (IT Botham 46 RC Russell 42 TS Curtis 41)

Match Draw4th Test at Old Trafford

July 27, 28, 29, 31 August 1
ENGLAND 260 (RA Smith 143 GF Lawson 6-72) and 264 (RC Russell 128* JE Emburey 64 TM Alderman 5-66)
AUSTRALIA 447 (SR Waugh 92 MA Taylor 85 AR Border 80 DM Jones 69 GR Marsh 47) and 81-1

AUSTRALIA WON BY 9 WICKETS

5th Test at Trent Bridge

August 10, 11, 12, 14
AUSTRALIA 602-6 dec (MA Taylor 219 GR Marsh 138 DC Boon 73 AR Border 65*)
ENGLAND 255 (RA Smith 101 TM Alderman 5-69) and 167 (MA Atherton 47)

AUSTRALIA WON BY AN INNINGS AND 180 RUNS

6th Test at The Oval

August 24, 25, 26, 28, 29
AUSTRALIA 468 (DM Jones 122 AR Border 76 MA Taylor 71 DC Boon 46 IA Healy 44 DR Pringle 4-70) and 219-4 dec (AR Border 51* DM Jones 50 MA Taylor 48)
ENGLAND 285 (DI Gower 79 GC Small 59 TM Alderman 5-66) and 143-5 (RA Smith 77*)

MATCH DRAWN

1990-91
AUSTRALIA WON SERIES 3-0

1st Test at Brisbane

November 23, 24, 25
ENGLAND 194 (DI Gower 61 BA Reid 4-53) and 114 (TM Alderman 6-47)
AUSTRALIA 152 and 157-0 (GR Marsh 72* MA Taylor 67*)

AUSTRALIA WON BY 10 WICKETS

2nd Test at Melbourne

December 26, 27, 28, 29, 30
ENGLAND 352 (DI Gower 100 AJ Stewart 79 W Larkins 64 BA Reid 4-97) and 150 (GA Gooch 58 W Larkins 54 BA Reid 7-51)
AUSTRALIA 306 (AR Border 62 MA Taylor 61 DM Jones 44 ARC Fraser 6-82) and 197-2 (DC Boon 94* GR Marsh 79*)

AUSTRALIA WON BY 8 WICKETS

3rd Test at Sydney

January 4, 5, 6, 7, 8
AUSTRALIA 518 (GRJ Matthews 128 DC Boon 97 AR Border 78 DM Jones 60 SR Waugh 48 DE Malcolm 4-128) and 205 (IA Healy 69 PCR Tufnell 5-61)
ENGLAND 469-8 dec (DI Gower 123 MA Atherton 105 AJ Stewart 91 GA Gooch 59) and 113-4 (GA Gooch 54)

MATCH DRAWN

4th Test at Adelaide

January 25, 26, 27, 28, 29
AUSTRALIA 386 (ME Waugh 138 GRJ Matthews 65 DC Boon 49 CJ McDermott 42* PAJ DeFreitas 4-56) and 314-6 dec (DC Boon 121 AR Border 83*)
ENGLAND 229 (GA Gooch 87 RA Smith 53 PAJ DeFreitas 45 CJ McDermott 5-97 BA

Reid 4-53) and 335-5 (GA Gooch 17 MA Atherton 87 AJ Lamb 53)

MATCH DRAWN

5th Test at Perth

February 1, 2, 3, 5
ENGLAND 244 (AJ Lamb 91 RA Smith 58 CJ McDermott 8-97) and 182 (RA Smith 43 PJ Newport 40*(MG Hughes 4-37)
AUSTRALIA 307 (DC Boon 64 GRJ Matthews 60* IA Healy 42) and 120-1 (GR Marsh 63*)

AUSTRALIA WON BY 9 WICKETS

1993
AUSTRALIA WON SERIES 4-1

1st Test at Old Trafford

June 3, 4, 5, 6, 7
AUSTRALIA 289 (MA Taylor 124 MJ Slater 58 PM Such 6-67) and 432-5 dec (IA Healy 102* DC Boon 93 SR Waugh 78* ME Waugh 64)
ENGLAND 210 (GA Gooch 65 MG Hughes 4-59 SK Warne 4-51) and 332 (GA Gooch 133 CC Lewis 43 MG Hughes 4-92 SK Warne 4-86)

AUSTRALIA WON BY 179 RUNS

2nd Test at Lord's

June 17, 18, 19, 20, 21
AUSTRALIA 632-4 dec (DC Boon 164* MJ Slater 152 MA Taylor 111 ME Waugh 99 AR Border 77)
ENGLAND 205 (MA Atherton 80 MG Hughes 4-52 SK Warne 4-57) and 365 (MA Atherton 99 GA Hick 64 AJ Stewart 62 MW Gatting 59 TBA May 4-81 SK Warne 4-102)

AUSTRALIA WON BY AN INNINGS AND 62 RUNS

3rd Test at Trent Bridge

July 1, 2, 3, 5, 6
ENGLAND 321 (RA Smith 86 N Hussain 71 MG Hughes 5-92) and 422-6 dec (GA Gooch 120 GP Thorpe 114* RA Smith 50 N Hussain 47*)
AUSTRALIA 373 (DC Boon 101 ME Waugh 70 MJ Slater 40 MJ McCague 4-121) and 202-6 (BP Julian 56* SR Waugh 47*)

MATCH DRAWN

4th Test at Headingley

July 22, 23, 24, 25, 26
AUSTRALIA 653-4 dec (AR Border 200* SR Waugh 157* DC Boon 107 MJ Slater 67 ME Waugh 52)
ENGLAND 200 (GA Gooch 59 MA Atherton 55 PR Reiffel 5-65) and 305 (AJ Stewart 78 MA Atherton 63 TBA May 4-65)

AUSTRALIA WON BY AN INNINGS AND 148 RUNS

5th Test at Edgbaston

August 5, 6, 7, 8, 9
ENGLAND 276 (MA Atherton 72 JE Emburey 55* AJ Stewart 45 PR Reiffel 6-71) and 251 (GP Thorpe 60 GA Gooch 48 TBA May 5-89 SK Warne 5-82)
AUSTRALIA 408 (ME Waugh 137 IA Healy 80 SR Waugh 59) and 120-2 (ME Waugh 62*)

AUSTRALIA WON BY 8 WICKETS

6th Test at The Oval

August 19, 20, 21, 22, 23
ENGLAND 380 (GA Hick 80 AJ Stewart 76 GA Gooch 56 MA Atherton 50) and 313 (GA Gooch 79 MR Ramprakash 64 MA Atherton 42)
AUSTRALIA 303 (IA Healy 83* MA Taylor 70 AR Border 48 ARC Fraser 5-87) and 229 (ME Waugh 49 PR Reiffel 42 SL Watkin 4-65)

ENGLAND WON BY 161 RUNS

1994-95
AUSTRALIA WON SERIES 3-1

1st Test at Brisbane

November 25, 26, 27, 28, 29
AUSTRALIA 426 (MJ Slater 176 ME Waugh 140 MA Taylor 59 DR Gough 4-107) and 248-8 dec (MA Taylor 58 IA Healy 45* MJ Slater 45 PCR Tufnell 4-79)
ENGLAND 167 (MA Atherton 54 CJ McDermott 6-53) and 323 (GA Hick 80 GP Thorpe 67 GA Gooch 56 SK Warne 8-71)

AUSTRALIA WON BY 184 RUNS

2nd Test at Melbourne

December 24, 26, 27, 28, 29
AUSTRALIA 279 (SR Waugh 94* ME Waugh 71 DR Gough 4-60) and 320-7 dec (DC Boon 131 MJ Slater 44)
ENGLAND 212 (GP Thorpe 51 MA Atherton 44 SK Warne 6-64) and 92 (CJ McDermott 5-42)

AUSTRALIA WON BY 295 RUNS

3rd Test at Sydney

January 1, 2, 3, 4, 5
ENGLAND 309 (MA Atherton 88 JP Crawley 72 DR Gough 51 CJ McDermott 5-101) and 255-2 dec (GA Hick 98* MA Atherton 67 GP Thorpe 47*)
AUSTRALIA 116 (MA Taylor 49 DR Gough 6-49) and 344-7 (MA Taylor 113 MJ Slater 103 ARC Fraser 5-73)

MATCH DRAWN

4th Test at Adelaide

January 26, 27, 28, 29, 30
ENGLAND 353 (MW Gatting 117 MA Atherton 8o) and 328 (PAJ DeFreitas 88 GP Thorpe 83 JP Crawley 71 ME Waugh 5-40)
AUSTRALIA 419 (GS Blewett 102* MA Taylor 90 IA Healy 74 MJ Slater 67) and 156 (IA Healy 51* CC Lewis 4-24 DE Malcolm 4-39)

ENGLAND WON BY 106 RUNS

5th Test at Perth

February 3, 4, 5, 6, 7
AUSTRALIA 402 (MJ Slater 124 SR Waugh 99* ME Waugh 88) and 3345-8 dec (GS Blewett 115 SR Waugh 80 MA Taylor 52)
ENGLAND 295 (GP Thorpe 123 MR Ramprakash 72) and 123 (MR Ramprakash 42 CJ McDermott 6-38)

AUSTRALIA WON BY 329 RUNS

1997
AUSTRALIA WON SERIES 3-2

1st Test at Edgbaston

June 5, 6, 7, 8
AUSTRALIA 118 (SK Warne 47 AR Caddick 5-50) and 477 (MA Taylor 129 GS Blewett 125 MTG Elliott 66)
ENGLAND 478-9 dec (N Hussain 207 GP Thorpe 138 MA Ealham 53* MS Kasprowicz 4-113) and 119-1 (MA Atherton 57* AJ Stewart 40*)

ENGLAND WON BY 9 WICKETS

2nd Test at Lord's

June 19 (no play), 20, 21, 22, 23
ENGLAND 77 (GD McGrath 8-38) and 266-4 dec (MA Butcher 87 MA Atherton 77)
AUSTRALIA 213-7 dec (MTG Elliott 112 AR Caddick 4-71)

MATCH DRAWN

3rd Test at Old Trafford

July 3, 4, 5, 6, 7
AUSTRALIA 235 (SR Waugh 108 DW Headley 4-72) and 395-8 dec (SR Waugh 116 ME Waugh 55 SK Warne 53 DW Headley 4-104)
ENGLAND 162 (MA Butcher 51 SK Warne 6-48) and 200 (JP Crawley 83 GD McGrath 4-46)

AUSTRALIA WON BY 268 RUNS

4th Test at Headingley

July 24, 25, 26, 27, 28
ENGLAND 172 (MA Atherton 41 JN Gillespie 7-37) and 268 (N Hussain 105 JP Crawley 72 PR Reiffel 5-49)
AUSTRALIA 501-9 dec (MTG Elliott 199 RT Ponting 127 PR Reiffel 54* DR Gough 5-149)

AUSTRALIA WON BY AN INNINGS AND 61 RUNS

5th Test at Trent Bridge

August 7, 8, 9, 10
AUSTRALIA 427 (MA Taylor 76 SR Waugh 75 MTG Elliott 69 ME Waugh 68 GS Blewett 50 DW Headley 4-87) and 336 (IA Healy 63 GS Blewett 60)
ENGLAND 313 (AJ Stewart 87 GP Thorpe 53 GD McGrath 4-71 SK Warne 4-86) and 186 (GP Thorpe 82*)

AUSTRALIA WON BY 264 RUNS

6th Test at The Oval

August 21, 22, 23
ENGLAND 180 (GD McGrath 7-76) and 163 (GP Thorpe 62 MR Ramprakash 48 MS Kasprowicz 7-36)
AUSTRALIA 220 (GS Blewett 47 PCR Tufnell 7-66) and 104 (AR Caddick 5-42 PCR Tufnell 4-27)

ENGLAND WON BY 19 RUNS

1998-99
AUSTRALIA WON SERIES 3-1

1st Test at Brisbane

November 20, 21, 22, 23, 24
AUSTRALIA 485 (IA Healy 134 SR Waugh 12 DW Fleming 71* AD Mulally 5-105) and 237-3 dec (MJ Slater 113 JL Langer 74)

ENGLAND 375 (MA Butcher 116 GP Thorpe 77 MR Ramprakash 69* N Hussain 59 GD McGrath 6-85) and 179-6 (N Hussain 47)

MATCH DRAWN

2nd Test at Perth

November 28, 29, 30
ENGLAND 112 (DW Fleming 5-46) and 191 (GA Hick 68 MR Ramprakash 47* JN Gillespie 5-88 DW Fleming 4-45)
AUSTRALIA 240 (MA Taylor 61 AJ Tudor 4-89) and 64-3

AUSTRALIA WON BY 7 WICKETS

3rd Test at Adelaide

December 11, 12, 13, 14, 15
AUSTRALIA 391 (JL Langer 179* MA Taylor 59 SR Waugh 59 DW Headley 4-97) and 278-5 dec(MJ Slater 103 JL Langer 52 ME Waugh 51*)
ENGLAND 227 (N Hussain 89* MR Ramprakash 61 SC MacGill 4-53) and 237 (AJ Stewart 63* MR Ramprakash 57 GD McGrath 4-50)

AUSTRALIA WON BY 205 RUNS

4th Test at Melbourne

December 26(no play), 27, 28, 29
ENGLAND 270 (AJ Stewart 107 MR Ramprakash 63 SC MacGill 4-61) and 244 (GA Hick 60 AJ Stewart 52 N Hussain 50)
AUSTRALIA 340 (SR Waugh 122* DR Gough 5-96) and 162 (ME Waugh 43 DW Headley 6-60)

ENGLAND WON BY 12 RUNS

5th Test at Sydney

January 2, 3, 4, 5
AUSTRALIA 322 (ME Waugh 121 SR Waugh 96 DW Headley 4-62) and 184 (MJ Slater 123 PM Such 5-81 DW Headley 4-40)
ENGLAND 220 (JP Crawley 44 SC MacGill 5-57) and 188 (N Hussain 53 SC MacGill 7-50)

AUSTRALIA WON BY 98 RUNS

2001
AUSTRALIA WON SERIES 4-1

1st Test at Edgbaston

July 5, 6, 7, 8
ENGLAND 294 (AJ Stewart 65 MA Atherton 57 SK Warne 5-71) and 164 (ME Trescothick 76 MA Butcher 41)
AUSTRALIA 576 (AC Gilchrist 152 SR Waugh 105 DR Martyn 105 MJ Slater 77 MA Butcher 4-42)

AUSTRALIA WON BY AN INNINGS AND 118 RUNS

2nd Test at Lord's

July 19, 20, 21, 22
ENGLAND 187 (GD McGrath 5-54) and 227 (MA Butcher 83 JN Gillespie 5-53)
AUSTRALIA 401 (ME Waugh 108 AC Gilchrist 90 AR Caddick 5-101) and 14-2

AUSTRALIA WON BY 8 WICKETS

3rd Test at Trent Bridge

August 2, 3, 4
ENGLAND 185 (ME Trescothick 69 AJ Stewart 46 GD McGrath 5-49) and 162 (MA Atherton 51 SK Warne 6-33)

AUSTRALIA 190 (AC Gilchrist 54 AJ Tudor 5-44) and 158-3 (ME Waugh 42* ML Hayden 42)

AUSTRALIA WON BY 7 WICKETS

4th Test at Headingley

August 16, 17, 18, 19, 20
AUSTRALIA 447 (RT Ponting 144 DR Martyn 118 ME Waugh 72 DR Gough 5-103) and 176-4 dec (RT Ponting 72)
ENGLAND 309 (AJ Stewart 76* MA Butcher 47 N Hussain 46 GD McGrath 7-76) and 315-4 (MA Butcher 173* N Hussain 55)

ENGLAND WON BY 6 WICKETS

5th Test at The Oval

August 23, 24, 25, 26, 27
AUSTRALIA 641-4 dec (SR Waugh 157* ME Waugh 1`20 JL Langer 102 ret hurt)
ENGLAND 432 (MR Ramprakash 133 ME Trescothick 55 N Hussain 52 SK Warne 7-165) and 184 (GD McGrath 5-43 SK Warne 4-64)

AUSTRALIA WON BY AN INNINGS AND 25 RUNS

2002-03
AUSTRALIA WON SERIES 4-1

1st Test at Brisbane

November 7, 8, 9, 10
AUSTRALIA 492 (ML Hayden 197 RT Ponting 123 AF Giles 4-101) and 296-5 dec (ML Hayden 103 DE Martyn 64 AC Gilchrist 60*)
ENGLAND 325 (ME Trescothick 72 JP Crawley 69* GD McGrath 4-87) and 79 (GD McGrath 4-36)

AUSTRALIA WON BY 384 RUNS

2nd Test at Adelaide

November 21, 22, 23, 24
ENGLAND 342 (MP Vaughan 177 JN Gillespie 4-78) and 159 (AJ Stewart 57 GD McGrath 4-41)
AUSTRALIA 552-9 dec (RT Ponting 154 DR Martyn 95 C White 4-106)
Captains N Hussain (E) SR Waugh (A)

AUSTRALIA WON BY AN INNINGS AND 51 RUNS

3rd Test at Perth

November 29, 30 December 1
ENGLAND 185 (RWT Key 47) and 223 (AJ Stewart 66* N Hussain 61)
AUSTRALIA 456 (DR Martyn 71 RT Ponting 68 SR Waugh 53 C White 5-127)

AUSTRALIA WON BY AN INNINGS AND 48 RUNS

4th Test at Melbourne

December 26, 27, 28, 29, 30
AUSTRALIA 551-6 dec (JL Langer 250 ML Hayden 102 SR Waugh 77 MI Love 62) and 107-5
ENGLAND 270 (C White 85* JN Gillespie 4-25) and 387 (MP Vaughan 145 RWT Key 52 SC MacGill 5-152)

AUSTRALIA WON BY 5 WICKETS

5th Test at Sydney

January 2, 3, 4, 5, 6
ENGLAND 362 (MA Butcher 124 N Hussain 75 AJ Stewart 71) and 452 (MP Vaughan 183 N Hussain 72)
AUSTRALIA 363 (AC Gilchrist 133 SR Waugh 102 MJ Hoggard 4-92) and 226 (AJ Bichel 49 B Lee 46 AR Caddick 7-94)

ENGLAND WON BY 225 RUNS

RECENT PERFORMANCES

I am writing this review of next summer's Ashes content just prior to the turn of the year. It is the time of year when England's hopes rise. But to be fair, they have good reason to be more optimistic than in previous years – the whitewashing of New Zealand and West Indies, the thrilling rise of Andrew Flintoff and Stephen Harmison, the discovery of Andrew Strauss and, of course, the Champions Trophy, when Vaughan and Trescothick led England to a resounding victory over Australia.

After Steve Harmison had destroyed the West Indies in the first Test at Kingston, taking 7 for 12 as the home side were bowled out for 47, the Durham destroyer continued in similar vein at Port-of-Spain with 6 for 61 in a seven-wicket victory. Matthew Hoggard's hat-trick in the third Test at Bridgetown gave England a third successive victory and secured their first series win in the Caribbean since 1967-68. This left them with a clear chance of becoming the first team to complete a clean sweep over the West Indies at home in the last match in Antigua. But an unbeaten 400 by Brian Lara in a total of 751 for 5 declared – the biggest England had ever conceded – meant that the game was drawn. For England to preserve their unbeaten record in the face of Lara's onslaught, however, was a good save and an achievement in itself.

ANDREW STRAUSS: CENTURION

Against New Zealand, Andrew Strauss became the fourth player to make a century on his Test debut at Lord's, and

England's fourth innings total of 282 was their highest successful run chase at Lord's and their fifth-highest anywhere in a seven-wicket win. At Headingley in the second Test, Geraint Jones became the 10th England wicket-keeper to score a Test century and England's victory by nine wickets was their eighth victory in their last 12 Tests and with it they com-

ANDREW 'FREDDIE' FLINTOFF HITS ANOTHER OF HIS TRADEMARK HUGE BOUNDARIES v WEST INDIES, SUMMER 2004

pleted their first series victory over New Zealand since 1996-97. However, in the third Test at Trent Bridge, the wounded Kiwis ruffled a few feathers and with Fleming and Styris both making centuries, New Zealand made 348. An England lead seemed a certainty, but inspired bowling by Chris Cairns ensured a lead for the tourists of 65 runs. Like the first two matches, advantage swayed back and forth as Harmison and Giles helped dismiss New Zealand for 218. Needing 284 for victory, England produced a crucial Sunday performance with Thorpe making an unbeaten 104.

GILES TAKES CHARGE

With England now rated second behind Australia on the ICC's updated Test Championship, the outcome of the first Test at Lord's was hardly surprising. The die was cast after Lara won the toss but then put England in and with Key making 221, Strauss 137 and Vaughan 103, the home side made 568. Chanderpaul then made 128, this after Rudi Koertzen had failed to detect his gloved first ball catch to short-leg off Giles. Vaughan made his second hundred of the match before Giles bowled England to a 210-run win, clean bowling Lara in the process to claim his 100th Test wicket. England won the second Test by 256 runs, after Flintoff had exuded power allied to control in an innings of 167 and Trescothick had made 105. The Somerset opener made another hundred in England's second innings before Giles again proved the pick of the home side's bowlers. In the third Test, England had to overcome not only a West Indian side that showed more heart than in the previous Tests, but also the Manchester weather. England again conceded a first innings lead and it would have been even more if Thorpe – batting with the little finger of his right-hand broken – hadn't made 114. Chasing 231 to win, Rob Key and Flintoff shared a match-clinching partner-

ENGLAND'S STEVE HARMISON IN ACTION v WEST INDIES, SUMMER 2004

ship for England of 120, to win by seven wickets. In the final test at The Oval, every England batsman reached double figures, including debutant Ian Bell (70) and Steve Harmison (36 not out). The Durham paceman then took 6 for 46 as West Indies were bowled out for 152 and as they followed on, James Anderson more than doubled his wickets for the series in a 10-wicket win. This was England's first home season to include two clean sweeps – a seventh successive win equalling their best runs of 1885-88 and 1928-29.●

THIS WAS ENGLANDS FIRST HOME SEASON TO INCLUDE TWO CLEAN SWEEPS

AUSTRALIA

GLENN McGRATH OF AUSTRALIA CELEBRATES AFTER RETURNING CAREER-BEST
BOWLING FIGURES OF 8 FOR 24 v PAKISTAN AT THE WACA, PERTH, 19 DECEMBER 2004

When Australia visited Sri Lanka in 2003, they began a Test series for the first time since 1992 without Steve Waugh and in those 12 years, they had gone from contenders to undisputed champions of the world. Waugh's side had just been held to a draw at home by India and as some were thinking that the Australian empire was crumbling, a 3-0 win in Sri Lanka, the first time they had been whitewashed at home in a three-match series, proved them wrong. However, this was a nail-biting 3-0 win, for in every Test, Australia conceded a first innings lead. At Galle, Australia trailed by 161 after the first innings, but with Matthew Hayden, Damien Martyn and Darren Lehmann all scoring hundreds, they declared, allowing Shane Warne (26 wickets in the series) and Stuart MacGill to run through the home side. At Kandy, Australia were bowled out for 120 with Muralitharan being the third man to take 500 Test wickets. With Martyn and Adam Gilchrist both hitting big hundreds, Sri Lanka were left chasing 352 to win. They made a fight of it, but Warne and Jason Gillespie made sure Australia won by 27 runs. In the final Test at Colombo, Lehmann made another hundred before Marvan Atapattu cancelled this out and early on the fourth day, Australia were 98 for 5. But Justin Langer, who made 166 and Simon Katich dug in and put on 218. On the last day, Sri Lanka got within eight balls of a draw but Warne, exerting relentless pressure, eventually found Sri Lankan weakness.

AUSTRALIA FIGHT BACK

Ricky Ponting missed his first test as captain on home soil when Sri Lanka visited Darwin for the first of two Tests, to attend his aunt's funeral. Conditions for batsman on the Marrara pitch were difficult though Martyn and Lehmann boosted Australia to 207. Sri Lanka were then skittled out for 97, their lowest-ever total against Australia. Acting captain Gilchrist exemplified the application Sri Lanka lacked and helped Australia to 201 in their second innings. Mike Kasprowicz, revelling in the Northern Territory sun, then hit the pitch hard to produce his best figures in Australia of 7 for 39. In the second Test at Cairns, Langer and Hayden put on 255 for the first wicket as Australia totalled 517. While Atapattu also reached three figures, Sri Lanka fell 62 runs adrift of the home side's score. Hayden then constructed his 20th Test hundred but Sri Lanka, despite Warne bowling an engrossing 37-over spell on the fifth day, hung on at 183 for 8 to draw.

GILCHRIST IN CONTROL

Against India in the first Test at Bangalore, a sublime century on debut from Michael Clarke and a glorious display of controlled aggression by Adam Gilchrist gave Australia early initiative as they totalled 474. McGrath dismissed Chopra and Dravid with neither batsman troubling the scorers and India were eventually bowled out for 246. Harbhajan Singh bowled superbly when Australia batted a second time, taking 7 for 41 but then despite a swashbuckling half-century from Pathan, India were beaten by 217 runs. The second Test at Chennai was beautifully poised as India ended the fourth day on 19-0, needing a total of 229 for victory. But unfortunately, the north-east monsoon washed out the entire final day. It was a fine match which could have turned into a great finish. India would have been favourites to square the series as even

Gilchrist admitted afterwards ! At Nagpur, Adam Gilchrist became the first Australian captain to win a series in India in 35 years – they not only beat the hosts but thrashed them by 342 runs. An injury to Shane Warne cost him his place in the final Test as the hosts reduced the series deficit with a win.

JUST THE BEER TALKING...?

Whilst England coach Duncan Fletcher's standing has risen sharply since the tour of Australia two years ago, his Ashes record is quite grim – Played 10 won 2 Lost 8! In those games England have averaged 278 all out and Australia 478, so while England can do quite a bit better than last time and still lose heavily, I predict – foolishly some may say – that England will in the summer of 2005, regain the Ashes!●

SRI LANKA GOT WITHIN EIGHT BALLS OF A DRAW BUT WARNE'S RELENTLESS PRESSURE EVENTUALLY FOUND WEAKNESS.

ADAM GILCHRIST IN TYPICALLY DESTRUCTIVE MOOD AGAINST DANIEL VETTORI OF NEW ZEALAND DURING THE RECENT TEST SERIES, NOVEMBER 2004

CURRENT SQUADS

ENGLAND

James Anderson

Born: Burnley 30 July 1982

County: Lancashire

Test Debut: 2003 vs. Zimbabwe

Batting Style: Left Hand Bat

Bowling Style: Right Arm Fast Medium

Lancashire paceman James Anderson was playing for the Academy in Australia after just one first-class season, when he was suddenly thrown to the lions at the MCG in his first one-day international. Perhaps his sweetest moment to date came during the World Cup in Cape Town against Pakistan when the spearing, swinging yorker which bowled Yousuf Youhana first ball became his hallmark. His hat-trick against the same opposition at The Oval in 2003 was the first in 373 England one-day games. He remains an important part of the England attack.

Ian Bell, who made an accomplished 70 for England on debut as a replacement for Graham Thorpe at The Oval last summer, has been considered an England player from an early age. The batsman was an automatic choice for the first intake of players for the National Academy since, like all good players, he plays the ball late and when he's really on form he plays it from right under his eyes. The Gold Award winner in 2002 he converted potential into performances to help Warwickshire win the County Championship.

Ian Bell

Born Walsgrave-on-Sowe 11 April 1982

County: Warwickshire

Test Debut: 2004 vs. West Indies

Batting Style: Left Hand Bat

Bowling Style: Right Arm Fast Medium

Mark Butcher

Born Croydon 23 August 1972

County: Surrey

Test Debut: 1997 vs. Australia

Batting Style: Left Hand Bat

Bowling Style: Right Arm Fast Medium

One of the most senior players in the England team, Mark Butcher, has scored six hundreds and 13 fifties since his return to the Test side in 2001. A middle-order without him is unthinkable and when Australia last visited England in 2001, he scored an unbeaten 173 at Headingley to guide the home side to their only win of the series. At Sydney when the two countries last met, he scored his eighth century in what was his 50th Test.

Paul Collingwood

Born Shotley Bridge 26 May 1976

County: Durham

Test Debut: 2003 vs.Sri Lanka

Batting Style: Right Hand Bat

Bowling Style: Right Arm Off Break, Right Arm Medium

Durham all-rounder Paul Collingwood is one of the first names on the England team sheet in one-day internationals, though he has yet to make his mark at Test level, having appeared just twice for his country. Energetic, assertive and hard-working, Collingwood, who has played in 59 one-day internationals, has proved to be exactly what England had been looking for – a finisher. One of the game's greatest fielders, last year's 12-month central contract is an indication that from now on, Paul Collingwood is going to be internationally involved in both forms of the game.

Andrew Flintoff

Born Preston 6 December 1977

County: Lancashire

Test Debut: 1998 vs.South Africa

Batting Style: Right Hand Bat

Bowling Style: Right Arm Fast Medium

The world's leading all-rounder, Andrew Flintoff can, like the mighty Ian Botham, change the course of a game with either bat or ball. Voted 'Young Player of the Year' in 1998, a long catalogue of injuries blunted his progress but in 2003 against South Africa, Flintoff delivered – at Test level – on all the promises that his prodigious talent had made for him. After hitting his maiden test hundred against New Zealand at Christchurch in March 2002, Flintoff has gone from strength to strength and last summer made a superb 167 in the white-wash of the West Indies – Australia beware !

Ashley Giles

Born Chertsey 19 March 1973

County: Lancashire

Test Debut: 2003 vs.Zimbabwe

Batting Style: Right Hand Bat

Bowling Style: Left Arm Slow

Last summer, the Warwickshire spinner had his most successful Test series, taking 22 wickets at 23.13 runs apiece in the 4-0 drubbing of the West Indies. Giles, who was Surrey's 'Young Cricketer of the Year' in 1990, left The Oval following a lack of opportunity and after joining Warwickshire, succeeded Phil Tufnell in the England side. He made a name for himself on the parched pitches of Pakistan in the autumn of 2000 – finishing the series with 17 wickets, a record for an England bowler in that country.

Steve Harmison

Born Ashington23 October1978

County: Durham

Test Debut: 2002 vs. India

Batting Style: Right Hand Bat

Bowling Style: Right Arm Fast

Under the captaincy of former Australian opener David Boon, Steve Harmison had two hugely successful seasons for Durham in 1998 and 1999. Selected for the 1999-2000 England 'A' tour, he withdrew injured and was gaining a reputation – deserved or not – as a shirker who lacked the toughness required for the top level. The last four winters, though, have all provided watershed moments in Harmison's career with last winter's display in the Caribbean – 7 for 12 in the first Test – being exemplary. Last summer in the third Test against the West Indies, he became the first bowler to take 50 wickets in 2004.

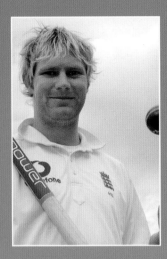

Matthew Hoggard

Born Leeds 31 December 1976

County: Yorkshire

Test Debut: 2000 vs. West Indies

Batting Style: Right Hand Bat

Bowling Style: Right Arm Fast Medium

A strong, powerful pace bowler, Matthew Hoggard has made rapid strides since he made the first of his 32 Test appearances against the West Indies at Lord's in 2000. During the early part of his career he spent two seasons as an overseas professional for Orange Free State, during which time he received special tuition from South African fast bowler Allan Donald. Now having taken 117 Test wickets, including a hat-trick against the West Indies at the Kensington Oval last April, his figures of 7 for 63 against New Zealand at Christchurch remain his best.

Geraint Jones

Born Kundiawa, Papua New Guinea 14 July 1976

County: Kent

Test Debut: 2004 vs. West Indies

Batting Style: Right Hand Bat

Wicket-keeper

If it were not for Adam Gilchrist, Geraint Jones would probably not be playing for England – Gilchrist's value coming in at No.7 set the agenda for all wicket-keepers. Jones, born to Welsh parents, was brought up in Brisbane where he took up wicket-keeping as it offered constant involvement with the game. Though his keeping is not quite up to that of Chris Read, he was given his Test debut at Antigua in April 2004 and in the West Indies total of 751 for 5 declared, took almost 200 overs before conceding a bye. Last summer he hit his maiden test century against New Zealand at Headingley.

Simon Jones

Born Swansea 25 December 1978

County: Glamorgan

Test Debut: 2002 vs. India

Batting Style: Left Hand Bat

Bowling Style: Right Arm Fast

Cricket is in Simon Jones' blood – his father Jeff took 44 wickets in 15 Test in the 1960s before his career was ended by an elbow injury. The Glamorgan fast bowler, who made his Test debut against India at Lord's in 2002 was playing for England against Australia in Brisbane in November of that year when he tore the anterior cruciate ligament to his right knee. He missed the whole of the 2003 County Championship season but returned to action at Test level in the Caribbean where he reeked of purpose and proved a fine foil to Harmison.

Robert Key

Born East Dulwich 12 May 1979

County: Kent

Test Debut: 2004 vs. West Indies

Batting Style: Right Hand Bat

Bowling Style: Right Arm Off Break

Kent middle-order batsman Robert Key's 221 against the West Indies at Lord's last summer was the third highest maiden Test century by an England batsman and the highest-ever score at Lord's for matches between England and the West Indies. In his early days in the game, Key captained the England Under 17 side to victory in the International Under 19 tournament in Bermuda and played for the victorious England side in the Under 19 World Cup in South Africa. Last summer, Robert Key was the first in the country to reach 1000 first-class runs.

Andrew Strauss

Born Johannesburg 2 March 1977
County: Middlesex
Test Debut: 2004 vs.New Zealand
Batting Style: Left Hand Bat
Bowling Style: Left Arm Fast Medium

South African-born Middlesex captain Andrew Strauss, a former student of Radley College and Durham University, where he read Economics, was offered a couple of jobs in the City at accountancy firms prior to playing first-class cricket. A lot of hard work brought him into the England side for the first Test against New Zealand last summer where he made 112 and 83 – the fourth player to make a century on debut. Now an automatic choice in the England team, he has scored 590 runs at the impressive average of 45.38 including another hundred against the West Indies.

Graham Thorpe

Born Farnham 1 August 1969
County: Surrey
Test Debut: 1993 vs.Australia
Batting Style: Left Hand Bat
Bowling Style: Right Arm Fast Medium

One of the world's best left-handed batsmen, Graham Thorpe made his Test debut against Australia at Trent Bridge in 1993, when he notched up an undefeated century. A Wisden Cricketer of the Year in 1998, he has scored 15 centuries in 93 Tests with a batting average of 45.35. Last summer in the match against the West Indies at Old Trafford, Thorpe occupied the crease for over six hours and, despite a fractured finger, made 14 – it was just another exemplary display of building an innings from one of the game's finest exponents of team batting.

Marcus Trescothick

Born Keynsham 25 December 1975
County: Somerset
Test Debut: 2000 vs.West Indies
Batting Style: Left Hand Bat
Bowling Style: Right Arm Fast Medium

Now firmly established at the head of the England batting order, the left-handed Somerset opener has impressed ever since making his Test debut against the West Indies at Old Trafford in 2000. During the early stages of his cricket career, Trescothick benefited from winter training in Perth, Western Australia under the guidance of Peter Wishart who has helped to develop his physique as well as the concentration needed to play long innings. Now having appeared in 53 Tests, Trescothick has scored 3982 runs at 42.81 with a highest score of 219 against South Africa at The Oval in 2003.

Michael Vaughan

Born Manchester 29 October 1974
County: Yorkshire
Test Debut: 1999 vs.South Africa
Batting Style: Right Hand Bat
Bowling Style: Right Arm Leg Spinner

England captain Michael Vaughan is a composed well-organised batsman, having now scored 3766 runs at 45.37 in his 50 Tests. The Yorkshire batsman was given a baptism of fire on his Test debut against South Africa in Johannesburg in November 1999. England were 2 for one run and Allan Donald was on a hat-trick when Vaughan walked to the crease. He survived to score 33. When England last met Australia for the Ashes, Vaughan scored 663 runs and hit three centuries. Last summer, hundreds in each innings of the first Test against the West Indies meant he became the second England captain to achieve the feat.

CURRENT SQUADS
AUSTRALIA

Michael Clarke

Born Liverpool NSW 2 April 1981

County: New South Wales

Test Debut: 2004 vs. India

Batting Style: Right Hand Bat

Bowling Style: Left Arm Off Break

An attacking right-handed middle-order batsman and useful left-arm orthodox spin, Clarke, Australia's Under 19 captain in the 2000 World Cup in Sri Lanka, moved quickly through the youth system making his NSW debut at 18. Graduating with honours from the Australian Academy, he had a season in the Lancashire League with Ramsbottom. Clarke has now assumed Ricky Ponting's tag as cricket Australia's golden boy – a buzz of expectation flies around the ground when he goes out to bat.

Adam Gilchrist

Born Bellingen NSW 11 April 1982

State: New South Wales

Test Debut: 1999 vs. Pakistan

Batting Style: Right Hand Bat Wicket-keeper

A dashing run-scoring batsman/wicket-keeper, Adam Gilchrist took over the gloves from Ian Healy and made his Test debut against Pakistan on Guy Fawkes Day 1999. When he first played Test cricket, he had been a one-day international for three years. He started his career with NSW but moved to Western Australia in 1994 to develop his wicket-keeping potential and in 1995-96 claimed a record 54 dismissals in the Sheffield Shield. Batting primarily at No.7 he has hit 10 centuries in his total of 3,485 Test runs at 52.80.

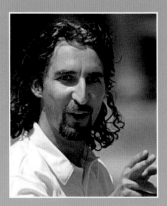

Jason Gillespie

Born: Darlinghurst, NSW 19 April 1975

State: South Australia

Test Debut: 1996 vs. West Indies

Batting Style: Right Hand Bat

Bowling Style: Right Arm Fast Medium

One of Australia's unluckiest cricketers who since arriving on the Test scene, has suffered a string of injury problems. After making his Test debut against West Indies at Sydney in December 1996, the wickets have tumbled – 189 at 25.24 – as the world's leading batsmen have struggled to tame his pace and nagging accuracy. After colliding with Steve Waugh in Kandy in September 1999, the injury left him with a broken leg and a weakened wrist but since then, he has demonstrated on numerous occasions just what he is capable of.

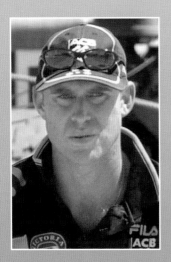

Matthew Hayden

Born Kingaroy, Queensland
29 October 1971

State: Queensland

Test Debut: 1994 vs South Africa

Batting Style: Left Hand Bat

Bowling Style: Right Arm
Medium

The big Queenslander, who has played county cricket for Hampshire and Northamptonshire, has since making his Test debut against South Africa in Johannesburg in 1994, had to survive fierce competition from Mark Taylor, Michael Slater, Matthew Elliott and Michael Hussey. But he now commands a regular spot in Australia's Test line-up and scores a hundred almost once every five times he goes out to bat. Having scored 4,488 runs at 58.28, he is also the eighth batsman ever to score a century in both innings of a Test more than once.

Brad Hodge

Born Sandringham, Victoria
29 December 1971

County: Lancashire

Test Debut: Yet to play

Batting Style: Right Hand Bat

Bowling Style: Right Arm Off
Break

Brad Hodge, who recently signed a two-year contract with Lancashire, has been given a glowing reference from Ricky Ponting. Hodge has never played international cricket but the Aussie captain believes that the former Leicestershire skipper is now the front runner for Test selection. Hogg was the leading scorer in the 2004 County Championship with 1,528 runs at just under 62 and led 'The Foxes' to victory in the Twenty 20 Cup with a superb 77 in the final. Last winter he plundered 1,282 runs at 67.47 with five hundreds in a golden season for Victoria.

Mike Kasprowicz

Born South Brisbane 10
February 1972

County: Glamorgan

Test Debut: 1996 vs.West Indies

Batting Style: Right Hand Bat

Bowling Style: Right Arm Fast
Medium

A right-arm fast bowler who has played for Queensland since 1989-90, he was desperately unlucky not to tour England in 1993 after taking 51 wickets in the Australian season. He joined Essex as their overseas player in 1994 and has also played county cricket for Leicestershire and more recently Glamorgan. Kasprowicz's best Test figures are 7 for 36 against England at The Oval in 1997 whilst for Queensland he performed the hat-trick in 1998-99 and for Glamorgan in 2003, he twice took nine wickets – 9 for 36 and 9 for 45 in the matches against Durham.

Simon Katich

Born Midland, Western
Australia 21 August 1975

State: Western Australia

Test Debut: 2001 vs England

Batting Style: Left Hand Bat

Bowling Style: Slow Left Arm
Chinaman

At one time tipped to be a future Australian captain, it is only recently that Katich has begun to put a run together in terms of Test appearances, though he made way for Darren Lehmann in the series against New Zealand. Having gained County Championship experience with both Durham and Hampshire, he will be looking if selected to hold down a regular spot, having experienced English conditions for a number of seasons. At one time, his progress was hampered by a debilitating mystery illness but he seems to have conquered this problem.

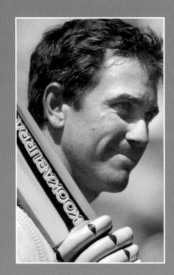

Justin Langer

Born Perth, Western Australia
21 November 1970

County: Lancashire

Test Debut: 1993 vs West Indies

Batting Style: Left Hand Bat

Bowling Style: Right Arm Fast Medium

An exceptionally gifted batsman, a product of the Australian Cricket Academy in Adelaide, he rose to fame as long ago as 1992 when he scored 149 in the Sheffield Shield final. A batsman for the big occasion, he almost carried Australia to victory on his debut with an heroic 54 but the West Indies won by one run! His perseverance allied to natural talent has made him a regular member of the Australian side, having scored 5,037 runs at 44.37 in 71 Tests.

Brett Lee

Born New South Wales
8 November 1976

State: New South Wales

Test Debut: 1999 vs India

Batting Style: Right Hand Bat

Bowling Style: Right Arm Fast

On his day, Brett Lee is probably the fastest bowler in the world. Very few new ball bowlers give batsmen a more torrid time at the crease. Playing state cricket for NSW, he made the first of his 37 Test appearances against India at Melbourne in December 1999 and celebrated the occasion with 5 for 47. Though these still remain his best figures in Test cricket, he remains a potent threat in the Australian attack.

Darren Lehmann

Born Gawler, South Australia
5 February 1970

State: South Australia

Test Debut: 1998 vs India

Batting Style: Left Hand Bat

Bowling Style: Left Arm Slow

Left-handed South Australian batsman Darren Lehmann, who also had a number of seasons playing for Victoria and played county cricket for Yorkshire has only recently forced himself into the Test side on a regular basis. Lehmann, whose top Test score is 177 against Bangladesh at Cairns in 2003 was named as a Wisden Cricketer of the Year in 2000 when he topped the Yorkshire batting averages with 1,47 runs at 67.13. The following season he again led the way with 1,416 runs at 83.29 as Yorkshire won the County Championship and since then, he has been captain of the white rose county.

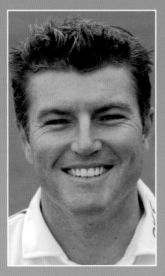

Stuart MacGill

Born Mount Lawley, Western
Australia 25 Australia 1971

County: Western Australia

Test Debut: 1998 vs South Africa

Batting Style: Right Hand Bat

Bowling Style: Left Arm Googly

Stuart MacGill, who bowls right-arm leg-breaks and googlies has always had to play second fiddle to the miraculous talents of Shane Warne, though he has made 30 Test appearances for Australia since making his debut in 1997-98. MacGill's best figures at Test level are 7 for 50 (12 for 107 in the match) against England at Sydney during the 1998-99 Ashes series. Beginning his career with Western Australia, he has played for NSW since 1996-97 and Nottinghamshire in the County Championship since 2002 and will be hoping that his experience on English wickets leads to his inclusion.

Glenn McGrath

Born Dubbo, NSW 9 February 1970

County: New South Wales

Test Debut: 1993 vs New Zealand

Batting Style: Right Hand Bat

Bowling Style: Right Arm Fast Medium

Known as the Enforcer, Glenn McGrath is a world-class performer. Though he preferred basketball to cricket until he was 16, only five years after taking up the sport, he was representing his country in the Test arena. His immaculate control was never better demonstrated when he took 8 for 38 in the Lord's Test of 1937 – the best single innings figures on that ground. Now having taken 430 Test wickets at 21.71 from 95 matches, he remains Australia's No.1 strike bowler.

Damien Martyn

Born Darwin 21 October 1971

State: Western Australia

Test Debut: 1992 vs West Indies

Batting Style: Right Hand Bat

Bowling Style: Right Arm Medium

An aggressive middle-order batsman who made his Test debut at the age of 21 against the West Indies at Brisbane in 1992, his career seemed to grind to a halt after just a handful of Tests and this despite a successful tour of England in 1993. A run glut for Western Australia earned him a recall six years later and though he has appeared in 143 one-day internationals, it is only recently that he has held down a regular place in Australia's Test side.

Ricky Ponting

Born Launceston, Tasmania 19 December 1974

State: Tasmania

Test Debut: 1995 vs Sri Lanka

Batting Style: Right Hand Bat

Bowling Style: Right Arm Fast Medium

A prodigious run-getter for Tasmania, Ricky Ponting is now Australian captain and brings his side to England on the back of series wins over New Zealand and India. Unlucky to be given out to a controversial lbw decision after scoring 96 on his Test debut against Sri Lanka at Perth in 1995 but has since gone on to score 5,821 runs at 55.97 in 75 Tests. A player who has matured a lot in the last few years – there is little doubt that Australian cricket is in safe hands whilst he is in charge.

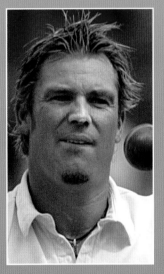

Shane Warne

Born Melbourne 13 September 1969

State: Victoria

Test Debut: 1992 vs India

Batting Style: Right Hand Bat

Bowling Style: Right Arm Leg Break

The highest wicket-taker in Test cricket history, Shane Warne arrived on the international scene in the Ashes series of 1993 when he took 34 wickets, conceding fewer than two an over. In November 1994 he took his best first-class figures of 8 for 71 against England at Brisbane and the following month performed a hat-trick against the same opposition. Named Man-of-the-Match in the 1999 World Cup Final at Lord's, the following year he was named as one of Wisden's Five Cricketers of the Century. Missed out on a much-desired century at Perth in December 2001, falling to New Zealand's Daniel Vettori on 99! Now back to his best after a drug ban.

THE VENUES

'Catches win matches' runs the old cricketing phrase, and while it is true that fielding is equally important as batting and bowling, there are two other factors that any good Test captain will take into account when deciding on the strategy for a particular match. One is the weather; the other is the ground where the match is being played. Whilst it is almost impossible to legislate for the weather – particularly in England – a knowledge of the various Test grounds around the country is invaluable. Here, then, is a condensed guide to the five Test grounds for the Ashes series of 2005, starting with the 'home of cricket', Lord's in London.

ANY GUIDE TO ENGLISH TEST MATCH GROUNDS MUST BEGIN AT HEADQUARTERS, HOME OF THE MCC – LORD'S

LORD'S

First Test
21-25 July 2005

Capacity
30,000

Ground Dimensions
The playing area at Lord's is 152 metres by 133 metres, within which the actual playing area is defined by a rope stretching to the appropriate dimensions depending on the position of the playing strip being used.

Ground Records (Test Matches)

Highest Total	
729-6 dec Australia v England 1930	
Lowest Total	
42 India v England 1974	
Highest Individual Innings	
333 GA Gooch(E) v India 1990	
Best Bowling(Innings)	
8-34 IT Botham(E) v Pakistan 1978	
Best Bowling(Match)	
16-137 RL Massie(A) v England 1972	

Lord's has traditionally been a happy hunting ground for Australia. It was not until 1884 that England met Australia in a Test match at Lord's, The Oval having led the way in staging Test cricket. England only managed to beat Australia once at Lord's during the 20th century. In 24 Tests during this period, Australia triumphed 10 times with 13 games drawn.

England's sole victory came in 1934 under the captaincy of Bob Wyatt. And prior to 1934, you have to go back to 1896 to find the previous England victory at Lord's.

When the two sides met in 1961, England had gone 18 Tests without defeat but the Lord's hoodoo was to strike again. Only one England batsman reached 50 as Australia won by five wickets. Not even winning the toss for a 12th consecutive match could help England !

Ray Illingworth's 1972 side retained the Ashes but suffered a mauling at Lord's where the hero was debutant Bob Massie who bagged 16 for 137.

In 1997 Glenn McGrath ripped through the England batting, taking 8 for 38 as the hosts were all out for 77. In England's second innings, Atherton (in his 42nd match as captain, breaking Peter May's record of 41) and Butcher enjoyed an opening partnership of 162 which together with the rain enabled the hosts to scrape a draw.

EDGBASTON

Second Test
4-8 August 2005

Capacity
20,000

Ground Dimensions
Though the ground dimensions are 148 metres by 145 metres, the actual playing area for a particular match will depend on the position of the playing strip selected and boundaries defined by ropes may vary. Test match boundaries will only vary between 68 and 70 metres.

Ground Records (Test Matches)

Highest Total
633-5 dec England v India 1979

Lowest Total
30 South Africa v England 1924

Highest Individual Innings
285 not out PBH May(E) v West Indies 1957

Best Bowling(Innings)
7-17 W Rhodes(E) v Australia 1902

Best Bowling(Match)
12-119 FS Trueman(E) v West Indies 1963

In 1902, Edgbaston was recognised as suitable for Test matches when England met Australia in the first Test of the series. Australia were bowled out for 36 with Wilfred Rhodes taking 7 for 17 in 11 overs. Test matches continued to be played until 1929, but there was a gap until 1946, since when it has remained a regular venue.

In 1981 Ian Botham was the scourge of the Aussies who needed only 146 to win the fourth Test and take a 2-1 lead in the series. The tourists reached 105 for 4, needing just 41 for victory on the fourth afternoon. But enter Botham, who took 5 for 11 in 14 overs as England scraped home by 29 runs.

Over the last decade or so, Edgbaston developed a reputation for low-scoring, so when Australia were bowled out for 118 inside three hours on the first morning in 1997, it appeared that another low-scoring contest was on the cards. But England made 478 for 9 declared thanks largely to a match-winning stand of 288 between Hussain (207) and Thorpe (138). But Australia made a fight of it with captain Mark Taylor (129) and Greg Blewett (125) putting on 194 for the second wicket in their second innings total of 477. England reached their target of 118 in less than 22 overs and with a day to spare.

OLD TRAFFORD

Third Test

11-15 August 2005

Capacity

18,500

Ground Dimensions

The playing area is flat and defined by a rope and advertising Boards and by a white metal fence in front of the pavilion. The pitch is 143 metres by 149 metres and approximately circular in shape.

Ground Records (Test Matches)

Highest Total

658-8 dec Australia v England 1964

Lowest Total

58 India v England 1952

Highest Individual Innings

311 RB Simpson(A) v England 1964

Best Bowling(Innings)

10-53 JC Laker(E) v Australia 1956

Best Bowling(Match)

19-90 JC Laker(E) v Australia 1956

Old Trafford's first day of Test cricket in July 1884 was, would you believe, washed out! In the Test of 1888, Yorkshire's Bobby Peel had match figures of 11 for 68 as Australia, bowled out for 81 in their first innings, were forced to follow-on in the wake of England's 172. After a disastrous start, at one point 7 for 6 until Turner and Lyons added 48. Even so, they lost by an innings and 21 runs shortly before lunch on the second day, making this the shortest Test match of all-time.

In 1902, Victor Trumper reached his century before lunch when Australia were 173 for 1 but the game known as 'Tate's match' ended when England's Fred Tate needed just four runs to win the game:

he was bowled by Saunders. It was at Old Trafford in 1909 that Frank Laver recorded the best bowling figures by an Australian in a Test match in England, taking 8 for 31 in a drawn rain-affected game. There can be few lovers of the game who have not heard of 'Laker's Match', that amazing example of spin bowling in which the England bowler took 10 wickets in one innings for 53 runs, and a match total of 19 for 90, taking all his wickets from the Stretford End.

In 1964, Bobby Simpson scored 311 for Australia out of their total of 656 for 8 declared while Ken Barrington (256) and Ted Dexter (174) replied for England in a game in which both sides passed the 600-run mark.

▶

TRENT BRIDGE

Fourth Test
25-29 August 2005

Capacity
15,000

Ground Dimensions
This is a large ground with a playing area extending to 160 metres by 150 metres but this is restricted on match days to about 141 metres by 144 metres.

Ground Records (Test Matches)

Highest Total
658-8 dec England v Australia 1938

Lowest Total
88 South Africa v England 1960

Highest Individual Innings
278 DCS Compton(E) v Pakistan 1954

Best Bowling(Innings)
8-107 BJ Bosanquet(E) v Australia 1905

Best Bowling(Match)
14-99 AV Bedser(E) v Australia 1953

The first Test match at Trent Bridge was played in 1899 against Australia. This was WG Grace's last match for England and when the match ended on 3rd June, he was 50 years and 320 days old. By coincidence the only Englishman to play Test cricket at an older age – Wilfred Rhodes – made his debut in this game, taking 4 for 58 and 3 for 60. Also making his debut was Victor Trumper, without doubt the finest Australian batsman in the pre-Bradman era.

The great Australian side of 1948 opened the Test series with an eight-wicket win. Early on the first day, England were reduced to 74 for 8, which seemed to set the tone for the entire five-match series – the tourists won 4-0. Australia topped 500 in the first innings as Don Bradman scored his 28th Test century on his final tour of England.

In 1993 Graham Thorpe became the first England batsman – since Frank Hayes in 1973 – to score a hundred on his Test debut. The Surrey left-hander hit an unbeaten 114 in his second innings and helped England end a run of seven straight Test defeats. England skipper Graham Gooch passed 8,000 Test runs during the game which ended in a draw.

THE OVAL

Fifth Test

8-12 September 2005

Capacity

23,000

Ground Dimensions

The playing area is very large, extending to 170 metres by 150 metres, within which the actual playing area is defined by a rope, stretched to the appropriate dimensions depending on the position of the playing strip being used, but usually about 137 metres by 140 metres.

Ground Records (Test Matches)

Highest Total

903-7 dec England v Australia 1938

Lowest Total

44 Australia v England 1896

Highest Individual Innings

364 L Hutton(E) v Australia 1938

Best Bowling(Innings)

9-57 DE Malcolm(E) v S.Africa 1994

Best Bowling(Match)

16-220 M Muralitharan(SL) v England1998

In 1880, The Oval was the venue for the first-ever meeting on English soil between the two oldest nations in Test cricket. WG Grace scored 152 for England and William Murdoch replied for Australia with 153 not out, yet it was the hosts who won by five wickets. The game was made famous with England fielding three brothers in their team, WG, EM and GF Grace !

In 1938, Len Hutton scored 364 in England's first innings total of 903 for 7 declared. Together with Maurice Leyland, Hutton put on 382 for the second wicket while occupying the crease for an amazing 13 hours and 17 minutes – England won by an innings and 579 runs.

Don Bradman was given a standing ovation when he walked out to bat on his last Test appearance in 1948. England had just been dismissed for 53. The home side, captained by Norman Yardley, gave him three cheers on his arrival at the crease. But two balls later, Bradman was walking back to the pavilion after being bowled by Eric Hollies for a duck. England lost by an innings and Bradman, who needed just four runs for a batting average of 100, never had the opportunity to bat again!

BEST XI'S

Selecting best-ever England and Australia XI's is a fascinating exercise but the results are bound to be highly provocative. The more I thought about all the players who have represented the two countries and their respective performances in the battle for the Ashes, the more difficult the

ENGLAND

JACK HOBBS

'The Master' was the supreme England batsman and though he set records which may never be surpassed, he was not especially interested in runs for the sake of runs and it was the sheer quality that made him such a delight for Surrey and England.

LEN HUTTON

A complete batsman on all types of wickets, Hutton's greatness was all the more amazing for the fact that he made a full recovery from a wartime accident, which shortened his left arm by two inches. He was also the first professional to captain England in 1952, since 1887.

WALLY HAMMOND

The greatest England batsman of his generation, Hammond set a record for most runs in Test cricket, passing Jack Hobbs' total of 5410 in 1937 and going on to be the first to score 6000 and 7000 runs. His 905 runs in the 1928-29 Ashes series were a record beaten only by Don Bradman.

KEN BARRINGTON

A highly productive and sound batsman, ever determined to sell his wicket dearly. England were very glad of his determination and consistency virtually throughout the 1960s. Perhaps his most vital contribution was his 582 runs at 72.75 against Australia in 1962-63.

DAVID GOWER

A sublime left-handed batsman, Gower charmed cricket watchers with his batting for many years. He never scored the mass of runs in first-class cricket of many other great batsmen but significantly his average was much higher in Tests than other matches.

IAN BOTHAM

The charismatic all-rounder who became a folk hero in England after his exploits in the 1981 Ashes series, could on his day turn any game with both bat and ball.

ALAN KNOTT

He was not simply a brilliant wicket-keeper, his five Test hundreds puts him in the category of one of England's finest all-rounders. Supremely fit and renowned for his on-field callisthenics, he made a record 65 appearances for England between 1968 and 1977.

ALEC BEDSER

His accurate in-swing bowling with a most effective leg-cutter was the mainstay of the England attack and at times he seemed to carry the attack almost single-handedly. He took 30 wickets at 16.06 against Australia in1950-51 and reached his peak effectiveness in the Ashes-winning series of 1953 when he took 39 wickets at 17.48 in the five Tests.

WILFRED RHODES

Rhodes was the greatest wicket-taker of all-time in first-class cricket and an all-rounder whose runs total is exceeded by only 15 batsmen. One of only three cricketers to have batted in every position in the order in Test matches!

DEREK UNDERWOOD

With his medium-pace left-arm spin bowling, Underwood fully lived up to his nickname of 'Deadly', for he was so on any sort of wicket that gave him some assistance. In an age when pace bowling dominated, he could and should have played more often for England.

SYDNEY BARNES

Regarded by many as the greatest of all bowlers, he played only 27 Tests, yet his 46-year-old career reached heights that will never again be attained. In all competitive matches, he claimed 6229 wickets at 8.33 apiece and took all 10 wickets in an innings 12 times!

task of selecting my best XI's became. How good a player is or has been is purely a matter of opinion and it is certainly true that figures seldom tell the true story, but perhaps the brief summary under each player, will go some way to explaining why I have chosen the players that I have!

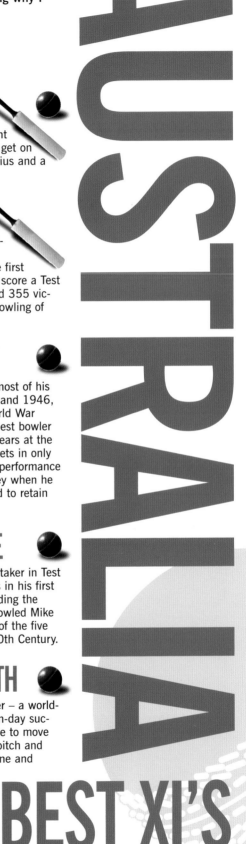

VICTOR TRUMPER

In his lifetime, Victor Trumper was the most charismatic figure in Australian cricket. He has become an Australian legend – his century before lunch on a sodden wicket at Old Trafford in 1902 helped Australia to win by 3 runs and take the series. As Pelham Warner once said: 'No-one ever played so naturally.'

ARTHUR MORRIS

A key member of the country's Test side for nearly a decade after the Second World War, he batted his side out of many a crisis, setting up numerous victories along the way and eight of his 12 Test centuries were made against England.

DON BRADMAN

Runs were what Bradman was all about and in 1930 he scored a record 974 runs. In 338 first-class innings he made 117 hundreds with a career average of 95.14: his 52 Tests would have yielded an average of 100 had he not been famously bowled just four runs short in his last match.

GREG CHAPPELL

An elegant batsman and highly successful Australian captain, he scored a century against England on his Test debut in 1970 and under his brother's leadership, continued to punish England with centuries in the 1972 series – at The Oval, he and his brother created history when they became the firs brothers to score hundreds in the same innings of a Test.

ALLAN BORDER

A tough determined left-hander, he was the basis of Australia's batting through the 1980s; in fact there were times when many believed he was the batting, such was the level of performance he maintained.

DENNIS LILLEE

Came back from the cricketing dead with real speed and fire to rival Sydney Barnes as the world's greatest bowler: this speaks volumes for his character and determination.

KEITH MILLER

Australia's finest all-round cricketer, who saw cricket as a game to be enjoyed. e was a magnificent batsman, always looking to get on with it, a fast bowler of genius and a great slip fieldsman.

ROD MARSH

Besides taking the most dismissals in a series – 28 in 1982-83 and becoming the first Australian wicket-keeper to score a Test century, he claimed a record 355 victims – 95 of them off the bowling of Dennis Lillee.

BILL O'REILLY

The records show that for most of his Test career – between 193 and 1946, with an interruption for World War Two, Bill O'Reilly was the best bowler in the world. In his seven years at the top, O'Reilly took 144 wickets in only 27 Tests. Perhaps his best performance came in 1934 at Headingley when he took 10 for 122 and helped to retain the Ashes.

SHANE WARNE

The world's leading wicket-taker in Test cricket. He took 34 wickets in his first Ashes series in 1993 including the 'Ball of the Century' that bowled Mike Gatting. Also voted as one of the five greatest cricketers of the 20th Century.

GLEN MCGRATH

Devastating new ball bowler – a world-class performer and modern-day successor to Dennis Lillee. Able to move the ball both ways off the pitch and can maintain a relentless line and length at pace.

AUSTRALIA BEST XI'S

ASHES STATISTICS: ENGLAND v AUSTRALIA 1876-77 to 2002-03

HIGHEST INNINGS TOTALS

England	in England	903-7 dec	The Oval	1938
	in Australia	636	Sydney	1928-29
Australia	in England	729-6 dec	Lord's	1930
	in Australia	659-8 dec	Sydney	1946-47

LOWEST INNINGS TOTALS

England	in England	52	The Oval	1948
	in Australia	45	Sydney	1886-87
Australia	in England	36	Edgbaston	1902
	in Australia	42	Sydney	1887-88

HIGHEST MATCH AGGREGATE

1753 for 40 wickets   Adelaide   1920-21

LOWEST MATCH AGGREGATE

291 for 40 wickets   Lord's   1888

HIGHEST INDIVIDUAL INNINGS

England	in England	364	L Hutton	The Oval	1938
	in Australia	287	RE Foster	Sydney	1903-04
Australia	in England	334	DG Bradman	Headingley	1930
	in Australia	307	RM Cowper	Melbourne	1965-66

HIGHEST AGGREGATE OF RUNS IN A SERIES

England	in England	732 (Av 81.33)	DI Gower	1985
	In Australia	905 (av 113.12)	WR Hammond	1928-29
Australia	in England	974 (av 139.14)	DG Bradman	1930
	In Australia	810 (av 90.00)	DG Bradman	1936-37

RECORD WICKET PARTNERSHIPS — ENGLAND

1st	323	JB Hobbs(178)/W Rhodes(179)	Melbourne	1911-12
2nd	382	L Hutton(364)/M Leyland (187)	The Oval	1938
3rd	262	WR Hammond(177)/DR Jardine(98)	Adelaide	1928-29
4th	288	N Hussain(207)/GP Thorpe(138)	Edgbaston	1997
5th	206	E Paynter(216*)/DCS Compton (102)	Trent Bridge	1938
6th	215	L Hutton(364)/J Hardstaff jnr(169*)	The Oval	1938
	215	G Boycott(107)/APE Knott(135)	Trent Bridge	1977
7th	143	FE Woolley(133*)/JJ Vine (36)	Sydney	1911-12
8th	124	EH Hendren(169)/H Larwood(70)	Brisbane	1928-29
9th	151	WH Scotton(90)/WW Read(117)	The Oval	1884
10th	130	RE Foster(287)/W Rhodes(40*)	Sydney	1903-04

RECORD WICKET PARTNERSHIPS — AUSTRALIA

1st	329	GR Marsh(138)/MA Taylor(219)	Trent Bridge	1989
2nd	451	WH Ponsford(266)/DG Bradman(244)	The Oval	1934
3rd	276	DG Bradman(187)/AL Hassett(128)	Brisbane	1946-47
4th	388	WH Ponsford(181)/DG Bradman(304)	Headingley	1934
5th	405	SG Barnes(234)/DG Bradman(234)	Sydney	1946-47
6th	346	JHW Fingleton(136)/DG Bradman(270)	Melbourne	1936-37
7th	165	C Hill(188)/H Trumble(46)	Melbourne	1897-98
8th	243	RJ Hartigan(16)/C Hill(160)	Adelaide	1907-08
9th	154	SE Gregory(201)/JMc Blackham(74)	Sydney	1894-95
10th	127	JM Taylor(108)/AA Mailey(46*)	Sydney	1924-25

BEST INNINGS BOWLING ANALYSIS

England	in England	10-53	JC Laker	Old Trafford	1956
	in Australia	8-35	GA Lohmann	Sydney	1886-87
Australia	in England	8-31	F Laver	Old Trafford	1909
	in Australia	9-121	AA Mailey	Melbourne	1920-21

BEST MATCH BOWLING ANALYSIS

England	in England	19-90	JC Laker	Old Trafford	1956
	in Australia	15-124	W Rhodes	Melbourne	1903-04
Australia	in England	16-137	RL Massie	Lord's	1972
	in Australia	13-77	MA Noble	Melbourne	1901-02

HIGHEST AGGREGATE OF WICKETS IN A SERIES

England	in England	46 (av 9.60)	JC Laker	1956
	in Australia	38 (av23.18)	MW Tate	1924-25
Australia	in England	42 (av 21.26)	TM Alderman	1981
	in Australia	41 (av 12.85)	RM Hogg	1978-79

HAT-TRICKS

England	W Bates	Melbourne	1882-83
	J Briggs	Sydney	1891-92
	JT Hearne	Headingley	1899
	DR Gough	Sydney	1998-99
Australia	FR Spofforth	Melbourne	1878-79
	H Trumble	Melbourne	1901-02
	H Trumble	Melbourne	1903-04
	SK Warne	Melbourne	1994-95

BATSMEN SCORING OVER 2000 RUNS IN ASHES TESTS

	Tests	Inns	No's	HSc	Runs	Avr	100	50
DG Bradman (A)	37	63	7	334	5028	89.78	19	12
JB Hobbs(E)	41	71	4	187	3636	54.26	12	15
AR Border(A)	47	82	19	200*	3548	56.31	8	21
DI Gower(E)	42	77	4	215	3269	44.78	9	12
SR Waugh(A)	46	73	18	177*	3200	58.18	10	14
G Boycott(E)	38	71	9	191	2945	47.50	7	14
WR Hammond(E)	33	58	3	251	2852	51.85	9	7
H Sutcliffe(E)	27	46	5	194	2741	66.85	8	16
C Hill(A)	41	76	1	188	2660	35.46	4	16
JH Edrich(E)	32	57	3	175	2644	48.96	7	13
GA Gooch(E)	42	79	0	196	2632	33.31	4	16
GS Chappell(A)	35	65	8	144	2619	45.94	9	12
MA Taylor(A)	33	61	2	219	2496	42.30	6	15
MC Cowdrey(E)	43	75	4	113	2433	34.26	5	11
L Hutton(E)	27	49	6	364	2428	56.46	5	14
RN Harvey(A)	37	68	5	167	2416	38.34	6	12
VT Trumper(A)	40	74	5	185*	2263	32.79	6	9
DC Boon(A)	31	57	8	184	2237	45.65	7	8
WM Lawry(A)	29	51	5	166	2233	48.54	7	13
ME Waugh(A)	29	51	7	140	2204	50.09	6	11
SE Gregory(A)	52	92	7	201	2193	25.80	4	8
WW Armstrong(A)	42	71	9	158	2172	35.03	4	6
IM Chappell(A)	30	56	4	192	2138	41.11	4	16
KF Barrington(E)	23	39	6	256	2111	63.96	5	13
AR Morris(A)	24	43	2	206	2080	50.73	8	8

BOWLERS TAKING OVER 100 WICKETS IN ASHES TESTS

	Tests	Balls	Runs	Wkts	Average	Best	5w	10w
DK Lillee(A)	29	8516	3507	167	21.00	7-89	11	4
IT Botham(E)	36	8479	4093	148	27.65	6-78	9	2
H Trumble(A)	31	7895	2945	141	20.88	8-65	9	3
SK Warne(A)	26	7792	3040	132	23.03	8-71	7	2
RGD Willis(E)	35	7294	3346	128	26.14	8-43	7	-
GD McGrath(A)	22	5241	2344	117	20.03	8-38	7	-
MA Noble(A)	39	6845	2860	15	24.86	7-17	9	2
RR Lindwall(A)	29	6728	2559	114	22.44	7-63	6	-
W Rhodes(E)	41	5791	2616	109	24.00	8-68	6	1
SF Barnes(E)	20	5749	2288	106	21.58	7-60	12	1
CV Grimmett(A)	22	9224	3439	106	32.44	6-37	11	2
DL Underwood(E)	29	8000	2770	105	26.38	7-50	4	2
AV Bedser(E)	21	7065	2859	104	27.49	7-44	7	2
G Giffen(A)	31	6457	2791	103	27.09	7-11	77	1
WJ O'Reilly(A)	19	7864	2587	102	25.36	7-54	8	3
R Peel(E)	20	5216	1715	101	16.98	7-31	5	1
CTB Turner(A)	17	5195	1670	101	16.53	7-43	11	2
TM Alderman(A)	17	4717	2117	100	21.17	6-47	11	1
JR Thomson(A)	21	4951	2418	100	24.18	6-46	5	-

75 WICKET-KEEPING DISMISSALS IN ASHES TESTS

	Tests	Caught	Stumped	Total
RW Marsh(A)	42	141	7	148
IA Healy(A)	33	123	12	135
APE Knott(E)	34	97	8	105
WAS Oldfield(A)	38	59	31	90
AFA Lilley(E)	32	65	19	84
ATW Grout(A)	22	69	7	76
TG Evans(E)	31	63	12	75

Captains

Season	England	Australia	Tests	Eng.	Aus.	Draw	Season	England	Australia	Tests	Eng.	Aus.	Draw
1876-77	James Lilywhite	DW Gregory	2	1	1	-	1938	WR Hammond	DG Bradman	4	1	1	2
1878-79	Lord Harris	DW Gregory	1	-	1	-	1946-47	WR Hammond	DG Bradman	5	-	3	2
1880	Lord Harris	WL Murdoch	1	1	-	-	1948	NWD Yardley	DG Bradman	5	-	4	1
1881-82	A Shaw	WL Murdoch	4	-	2	2	1950-51	FR Brown	AL Hassett	5	1	4	-
1882	AN Hornby	WL Murdoch	1	-	1	-	1953	L Hutton	AL Hassett	5	1	-	4
1882-83	Hon Ivo Bligh	WL Murdoch	4	2	2	-	1954-55	L Hutton	IW Johnson	5	3	1	1
1884	Lord Harris	WL Murdoch	3	1	-	2	1956	PBH May	IW Johnson	5	2	1	2
1884-85	A Shrewsbury	T Horan	5	3	2	-	1958-59	PBH May	R Benaud	5	-	4	1
1886	AG Steel	HJH Scott	3	3	-	-	1961	PBH May	R Benaud	5	1	2	2
1886-87	A Shrewsbury	PS McDonnell	2	2	-	-	1962-63	ER Dexter	R Benaud	5	1	1	3
1887-88	WW Read	PS McDonnell	1	1	-	-	1964	ER Dexter	RB Simpson	5	-	1	4
1888	WG Grace	PS McDonnell	3	2	1	-	1965-66	MJK Smith	RB Simpson	5	1	1	3
1890	WG Grace	WL Murdoch	2	2	-	-	1968	MC Cowdrey	WM Lawry	5	1	1	3
1891-92	WG Grace	JMc Blackham	3	1	2	-	1970-71	R Illingworth	WM Lawry	6	2	-	4
1893	WG Grace	JMc Blackham	3	1	-	2	1972	R Illingworth	IM Chappell	5	2	2	1
1894-95	AE Stoddart	C Giffen	5	3	2	-	1974-75	MH Denness	IM Chappell	6	1	4	1
1896	WG Grace	GHS Trott	3	2	1	-	1975	AW Greig	IM Chappell	4	-	1	3
1897-98	AE Stoddart	GHS Trott	5	1	4	-	1976-77	AW Greig	GS Chappell	1	-	1	-
1899	AC MacLaren	J Darling	5	-	1	4	1977	JM Brearley	GS Chappell	5	3	-	2
1901-02	AC MacLaren	J Darling	5	1	4	-	1978-79	JM Brearley	GN Yallop	6	5	1	-
1902	AC MacLaren	J Darling	5	1	2	2	1979-80	JM Brearley	GS Chappell	3	-	3	-
1903-04	PF Warner	MA Noble	5	3	2	-	1980	IT Botham	GS Chappell	1	-	-	1
1905	Hon FS Jackson	J Darling	5	2	-	3	1981	IT Botham	KJ Hughes	6	3	1	2
1907-08	AO Jones	MA Noble	5	1	4	-	1982-83	RGD Willis	GS Chappell	5	1	2	2
1909	AC MacLaren	MA Noble	5	1	2	2	1985	DI Gower	AR Border	6	3	1	2
1911-12	JWHT Douglas	C Hill	5	4	1	-	1986-87	MW Gatting	AR Border	5	2	1	2
1912	CB Fry	SE Gregory	3	1	-	2	1987-88	MW Gatting	AR Border	1	-	-	1
1920-21	JWHT Douglas	WW Armstrong	5	-	5	-	1989	DI Gower	AR Border	6	-	4	2
1921	Hon LH Tennyson	WW Armstrong	5	-	3	2	1990-91	GA Gooch	AR Border	5	-	3	2
1924-25	AER Gilligan	HL Collins	5	1	4	-	1993	GA Gooch	AR Border	6	1	4	2
1926	AW Carr	HL Collins	5	1	-	4	1994-95	MA Atherton	MA Taylor	5	1	3	1
1928-29	APF Chapman	J Ryder	5	4	1	-	1997	MA Atherton	MA Taylor	6	2	3	1
1930	APF Chapman	WM Woodfull	5	1	2	2	1998-99	AJ Stewart	MA Taylor	5	1	3	1
1932-33	DR Jardine	WM Woodfull	5	4	1	-	2001	N Hussain	SR Waugh	5	1	4	-
1934	RES Wyatt	WM Woodfull	5	1	2	2	2002-03	N Hussain	SR Waugh	5	1	4	-
1936-37	GOB Allen	DG Bradman	5	2	3	-							

VENUES

???	Tests	Eng.	Aus.	Draw		Tests	Eng.	Aus.	Draw
The Oval	33	15	6	12	Melbourne	52	18	27	7
Old Trafford	27	7	7	13	Sydney	52	21	24	7
Lord's	32	5	13	14	Adelaide	28	8	15	5
Trent Bridge	19	3	7	9	Brisbane	18	5	9	4
Headingley	23	7	8	8	Perth	10	1	6	3
Edgbaston	11	4	3	4	In England	146	41	45	60
Bramall Lane	1	0	1	0	In Australia	160	53	81	26
					Total	306	94	126	86